THE ISLAMIC UNDERSTANDING OF DEATH AND RESURRECTION

The Islamic Understanding of Death and Resurrection

Jane Idleman Smith
Yvonne Yazbeck Haddad

STATE UNIVERSITY OF NEW YORK PRESS
ALBANY

Published by
State University of New York Press, Albany

Printed in the United States of America

For information, address State University of New York Press, State University Plaza, Albany, N.Y., 12246

Library of Congress Cataloging in Publication Data

Smith, Jane I
The Islamic understanding of death and resurrection.

Bibliography: p.245
Includes index.
1. Eschatology, Islamic. I. Haddad, Yvonne Y., 1935– joint author.
BP166.8.S55 297'.23 80-21303
ISBN 0-87395-506-4
0-87395-507-2 (pbk)

Contents

Preface

Western observers of Islam have long been intrigued with Muslim conceptions of the life to come, particularly in light of the specifics of the future abodes of recompense portrayed so graphically in the Qur'ān. Numerous studies have been made of the revelations of the Qur'ān and of the importance of the concept of resurrection and judgment in Muslim theological understanding.

Nonetheless it is not an easy matter for Westerners to get a clear overview of all of the component elements making up the Islamic eschatological picture. While the Qur'ān itself describes the judgment and the habitations of the Fire and the Garden in exquisite detail, it makes little if any mention of the intermediate state between death and resurrection. The traditional material of the eschatological manuals, which affords a wealth of commentary on these circumstances, is generally unavailable in English. In the case of contemporary responses to questions of life after death, while much of the writing from the Indo-Pakistani subcontinent is in English, little has been translated from the Arabic works of Middle Eastern Muslims.

In this volume we have attempted to give as broad an overview as possible of the Islamic eschatological narrative, describing the understanding of the events beginning with the death of the individual and ending with habitation in the final abodes of recompense. Material has been taken from traditions, creeds, Qur'ān commentaries [*tafsīrs*] and other theological writing, balanced, whenever possible by the specifics (or lack thereof) presented in the Qur'ān. Our original intention was to consider both Sunnī and Shī'ī writings as well as works from the major schools and thinkers of Islamic philosophy and Sufism. Because of the wealth of material, however, and in the interests of feasibility, we were forced to limit our research and presentation primarily to works within the Sunnī tradition, both classical and modern. Our intent is not to ignore the significance of the rich resources of other branches of Islamic interpretation; we hope that other scholars more specifically trained in the disciplines of Shīʿī thought as well as philosophical and mystical interpretation might make available to English-speaking students these perspectives on issues of death, resurrection, and judgment.

Even within the Sunnī tradition, of course, there is so much material that we can only hope to provide a kind of representative sampling. In the chapters on classical Islam we have relied heavily on five manuals of eschatology generally recognized as among the most popular works of that genre. Such manuals are often little more than an ordering of a great number of reports, although Ibn Qayyim al-Jawzīya (*Kitāb al-rūḥ*) and Abū Ḥāmid al-Ghazālī (*al-Durra al-fākhira fī kashf ʿulūm al-ākhira)* both put the traditions in the context of their own discussions and analyses. In addition we have made frequent reference to the major collections of *hadīths* (narrative reports). So many traditions concerning the affairs of the eschaton are attributed to the Prophet that in general it is impossible to do more than allude to them by category. In many cases it is difficult to determine the relative authenticity of these reports, and as is true of the *ḥadīths* on any topic, it is clear that the companions and later followers of the Prophet filled in certain of the gaps left in these narratives. From the third Islamic century traditionalists amplified the eschatological material enormously, particularly in those areas on which the Qur'ān is relatively silent.[1] For the purpose of understanding the faith of many centuries of Muslims—and much of contemporary Islam still holds to the particulars of tradition—it is less important to determine whether or not reports are sound than to see their influence on the popular masses, as has been our concern here.

The first chapter of this work sets the theological scene, so to speak, for the details to follow, providing a general background of Islamic thought based on the Qur'ān and viewing in particular those issues to which concepts of death and afterlife specifically relate. Chapters Two and Three deal with classical Islamic understandings of death and resurrection, divided in terms of the chronological ordering of the material. In the former, traditional accounts of the specific events to occur to individuals from the time of death to the coming of the day of resurrection are surveyed. Continuing the sequence of afterdeath events, Chapter Three considers the traditional understanding of occurrences from the time of the signs portending the coming of the Hour through the various happenings of the day of judgment. The last two chapters attempt to view the ways in which Muslim thinkers of the twentieth century have understood issues of life, death, and the eschaton. Particular attention is given to afterlife concerns in the context of the questions with which Muslims are dealing in terms of this life and the struggle to re-define the nature of the Muslim community. Three general topics relating to life after death in the Islamic understanding are treated in the appendices. The material in each is relevant to the overall concern of the study, but specific enough in nature to have been placed in a separate section rather than incorporated into the text.

All translations from the Arabic, including Qur'ān passages, are the authors' own unless otherwise stipulated. Qur'ān verses are set off in brackets { ... }, in order to be immediately recognizable; verse references are preceded by a capital S for Sura or chapter. The following reference works are cited in abbreviation: the *Encyclopaedia of Islam* (*EI*); the *Shorter Encyclopaedia of Islam* (*SEI*); the *Encyclopaedia of Religion and Ethics* (*ERE*). Classical collections of traditions are abbreviated according to the name of the author: Abū Dā'ūd al-Sijistānī, *Sunan Abī Dā'ūd* (Cairo, 1952) (A.D.); Abū 'Abd Allāh al-Bukhārī, *al-Jāmi' al-ṣaḥīḥ* (Cairo, 1966) (Bu.); Abū Muḥammad al-Dārimī, *Sunan al-Dārimī* (Damascus, 1931) (Dā.); Aḥmad ibn Hanbal, *Musnad* (Cairo, 1895) (A.b.Ḥ.); Muḥammad Ibn Māja, *al-Sunan* (Cairo, 1952) (I.M.); Mālik ibn Anas, *al-Muwaṭṭa'* (Cairo, 1959) (Mā.); Muslim b. al-Ḥajjāj, *Ṣaḥīḥ Muslim* (Cairo, 1955–56), (Mu.); Abū 'Abd al-Raḥmān al-Nasā'ī, *al-Sunan al-musammá bi'l-mujtabá* (Cairo, 1894) (Nas.); Muḥammad b. Ja'far al-Tayālisī, *Musnad al-Tayālisī* (Haydarābād, 1904) (Ṭay.); Abū 'Īsá al-Tirmidhī, *al-Jāmi' al-ṣaḥīḥ* (Cairo, 1937) (Tir.).

We hope that one of the contributions of this work, aside from presenting an overall picture of how Sunnī Islam has viewed issues of death and afterlife, will be to demonstrate the continuing importance of the promise of resurrection for contemporary Islam. Despite certain variations in interpretation among modernists and traditionalists, the basic message to which all contemporary Muslims attest is that God has created humanity for a purpose, for the continuation of life and for ultimate accountability. In the next world injustices will be corrected and God will lead us to a perfected existence.

What the Qur'ān describes in terms of fear, hope, and finally as a matter of faith rather than of intellectual assent is understood by modern Islam as a matter of utter reasonableness. As expressed by Abū A'lá al-Mawdūdī:

> The fact is that whatever Muhammad (peace be upon him) has told us about life after death is clearly borne out by reason. Although our belief in that Day is based upon our implicit trust in the Messenger of God, rational reflection not only confirms this belief but it also reveals that Muhammad's (peace be upon him) teachings in this respect are much more reasonable and understandable than all other view-points about life after death.[2]

Many Muslim commentaries, especially contemporary works, do not deal directly with issues of life after death because they see the basic affirmation of the Qur'ān as so natural and reasonable as to require no defense or elaboration. To the extent to which authors do discuss and write about such issues, it is generally to remind themselves that Muslims must not fall prey to the lures of worldly materialism as has the West, and to affirm to the Muslim community and the world at large that the strength of Islam lies in the faith that the fruits of today's labor will be reaped in the hereafter, and that God will reward all in justice and mercy in the world to come.

The authors express their gratitude to all the friends here and in the Middle East who have assisted in the collection of this material. Particularly helpful were conversations with the following persons in the spring of 1976, in many cases followed up by lengthy correspondence: Dr. Maḥmūd Ibrāhīm, Dean of the Faculty of Arabic at The University of Jordan; Dr. Aḥmad 'Abd al-Majīd Ḥarīdī of Dār al-Kutub in Cairo; Dr. Ibrāhīm Ja'far and Dr. Aḥmad Shalabī, Kulliyat Dār al-'Ulūm, University of Cairo; Dr. 'Iffat Sharqāwī, Department of Arabic Studies, Ain Shams University in Cairo; Dr. Abd al-Wadūd Shalabī, Idārat al-Azhar, then Editor-in-Chief of *Majallat al-Azhar*; Sheikh Khalaf al-Sayyid 'Alī, Head of the Islamic Studies Division of the Azhar; Dr. Ahmed M. Sobhy, Professor of Philosophy and Theology at Alexandria University (now at San'ā' University in the Yemen); Dr. 'Abd al-Ḥalīm Maḥmūd, Shaykh al-Azhar; Professors John A. Williams, Sausan al-Missiri, and Muḥammad Nuwaihi of the American University of Cairo; Dr. Sa'īd Ramaḍān, Dean of the Kulliyat al-Shari'a, University of Damascus; Aḥmad Kaftāro, al-Muftī al-'Ām of Syria; Dr. Muḥammad Muḥammadī, Dean of the Faculty of Theology and Islamic Studies, Tehran University. We are also grateful to the Center for the Study of World Religions at Harvard University, under whose auspices travel in the Middle East in 1976 was possible, and the American Research Center in Egypt, Inc., for its assistance and support.

We hope that the form of presentation of this material concerning the Islamic understanding of death and resurrection will reflect as accurately and appreciatively as possible our understanding of the enormous significance that these doctrines have had in the lives of Muslims throughout the centuries, and that students of Islam and of comparative religion in general might be enriched through this brief look at one of the vital components of the living faith of Islam.

Jane I. Smith
Yvonne Y. Haddad

Chapter One
Considerations of God, Man, Time and Eternity

Time, History, and the Chronological Order

{They swear by God to the very limit of their oaths that God will not raise him who dies . . .} [S 16:38].

{They say, Are we to be returned to our former state when we have become decayed bones? They say, that would be a detrimental return!} [S 79:10–12].

Disbelief, rejection, and ridicule—thus the Qur'ān portrays the response of the Meccan community to the message delivered by the Prophet Muḥammad concerning the day of resurrection and the universal judgment.[1] For every mention of this scorn, however, the Qur'ān offers a multitude of assurances that God can and will raise the dead and that such a resurrection is an indispensable part of His plan for each individual and for all creation:

{O you people: If you are in doubt concerning the resurrection, know that We created you from dust, then from a sperm-drop, then from a blood-clot, then from an embryo partly formed and partly unformed, in order to make clear to you. We establish in the wombs whatever We wish for an appointed time, then We bring you out as an infant, then [sustain you] until you reach maturity. And among you are those who die and those who return to the infirmity of old age so that, after having been knowledgeable, they now have little understanding. You saw the earth lifeless, and then We poured down upon it water and it quivers and grows and sprouts forth all kinds of beautiful pairs. That is because God is the ultimately real [*al-ḥaqq*]. He it is Who gives life to what is dead; He it is Who has power over all things. Truly the Hour is coming—there is no doubt of it—when God will resurrect those who are in the graves} [S 22:5–7].

So intense is the Qur'ānic concern for and insistence on the day to come when all will be held accountable for their faith and their actions, that the ethical teachings contained in the Book must be understood in the light of this reality. Faith in the day of resurrection for the Muslim is his specific affirmation of God's omnipotence, the recognition of human accountability as a commitment to the divine unicity.

That God is the absolute Creator of all dominates the Qur'ānic message: {He Who originated the heavens and the earth; when He decrees a matter, He says to it, BE! and it is} [S 2:117]. In the Islamic conception, God as the Creator and Originator of all things has not only ultimate but also sole authority over the beginning, duration, and final dispensation of all things. His power is such that the mere command BE is sufficient to bring into existence all which He, in His supreme wisdom and according to His overall plan for the universe, chooses to create. All questions relating to the nature and purpose of life must be framed within this divine perspective. His omnipotence, His freely determined mercy and compassion, His guidance, and His justice are the ultimate determinants of the affairs of this world and the next. Basic to Islamic theological discussions of the nature of humankind, the structure and order of the universe, and the course of human history as part of the eschatological story of Islam is the primary consideration of whether or not specific formulations are consonant with the Qur'ānic understanding of the essential oneness of the divine.

The idea of creation was, of course, not unknown to the Arabs of the pre-Qur'ānic *jāhilīya* days (time of ignorance), but its significance for human life was then quite different. In the pre-Islamic conception, God created humankind and then retreated, in effect, from interference in or direction of their affairs. Humanity was seen as left to the mercy of an inexorable fate that determines the course of life. This fate was understood to be abstract time itself [*dahr, zamān*], the driving force dictating the continuing destinies of all persons. Combined with a recognition of the readily apparent difficulties of Bedouin existence, such a view led to a fatalism which concluded that the plan of one's life is set and cannot be altered by individual hope or action. (The vestiges of this attitude are recognizable in the long-standing Islamic view of destiny or foreordainment [*qadar*].[2] Such a fatalistic outlook is expressed, for example, in S 45:24: {They [the pagan Arabs] assert, There is nothing but our life in this present world; we die, we live, and nothing destroys us but time.}[3]

Even the often-repeated references to eternity in *jāhilīya* poetry are to be seen in the context of this world; *khulūd*, eternity, was literally understood as long life.[4] The Qur'ān draws an entirely different picture of life and death. Replacing the pessimistic world view of a people who felt themselves under the sway of an impersonal force leading inevitably and only to personal death came the conception that life has a purpose, that the events of human history, both individual and communal, are in the hands of a just and merciful God, and that death is not the end but the passage into a new and eternal existence.

Along with this sense of the purposeful direction of human events, the Qur'ān posits an understanding of meaning and significance to the flow of time and history. Arab history before the time of the Prophet had been concerned primarily with genealogies and the relationship of one individual to other members of his tribe, the unit through which he found his personal identity. There was not, however, a sense of the larger whole, in which individuals were understood to be members of the community of humankind. The Qur'ān clearly reflects the Arab concern for specific and seemingly isolated events and persons, yet in its overall narrative these events are related so as to reveal a common theme and pattern. The prophets came for a purpose and with a message to deliver; the consequences of heeding that message, both for communities and for individuals, have already been realized (as is evident in the fates of earlier peoples) and will be reaped again in the final day to come. The prophetic event is directly linked to the eschatological event. Both in this world and in the next the message of the prophets is validated by specific and immediate rewards for those who heed it, and by calamitous consequences for those who do not. Temporal disaster serves as a signal and a warning of the ultimate recompense to come.

With the transition from impersonal fate to divine direction, then, came a lifting of the dread of inevitable demise. Not that the element of fear is absent from the Qur'ān; verse after verse enjoins the hearers to fear the day of the Lord and the recompense to befall wrongdoers and hypocrites and those who reject the message of God. But fear is different from an unmitigated pessimism in which one sees no alternative to the destruction of individual existence. The opposite of fear is hope, and as abundant as the Qur'ānic references to take heed are those promising not only eternity of existence, but also eternity of felicity to persons who have faith and manifest the fruits of that faith.

God's action in history is illustrated most clearly in His sending of prophets with the message of joy and hope for all who will listen and heed. History itself is the arena in which the destruction of the faithless portends ultimate recompense and in which the faithful receive the assistance they need to live lives deserving of future reward. It is the context in which God's past acts manifest the pattern of His present and future acts, and in which His signs are sufficient instruction for men to know His expectations and to understand His justice. The Qur'ān does not present a complete record of human events and in that sense is not a book of history; rather it illustrates by means of specific cases the kinds of interaction between individuals, communities, and God that have characterized human history since the creation and whose significance will ultimately be seen in the events of the last hour and final judgment.

History is the framework in which God makes manifest His signs and His commands, and at the same time it is the arena in which humanity exhibits its acceptance or rejection of those signs. God's laws are thus evidenced in the flow of historical time just as they are revealed in the signs of nature. Civilizations come into being, grow and flourish, and pass away, all in the context of divine direction, illustrating in their success or demise the degree to which they have adhered to His laws. Some medieval theologians who followed al-Ash'arī's concern for affirming divine determinism saw time as a series of discontinuous instants created separately and individually by the One Who creates all things. Each instant was in itself the context for the revelation of one of God's signs and for the possibility of response to that revelation.[5] In Islamic theological parlance this came to be known as atomism, the intent of which is not a description of time or space as such but another expression of absolute divine control and prerogative. In the traditional Muslim view, however, time is generally understood to represent one continuous span from creation to the present (and by implication extending to the day of resurrection).

As will be seen in the succeeding chapters, time in the overall perspective has a beginning and an end. The starting point, of course, is the creation of the world, the heavens, and humankind: {We have placed the stars in the heavens and made them beautiful to the beholder . . . and We have spread out the earth and set on it the great mountains, and caused all things to grow there in harmony} [S 15:16, 19–20]. During the course of its flow, from one instant to the next, time itself is at the behest of God as are moments in the lives of individuals. God constantly acts to maintain and support the existence of all that He has brought into being, and in that sense time and history are actually a continuation of creation itself. The end of time is the beginning of a new state of existence, the ultimate manifestation of God's creative act in the transformation of the world after its destruction and the re-creation of human beings as total living bodies.

Islamic tradition provides some speculation on the precise time of the arrival of the day of judgment, and as we shall see, some contemporary thinkers interpret the degeneration of the present age as a clear sign of the imminence of the Hour. In the Qur'ān it is portrayed as being possibly very near at hand, but always as coming when God so chooses and according to His knowledge alone. As God appoints and determines the life span of every individual, so He determines the fixed limit of the earth and the duration of humanity as a whole upon it. At each instant we are drawing nearer to the climax of time and history when all will be brought into the awesome presence of the Creator. The unreality of time as a specific duration is demonstrated on the day of resurrection, when our time on earth will seem an extremely short period: {Say: How long did you dwell on the earth in number of years? They will reply, We remained only a day or part of a day . . .} S 23:112–113]; {On the day when He gathers them [it will seem as if] they did not remain but an hour of the day . . .} [S 10:45].

All of human history, then, moves from the creation to the eschaton. Preceding the final judgment will come signs (both cosmic and moral) signaling the arrival of the Hour as well as the specific events of the resurrection and assessment. Within this overall structure is the individual cycle which specifies the events of creation, death, and resurrection. Part of the fatalistic determinism of the pre-Islamic Arabs was their sense that each human life is for a fixed term or *ajal*. It is immutably set; on the appointed day one's life comes to an end. This idea of an *ajal* is repeated in the Qur'ān, both for individuals [S 6:2, 7:34, 16:61, 20:129] and for nations [S 10:49, 15:4–5]. Here, however, the emphasis is not on an impersonal determinism but on divine prerogative; God ascertains the life-spans of persons and of communities, and in His hands lies the fate of all that He has brought into being.[6]

Creation, then, is both the creation of the world and humankind as a generic whole, and the creation of every individual in the womb of his mother. Immediately before the resurrection will come the absolute destruction of the earth and all that lives on it [S 55:26–27]; this cosmic "death" is, of course, preceded by the death of each individual at the conclusion of his or her *ajal*. This concept has led to considerable speculation within the Islamic community about the time between individual death and resurrection, its duration, and the nature of those awaiting the resurrection. If we look structurally at the overall conception of time in the Islamic understanding, we see one pattern juxtaposed over another, individual time set within the context of collective time:

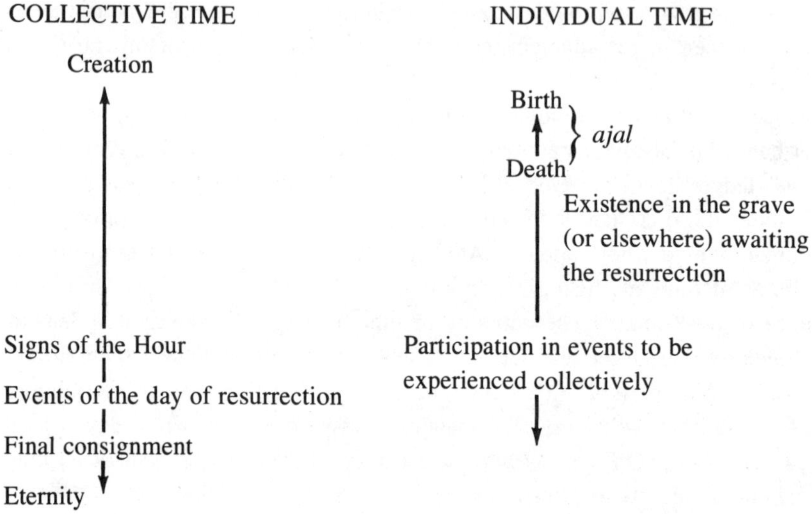

The events from the signs of the Hour through the final consignment are a linking of the temporal and the eternal, or to use the language of the Qur'ān, of the *dunyá* and the *ākhira*.[7] *Dunyá* literally means the closer or lower, and refers to things relating to the life of this world as we know it.[8] *Ākhira*, the hereafter, moves beyond or exists apart from the measure of time. In the eschatological vision of Islam one finds repeated instances of the overlapping of temporal and spatial concepts. The manuals contain descriptions of the approach of the Fire on the day of resurrection, for instance, measuring its distance from the community of the faithful in terms of years rather than in spatial units. The terms *dunyá* and *ākhira* themselves are related both to time and to space: *dunyá* is the earth in the physical sense but at the same time refers to the period every individual spends on earth, related to its activities, as well as to the total time frame continuing until the coming of the hour of judgment. *Ākhira* correspondingly refers both to the heavens, *samāwāt*, as the specific abodes of the angels and of the saved, and to the antithesis of *dunyá*, the hereafter or eternity. The very term used repeatedly in the Qur'ān for eternity is the *dār al-ākhira*, the "abode" of the hereafter, in itself illustrating the coincidence of the spatial and the temporal.

In the Qur'ān *dunyá* and *ākhira* are related both in the sense of "now" and "later," and in the specifically moral juxtaposition of negative and positive. The earth in a general sense is good insofar as it is created to provide sustenance and even comfort for man, and as it is the context for the revelation of God's creative power and maintenance through His specific signs [*āyāt*]. In this sense *dunyá* is the first and necessary arena for carrying out the divine will: {Ordain for us the good in this world [*al-dunyá*] and in the hereafter [*al-ākhira*]} [S 7:156]; {You [God] are my Friend [*walī*] in this world and the next . . .} [S 12:101].[9] In the usual contrast between *dunyá* and *ākhira*, however, the concepts are seen as two clear moral alternatives; the individual is enjoined to choose one abode over the other as the focal point of his or her attention and activity. *Dunyá*, when balanced against *ākhira* in this sense, is as the negative to the positive.[10] One's choice of this world over the next will earn him a sure recompense of woe; to choose the world is to forgo the joy of the hereafter: {Whosoever desires the harvest of the *ākhira*, We will increase for him this harvest. And whoever desires the harvest of the *dunyá*, We will give it to him, but he will have no share in the hereafter} [S 42:20]; {Life in the *dunyá* is nothing but a distraction and a sport, but in the *dār al-ākhira* is life, if only they knew} [S 29:64]. The world per se is not to be rejected—the reward of the hereafter is for those who do not neglect their duties in the world—but one's vision should focus on the things to come.

While on the one hand the contrast between *dunyá* and *ākhira* is absolute, that which passes away versus that which is the sphere of eternal existence, it is also true that only in the light of one can the other attain its full meaning. *Dunyá* must be seen in harmony with *ākhira*. How one lives on earth is both prescribed and assessed in terms of the relationship of now to the eternal. As people choose in the *dunyá*, so will they be rewarded both in the *dunyá* and, in greater magnitude, in the *ākhira*. Contemporary Islamic thinkers place great stress on the necessity of understanding the significance of the next life in providing a context and sanction for the moral imperative in this life.

The time chart above indicates that each individual span (except, presumably, for those alive in the last days) includes a period between death and resurrection in which one awaits the coming of the Hour. The relative conditions of individuals in this suspended state will be examined in detail below. In one sense the death of the body by definition means a cessation of involvement with *dunyá*, and thus a necessary entry into the sphere of the *ākhira*. In another sense the circumstance of the decreased awaiting resurrection forms a third possibility, which came to be considered as such in the later development of Islamic thought, and which provides another instance of the coincidence of time and space. The name that eventually was applied to that circumstance was *barzakh*, taken primarily from S 23:100, which expresses the inability of the departed to return to earth: {. . . behind them is a barrier [*barzakh*] until the day when they are resurrected.}[11] Belief in some kind of life in the grave was ancient and common, part of Islamic understanding from the earliest times. The *barzakh* conception developed in its fuller sense later (there are no references to *barzakh* in the canonical traditions[12]) and came to be understood as simultaneously the *time* every individual must wait between death and resurrection and the *place* or abode of that waiting.[13]

The clear intention of S 23:100 is that persons who have died will in no way be able to return to this earth. The entire message of the Qur'ān supports the idea that we have only one life on earth and that our assessment will be of the ways in which we have chosen to live in terms of God's specifications. Life may continue in some form either in the grave or in another condition, but we are assured the resurrection of our bodies and eternal life as fully constituted individuals. Nonetheless, we have but one opportunity—that of this world—to earn the recompense that will determine our eternal existence (the question of God's mercy temporarily aside). On the whole, then, Islam has rejected completely the suggestion that human souls will or could be reincarnated in different bodies for the purpose of improving their previous records of performance.

Some voices, not surprisingly, are raised in exception. Metempsychosis [*tanāsukh*] and incarnation of spirits in other bodies [*ḥulūl*] have been upheld by some individuals and some schools in the history of Islam. The doctrine of metempsychosis came originally to Islam from India and gained credence in a number of sects considered outside the orthodox fold. Some persons associated with the Mu'tazila held that God's justice necessitates another opportunity for those whose good and bad deeds are equal and who thus merit neither the Fire nor the Garden.[14] Many of the Shī'a, such as the Ismā'īlia, Bāṭinīya and others, applied the doctrine of metempsychosis both to the Imam and to individual believers. Most Sufis, like most orthodox Muslims, have rejected transmigration,[15] although a few accept it as a means of achieving spiritual perfection. In 1927 Nadarbek K. Mirza, a Karachi lawyer, wrote a little book called *Reincarnation and Islam*. In this he suggests that the Qur'ānic implication that the human soul progresses until it reaches the Divine necessitates an acceptance of the idea of reincarnation. Islam as the culmination of all religion incorporates the philosophies of older religions, he says, and the reference to *barzakh* in S 23:100 simply means that the barrier will not be raised until the next birth.[16] Such latitude in interpretation of a verse that almost all others have seen as proof of the opposite point suggests the ways in which different groups and sects have been able eisegetically to justify a wide range of different understandings. The body of Islam, however, admits of only one life on this earth and insists on the absolute imperative of that life being lived in faith, obedience, and submission.

As the issue of time in Islamic understanding is not one of chronology per se as much as a means of expressing God's provenance over the affairs of the world and human responsibility within it, so the descriptions of space and cosmology provide another dimension to what are basically theological concerns. Cosmic structure and the site of ultimate recompense are of interest only insofar as they provide support for the basic issue of divine guidance and human accountability. Much of Islamic cosmology came from earlier world views—the circles of damnation, the general location of the fires of purgation below the earth, the seven layers of heaven above the earth—either justified by or accepted in addition to references in the Qur'ān: {It is God Who created seven heavens, and of the earth that which is similar to it . . .} [S 65:12].[17] The *ḥadīths* contain many more details, sometimes elaborated in a wealth of picturesque specifics. God seated upon His Throne, borne by angels, is above the topmost layer of heaven; in the seven descending levels are to be found various angels and former messengers awaiting the day of resurrection but already partaking of the pleasures of the hereafter.

Corresponding to the layers of heaven[18] are the seven descending depths of the Fire, like a vast funnel. Across the top of the uppermost layer, Gehenna, is the bridge over which all must pass on the day of judgment. At each descending level the punishments for the damned are more severe and the suffering more intense. The lote-tree at the boundary of paradise, sometimes known as the Tubbá tree shading all of the Garden, is paralleled by the tree of Zaqqūm at the pit of hell, with its bitter smell and flowers like the heads of demons. S 7:46–50 describes a partition between the Garden and the Fire on whose heights [*a'rāf*] sits a band of men. Their precise function, as we shall see, is disputed, but the verses do indicate that there is a place from which the inhabitants of both the Garden and the Fire will clearly be seen. The symbolism of this wall or barrier is much like that of *barzakh*; while one separates the *dunyá* and the *ākhira*, the abode of preparation from the abode of realization, the other divides humanity on the basis of the recompense meted out as a result of action in the *dār al-dunyá*. In each case there is a clear and sharp distinction, and in the long run the choice of one abode precludes participation in the other.

Traditional eschatological narrative, as we shall see in the following chapter, describes among the events occurring immediately after the death of the individual a journey through the seven heavens in the company of the archangel Gabriel. (In the case of one who has lived a disreputable life, the description is rather of the frustrated attempt at such a journey.) This ascent, in the course of which the newly departed soul sees and talks with the inhabitants of each successive level, quite obviously parallels the ascent of Gabriel and the Prophet Muḥammad in what is known as the *mi'rāj* or ascension in the heavenly night journey [*isrā'*]: {Praise be to God Who took His servant by night for a journey from the sacred place of worship to the far distant place of worship, whose surroundings We have blessed, in order to show him Our signs . . .} [S 17:1]. From this reference grew the account of the Prophet Muḥammad traveling through the layers of the Fire and the Garden, seeing in an experience which was really atemporal the circumstances of the damned and the saved as they will be after the day of judgment.[19]

Great debate has developed over the location of the ascent (Mecca or Medina), the nature of the experience (physical, psychological, out of the body, dream[20]), the Prophet's purported vision of and conversation with God, and the implications for the question of whether or not the Garden and the Fire are already created. The signs encountered by the Prophet, seated on his winged horse Burāq and led by Gabriel, have inspired some of the most graphic portrayals of Islamic eschatological art and painting. Few details are consistent in the many reports of this ascent, and its use in helping construct a balanced and coherent picture of Islamic cosmology is greatly limited. Islamic mysticism has used this prototypical journey as a model for the spiritual journey of each soul towards God, rising from the world of the senses or earthly realm [*'ālam al-dunyá*] through the intermediate or celestial world [*'ālam al-jabarūt*].[21] To the great body of Muslims this journey has served to verify both the role of the Prophet as the chosen one and the reality of the future abodes. To many contemporary writers, however, it is taken as another reference to the possibility of human progress in this world. The journey serves as a means of ethical instruction rather than as the model for mystical progression, while the afterlife references serve as an imperative for living a moral and spiritual existence, a dominant theme in contemporary Islamic consideration of this life and the life to come.[22]

Modern Muslim writers have also suggested some interesting ways in which to understand the seven layers of the heavens and hells described by traditional Islam. Concerned with Qur'ānic prescience of the findings of modern scientific endeavor, some have attempted to see the variable of seven as related to such things as the colors in the spectrum or the notes of the musical scale,[23] or have suggested that the torments associated with the idea of hell will be experienced through the seven senses of sight, hearing, smell, taste, touch, the feeling of heat and cold, and the feeling of fatigue.[24] Spiritualists have suggested that there are seven spiritual worlds with varying vibrations and thus varying degrees of elevation, arranged like saucers over the earth in pyramid shape.[25] Even the psychological sciences are employed in the occasional attempt to see the Garden and the Fire not as localities but as states of mind and stages in a continuing corrective experience. Most contemporary writers, of course, do not specifically address the question of how the details of the Garden and the Fire should be interpreted. Those who do address it tend simply to affirm the existence of these abodes, repeating the specifics of the Qur'ān or the commonly accepted traditional elaborations.

Humanity: Nature, Role, and Responsibility

As part of God's creation man can be assured of two things: first, that the difference between himself as the created and God as the creator is virtually without limit, and thus his best effort is crowned with success only insofar as that is within the scope of God's will and choice; second, that behind the flow of events, both in the natural and the human orders, is a divine plan, and that all of man's life from birth to death is a microcosmic part of that overall macrocosmic scheme.

The Quar'ānic picture of the totality of the flow of life and illustrates clearly and unquestionably the structure of God's divine plan for His human creation. Man, says the Qur'ān, is created from clay and put on the earth for a specified time [*ajal*], the diminution or extensions of which is completely beyond his own control. He is, nonetheless, far from a creature to be despised. As the son of Adam, he is instructed by God in the true nature of things and designated as His vicegerent [*khalīfa*]; for man all that is on earth and in the heavens has been created [S 2:29–30]. But with this honor comes responsibility. All will ultimately be returned to God and called to account for individual deeds of commission and omission in a reckoning that takes absolutely seriously the reality of human liability. In S 32:7–11 we see a general outline of the process of the creation of man, culminating in a guarantee of the final return of God:

> {He has made all that He has created good. And He began the creation of man from clay, then made his offspring from a drop of fluid despised, then He formed him and breathed into him of His spirit. And He gave you hearing and

sight and feeling, though you give little thanks. They say, When we are lost in the earth, will we be created anew? and they deny the meeting with their Lord. But you say: The angel of death, who has charge over you, will take you unto Him, and you will be returned to your Lord.}

As we were created responsible, so shall we be held accountable, each person for himself and no soul answerable for the actions and beliefs of any other. When God so pleases, we humans will be brought into His presence and judgment will be rendered in terms of the ways in which we have chosen to live our lives. The reality of the eschaton, the arrival of the day of judgment, is consonant with the return to God, return being essential to the completion of God's plan for all of creation.

The eschatological manuals contain a great deal of highly imaginative material concerning the creation of man, most of which is beyond the scope of this work. Many discuss the nature and circumstances of souls after the time that God originally brings them into existence. The Qur'ān makes no mention of the pre-existence of souls aside from the rather ambiguous reference in S 7:172: {When your Lord took from Banī Ādam their progeny from their loins and made them testify concerning themselves, Am I not your Lord? They replied, Yes! we do testify. That you may not say on the day of resurrection, Truly we were ignorant of this.}

Traditional Islam saw in this reference the occasion to affirm the idea of pre-existence. While as a subject for conjecture it does not occupy the attention of the traditionalists or the theologians anywhere near the extent that eschatology does, some of the collections of *ḥadīths* contain narratives concerning the location of souls between the time of their creation from Adam's loins and their placement in the wombs of their mothers. Often God is said to have these pre-existent souls with Him in one of the treasure-houses attached to the Throne. Rather than the idea of pre-existence, the contemporary understanding of this verse stresses its ethical content, i.e. the nature of the primordial covenant made between God and man to which man must continue to be responsible. Because people are created by nature to know the truth, there is no escape from individual accountability at the eschaton. God has created humanity with the natural disposition [*fiṭra*] to be truly Muslim; thus there will be no excuse in the last days for not having known the truth and conducted one's life in accordance with it and with God's divine commands.[26]

Two of the earliest messages transmitted by the angel Gabriel to the Prophet Muḥammad were of the absolute oneness [*tawḥīd*] of God and of the inevitability of the coming of the Hour at which judgment on human accountability will take place. To recognize that the full impact of each of these articles of faith can only be understood in light of the other is to begin to comprehend the fullness of the Islamic conception of the absolute unity of all being and of all action. God is one; the recognition of that oneness is the ultimate charge for each individual; the *content* of that recognition is the living of an ethically integrated existence, i.e. one of integrity. There is, in other words, a direct and clear relationship between recognizing God's oneness and unity, which is the full meaning of the term *tawḥīd*, and living a life of complete moral responsibility. According to the degree to which this responsibility has been discharged, God's word of judgment will be passed and final felicity or purgation accorded. (The centrality of the idea of unity, both of the divine and of human response to the divine, is also reflected in the importance of the community in Islamic understanding. The earliest questions of Islamic theology were framed in terms of their implications for the community as a whole, and one of the great tragedies of Islam is that often this very concern for preserving the integrity of the *umma* led to ruptures within it.)

Faced with the fact of human accountability, then, Muslims have had to deal with the extremely thorny question of relating accountability to the equally fundamental understanding of the Qur'ān that all matters lie entirely in the hands of God and that nothing that occurs does so against His omnipotent will. The dilemma of human responsibility, seemingly by definition implying a measure of human freedom to make choices, in the light of God's absolute authority and knowledge of all that has happened and will happen, is not unique to Islam. Searching for some resolution, Muslims have had the divine revelation of the Qur'ān as a guide, but even there the matter is complex, and varying interpretations of the meaning of human responsibility can be discerned: {God does not change the condition of a people until they change what is in their own souls; and if God wishes ill for a people, there is no avoiding it . . .} [S 13:11]; {Let any one who will, remember [the day of resurrection]; but none will remember it except as God wills . . .} [S 74:55–56]; {No soul can have faith except by the leave of God; He puts uncleanness [*rijs*] upon those who do not understand} [S 10:100].

What is most striking in the eschatological story of Islam is that in spite of the fact that the verses of the Qur'ān can lend themselves to different understandings of the extent to which man is the author of his own acts, never is the underlying theme of human accountability compromised. The battle over human free will was waged *not* on the grounds of whether or not we will be called to account at the final rendering—an issue never debated—but rather of whether or not the implication of free choice in any way impugns the understanding of God as absolutely free in His own actions and knowledge. This is of crucial importance in looking at the overall picture Islam has drawn of the events occurring from bodily death to the final dispensation. As the story unfolds, one sees at every step a clear indication that individuals are held to account for their deeds and for the degree of their faith. The very process of dying illustrates this accountability, as do the events of the questioning of the grave, the situation in which one finds himself while awaiting the resurrection, and the various occurrences of the day of judgment itself.

Given the fact of human responsibility, then, what can we say about the Islamic understanding of man in terms of his natural inclinations? There is not in Islam, as in at least some schools of Christian interpretation, a doctrine of original sin as such. The common Christian conception has been that Adam was expelled from paradise because of his sin, and due to this original act of disobedience the succession of humanity is tainted. While the Qur'ān contains the narrative of Adam's expulsion from the Garden [S 2:35–39], the expulsion is the result of satanic deception, immediately pardoned, rather than a progenitive act of disobedience with ramifications for the rest of humanity. Adam's act is generally felt to have been foreign to his real nature, for the recovery of which God sent him into the world.[27] This is not to say, however, that in Islamic understanding humanity does not exhibit certain tendencies toward base responses. If we look at the overall presentation of the Qur'ān and the commentary it provides about the nature of man, a very interesting picture emerges.

In the first place, as observed above, man has been placed on the earth to be the vicegerent of God, both in the singular references to Adam [S 2:30] and the plural suggestion that all of humanity are the inheritors of the earth [S 6:165]. The sons of Adam are placed in an honored position because of their rational abilities [S 2:31] and are given all good things necessary for the maintenance of life [S 17:70, 16:5–8]; God created man in the best of molds [S 15:4]. There is thus nothing inherently debased about man; he has been given every natural opportunity to live a life of well-being and honor. (All of this, of course, presupposes the understanding that man in relation to God is *'abd*, servant, whose fundamental response is worship and submission to His will and prerogative.)

It is clear, however, that man must stand the test of his ability to make right choices and to live according to the will of the One who placed him in this inherently favorable position vis-á-vis the rest of creation. Here the

Qur'ān recognizes that there is nothing automatic about choosing the right, and that in fact man by his very nature finds obedience and gratitude to his Maker a difficult task. {Man has been created weak}, says S 4:28. S 90:4 states that God created man in affliction, and 84:6 that man's toil toward God is a painful struggle. There is no assuming, in other words, that because God ordered even the angels to bow down to Adam, man will by definition find life unburdened or obedience an easy and natural response.

The truly powerful contrast the Qur'ān draws in relation to man, however—and it is repeated throughout the Suras of the Book—is that between his actual creation from base elements and his innate lack of gratitude for that creation and for all that has been provided for him. In verse after verse we hear of man having been brought to life from such lowly constituents as clay, mud, dust, earth, sperm, and a bloodclot.[28] Yet in spite of the wonder that from such mean beginnings he has been given life and raised to his stated rank among creation, man consistently refuses to honor his Lord with the gratitude due from such a gift: {Truly man is ungrateful to his Lord, and he bears witness to that} [S 100:6–7]. Even though humankind has been given authority in the earth and provided with every means for life's fulfillment, thanks are not rendered [S 7:10]. A number of verses relate the theme that men in trouble cry out to God, but that when circumstances improve they are heedless of Him and forget to give thanks for His assistance.[29]

The Qur'ānic insistence on human ingratitude does not mean that man is inherently ungrateful with no choice in the matter. That he inclines toward such forgetfulness and perversity is also a fact. We have shown him the way, says S 76:3, and whether he is grateful or ungrateful is up to him. Very few references in the Qur'ān describe man in general as living up to the promise of the exalted position in which God has placed him. As well as being ungrateful, he is also impatient, fretful, and stingy [S 70:19–21], greedy [S 74:15], and violent in his pursuit of wealth [S 100:8]. Full of pride and self-conceit, he forgets that his position and all things afforded to him are by the grace of God[30] and in rebelling against God thinks of himself as self-sufficient [S 96:6–7]. Hasty and heedless in his actions, he often mistakes the bad for the good (or consciously opts for the wrong), so that the prayer he should offer for good he makes instead for evil [S 17:11].

The picture of man as tending toward ingratitude and pride does not indicate, however, that he is irredeemable. He is capable of movement from the lower to the higher states, as the Qur'ān says: {You shall surely move from stage to stage} [S 84:19]. Islamic theology, in attempting to outline the general levels on this path of upward movement, has looked to three specific

Qur'ānic references as indicative of the three dispositions of the human soul. In these it has seen the potential for development in the nature of man as a being fully responsive to the commandments of God:

1. In the story of the attempted seduction of Joseph by the wife of the Egyptian 'Azīz, these words are put into her mouth as she blames her actions on her own nature: {I do not absolve myself; truly the soul [*nafs*] is prone to evil [*ammāra bi'l-sū'*], except as my Lord shows mercy . . .} [S 12:53]. What is indicated here is not a recognition of basic human sinfulness, but rather of the inclination inherent in every individual toward those responses of a lower or more animal-like nature, responding to the physical appetites. These inclinations are sometimes understood to be brought about by the lurings of that class of beings called the *shayāṭīn* or satans, immoral spirits ambiguously related to the fallen angels, at whose head is Iblīs.[31] More psychological interpretations, not surprisingly, see the satans as personifications of the workings of the human mind or the inclinations of the soul.

2. In the Sura entitled *qiyāma*, the first two verses witness to the reality of the resurrection through testimony first to the day of resurrection itself, and second to the human soul described as self-reproaching or blameworthy [*al-nafs al-lawwāma*]. This is usually seen as the next stage of development of the soul; in this condition one is aware of the temptation to wrongdoing and strives actively to overcome it with the assistance of God.

3. In a passage describing the contrast between the person doomed to the Fire and the one judged worthy of the Garden [S 89:25–30], the latter is characterized as the soul at peace [*al-nafs al-muṭma'inna*]. This phrase has been interpreted to refer to the soul in its fullest stage of development, the condition in which all base instincts are removed and it is utterly calm, at rest and at peace with itself and with God. Although some Sufis attest to the attainment of *al-nafs al-muṭma'inna* as a possiblity while still on this earth, the more common understanding is that this condition can only be reached when one abides finally in the Garden in the presence of God.[32]

In this conception of the full range of possibilities for the human person one finds another illustration of the divine balance in which the natural extremes are blended into one symmetrical whole. As humans we are disposed to opposite inclinations, but our potential is for progress toward a unified totality in which the *tawḥīd* of God is both expressed and in a microcosmic way paralleled. In the same way the very linking together of human ethical responsibility in this world [*al-dunyá*] with the full accounting and recompense in the next [*al-ākhira*] reveals the unity in God's overall plan for humanity. The awareness of the full range of life, the continuity between the present and the time to come, provides for man both the impetus for living a life of integrity—of which he is inherently capable—and the means and direction for living such a life. Recognizing the certainty of human fallibility and the limitations of human understandings, Islam in interpreting the words of the Qur'ān nonetheless holds the guarantee that through God's mercy one can overcome these limitations. As God brings back all to Him in a circle of unity, so He guides and supports the upward movement of the human soul in the progression which leads to the *nafs al-muṭma'inna* in the peace of the Garden of Eternity.

From an ethical perspective the message of the Qur'ān is clear. What it clarifies on almost every page, what all Muslims from the earliest days to the present have been fully cognizant of, is that humanity stands responsible for its actions before the divine. Semantic, philosophical, and other technical questions aside, it is abundantly clear that when God so pleases, we all will be revivified in the totality of being and will be brought before Him for a full accounting of the ways in which we have chosen to live our lives.

While on the one hand this is really all man needs to know in order to fulfill the ethico-religious responsibilities placed on him, on the other hand the complex and curious human mind has located additional concerns as Muslims have considered the nature of man. In the verses cited earlier (S 32:7–11) about the creation of man, we saw a description of the process by which God enlivens the material aspect of man by breathing into him the divine spirit, the *rūḥ*, which is the literal breath of life. What the Qur'ān does not explain here, and in fact nowhere clearly delineates, is the relationship between *rūḥ* and the other element in the human constitution differentiated from the purely physical body [*jism* or *badan*], that called the *nafs* or soul.

The issue of the immortality of the soul was generally of less concern to orthodox Islam than the affirmation of the resurrection of the body. Nonetheless the understanding of the relationship between body, soul, and spirit has been of interest to many Muslims, and their discussions have been influenced by various kinds of philosophical and mystical perspectives. The aspect of this debate most relevant to our present endeavors is the question of how Islam has understood the nature of the human person in terms of what survives the death of the body at the conclusion of one's *ajal*. What, in other words, lives beyond the physical death and awaits in some form the coming of the eschaton when it will again be joined to the resurrected body? By what terminology is that remaining individuality to be understood?

We will see in the succeeding analyses of some of the more popular eschatological manuals that many writers—theologians as well as traditionists—have failed to distinguish between the terms *nafs* and *rūḥ*, soul and spirit, either interchanging them or using one to the exclusion of the other. This tendency also characterizes much of contemporary analysis. The question of how to name and understand the nature of the human personality is sufficiently complex that many contemporary writers assert outright that they are very reluctant to deal with it.[33] The Qur'ān verse most frequently cited as a sanction against excessive speculation on the nature of the spirit is 17:85: {They ask you about the *rūḥ*, Say: The spirit is the affair of my Lord. Only a little knowledge is given to you.} Knowledge of the reality of the spirit is God's concern alone, and human knowledge when measured against the standard of God is pitiful indeed.[34]

Other writers, both classical and modern, have attempted to draw a clear distinction between the terms *nafs* and *rūḥ*, particularly as the occasion is provided in exegesis of certain verses of the Qur'ān. In the opinion of some contemporaries a clarification is not only legitimate but also necessary; the Qur'ān itself, they argue, uses *nafs* and *rūḥ* in very different ways, and to confuse or unnecessarily interchange them is to be inaccurate in terms of the Qur'ānic intention.

Nafs, following the usage of pre-Islamic poetry in the Qur'ān, refers primarily to the individual self in a reflexive sense. It also designates the soul (as in the three descriptions of *nafs* referred to above) and is found in both the singular and the plural. *Rūḥ*, appearing only in the singular, never refers to the human soul. Its usages are many;[35] of them the only ones suggesting the relation of the divine spirit to the human person speak of the "breathing in" of God's *rūḥ* (in addition to S 32:8 cited above, see 15:29, 38:72).[36]

Despite the quite distinct usages of the terms *nafs* and *rūḥ* employed in the Qur'ān, they were early the subject of intricate debate and speculation on the part of theologians and metaphysicians on the one hand, and quite clearly interchanged in the general parlance of Islam on the other. (There is some evidence that *nafs* was first used specifically for the human soul in Umayyad poetry.[37]) There was, in fact, relatively little distinction in the early understanding between soul and spirit. That is, both the body and the spirit (or soul) were considered to be of a material nature, the difference between them more quantitative than qualitative. The material nature of the body, however, was understood as gross and that of the soul/spirit as subtle or highly refined. The spiritual substance was thought to be diffused in the material body as its animating and controlling principle.[38]

Other voices in the community of Islam, such as those influenced by Greek philosophy, some of the Mu'tazila, Shī'a, and Sufis, denied that the spirit is in any way identified with matter. It is, they said, a purely spiritual substance, and unlike the atomist theologians they affirmed its immortal nature. The common Semitic view sees man as a union of body and soul/spirit; in contrast this spiritualist school of interpretation, with some real variations in understanding, held that man is essentially a spirit temporarily associated with a human body which comes into its own true nature after separation from the body at death. Soul or *nafs* in this view, while still sometimes identified with *rūḥ*, more commonly was seen as inferior to it and of a more animal nature. Those, of course, who held to this spiritualist perspective often disavowed the idea of a physical resurrection of the body. (We will see in the succeeding chapter dealing with the resurrection some of the ways in which classical Islamic orthodoxy understood this issue, as well as the kinds of responses to it made by contemporary Islam.) The interpretation of the spirit as espoused by philosophers, rationalists, Shī'a and others did have some effect on classical Islamic theology [*kalām*]. While an insistence on the generally material nature of body, soul, and spirit was never fully disregarded, *kalām* came to accept the notion that some aspect of the human person will survive the death of the body until the day of resurrection. Chapter Two below treats the different understandings of classical Islam concerning the state (or location) of the soul/spirit during this waiting period after death.

One of the specific references in the Qur'ān to that aspect of the human person which survives death is in S 39:42: {God takes unto Himself the souls [*al-anfus*] at their deaths, and that which has not died [He takes] in its sleep. He keeps that for which He has ordained death and sends the other to its appointed term. In that are signs for a thoughtful people.} Among attempts to interpret this verse, i.e. to determine the difference, if any, between the departure of souls at death and during sleep, one frequently also finds analyses of the distinction between *nafs* and *rūḥ* as they apply to that aspect of humanity surviving death.[39] Here it is evident that despite the common tendency to interchange these terms, when pressed to define the nature of sleep and death many of the exegetes both classical and modern do, in fact, draw a distinction between them. That taken by God during sleep is generally understood to be the *nafs al-'aql wa'l-tamyīz*, the soul possessing the rational faculties of intelligence and discrimination. The *rūḥ*, which in the condition of sleep remains attached to the body, is sometimes referred to as the *nafs al-ḥayāt wa'l ḥaraka* (the soul possessing life and movement), that by which life is bestowed on the individual. At death the connection of the spirit with the body is severed completely, although the spirit does not die. By implication the *nafs al-aql wa'l-tamyīz* is seen to be extinguished at death, the time at which independent action and other attendant faculties related to the functioning of the body cease. Thus while the terminology sometimes differentiates between *nafs* and *rūḥ* and sometimes suggests two varieties of *nafs*, there is a general understanding in both the classical and modern writings that the rational soul, which directs the activities of the body, perishes at physical death, while the life-infusing soul or spirit continues and awaits the coming of the Hour.[40]

Some modern writers say that as the long heritage of interchanged usage indicates, there is really no difference between the *nafs* and the *rūḥ*; they are to be seen simply as two different terms for one element. According to this understanding *nafs* is more appropriate as a term applied to that which directs one's activities while attached to the body, i.e. during life, while *rūḥ* is the term for this same element when it is separated from the body after death.[41] Others, however, see these parts of the human constitution as substantially different. *Nafs*, as that to which perception and consciousness belong, is lost partly during sleep and altogether at death. *Rūḥ* accompanies the body during life and departs at death. In this view, then, only the *nafs* can be subject to death, and the *rūḥ* remains alive.[42] Despite this kind of clarification, we must keep in mind that the most common view held by classical Islam and in general still underlying much of contemporary thought is that expressed earlier: Soul and spirit, *nafs* and *rūḥ*, are a *jism laṭīf*, a subtle body in some way inhabiting or infusing the material body, *badan*, and this substance, regardless of the degree of spirituality which one chooses to ascribe to it, is taken by God at death.[43]

The understanding of the material nature of the soul/spirit led many of the doctors of *kalām* to affirm that the resurrection of the body is to be understood as a corporeal resurrection only. That is, the soul will be part of the revivified body but not a separate spiritual substance in some way joined with it. Others in the Islamic community, of course, held different opinions. Some of the philosophers affirmed only a spiritual return; others such as al-Ghazālī held to the idea of a resurrection of both the material and the spiritual elements. Still others maintained that God alone knows the precise nature of that which is resurrected, a position which we will see is characteristic of much contemporary Muslim thought. For the majority of Muslims, however, the subtle body which is the *nafs* dies with the physical body [*badan*] and is resurrected with it at the final day. (As we have observed, this belief did not negate the general understanding that some part of the human person will remain alive and cognizant between the time of death and the resurrection, in some degree of pleasure or pain.)

Various questions concerning the nature of the resurrected body still remained even for those who understood it as essentially corporeal. Is it returned with or without its accidents or descriptive characteristics? If the former, can primary and secondary accidents be distinguished? Or in other words, will the body be brought back to life in exactly the same form it had while on this earth? As Ash'arī theology affirmed the theory of atomism, or continual creation and recreation, the question was naturally raised as to whether one essential self is raised up or rather a kind of accumulation of all the various selves. Again opinions differed, but in general the majority of Muslims understand that the permanence of one being underlies the succession of instantaneous creations. To the best of our knowledge that self is the self we know now on earth, and it will be raised again after death, after the great annihilation of the Hour signaling the return to life of all humanity.[44]

Divine Ordination: Issues of Justice and Mercy

The Islamic view of humanity in relation to the affairs of the afterlife must be investigated, then, in a variety of aspects. We have considered the constitution of man, both in its essence and from the perspective of its natural inclinations in light of God's expectations, as well as in relation to the dominant Islamic theme of human responsibility and accountability. That man is expected to do "right" and will be recompensed in accord with the degree of his success or failure in doing it is evident. As Islamic thinkers began to consider more closely the exact nature of those human responses which lead to reward or punishment in the hereafter, however, they raised a number of questions. The answers, as we shall see, often differed from one school of thought to another, although the responses given were always made in light of what we can understand about God and His omnipotence. Without going into lengthy analysis of issues with which *kalām* (speculative theology) dealt in very intricate fashion, let us consider some of the kinds of discussions held in the early Islamic community, the ramifications of which were far-reaching for the common understanding of who will be saved and damned on the day of resurrection.

As suggested earlier, a crucial question for the early community was whether or not human free will in any degree can be affirmed in light of divine will and power. The history of the Islamic controversy over the question of what has been called predestination, *taqdīr,* is detailed and complex. Even though some verses of the Qur'ān apparently suggest an understanding of human free will, the dominant picture is that the affairs of mankind, like all other matters, are completely under God's control. In the traditions this picture is even clearer, and one is hard put to find any *ḥadīths* supportive of human prerogative.[45] God's *qadar* or will is absolute, and His specific ordinances are sometimes said in the reports to be already inscribed in a heavenly tome. Theology struggled at length over the issue of *taqdīr*. Those who held to the necessity of human free will as a guarantee of divine justice were called Qadarīya, of whom the Mu'tazila were the best known exponents. The discussions in the early community were political as well as theological; the Ummayads, entrenched in power, not surprisingly supported the idea that events are predestined by God, while the Shī'a, who did not have political power, supported the Mu'tazilī opposition to that doctrine. The Mu'tazilī affirmation of human free will expressed a concern not only for testifying to God's justice, but also for avoiding the conclusion that He is in any way associated with acts of disobedience or *kufr*.

The "compromise" put forward by the school of al-Ash'arī is a rather complex piece of intellectual argumentation propounded in an attempt to safeguard the assurance of both divine omnipotence and human responsibility. This formula suggests that while God is the creator of human acts, man himself acquires or appropriates them, expressed by the term *kasb*. Human acts are predestined by God from all eternity; they are placed into the human heart in the course of time, making those who receive them fully responsible for them.

Another issue of crucial concern to early Islam was the understanding of the nature of good and bad deeds [*al-ṣāliḥāt* and *al-ma'ṣiyāt*].[46] The focal point of definition, based on references from the Qur'ān, is obedience [*ṭā'a*] or the lack of it. Failure to obey the divine prescriptions will be punished, just as obedience to them will be rewarded. On this most have agreed. Problems arose, however, in attempts to delineate precisely the content of *al-ṣāliḥāt* and *al-ma'ṣiyāt*, particularly the nature of disobedient deeds. Writers made the distinction between grave sins [*kabā'ir*] and lesser sins [*saghā'ir*], although they could not always agree how these were to be defined. The Muslim is certain that the one unpardonable sin, that for which the pain of the Fire is assured, is refusal to testify to the *tawḥīd* of God, called either *kufr* or *shirk*.[47] (It has been observed that this may have been almost the only point on which Muslim thinkers completely agreed.[48])

Since only grave sins are said to justify punishment to any extent in the

Fire—{If you avoid the major things [*kabā'ir*] that are forbidden to you, We shall grant remission of your evil deeds and give you entrance to a gate of honor} [S 4:31]—it was very important that some understanding be reached of what constituted this kind of offense. General consensus on this issue, however, was never attained, primarily because the Qur'ān is never absolutely explicit. The Prophet is said to have commented that the greatest sin is *shirk*, and after that comes the killing of one's child or treating parents in an inhuman way, followed by adultery or bearing false witness. Another tradition cites the Prophet as having enumerated several deadly sins, namely *shirk*, magic, murder, robbing orphans, usury, apostasy, and slander against faithful women.[49]

Along with the question of the definition of grave and lesser sins came the issue of how one's acts of obedience and disobedience will be measured at the day of resurrection. The great *mīzān* or balance will be the instrument by which the measure is taken at that day, although the Qur'ānic references to *mīzān* are less obviously to this particularly eschatological feature than to the entire system of balances by which the natural order is maintained. Contemporary Islamic exegesis of these verses emphasizes the coordination of justice in this world (the specific performance of acts of obedience that reflect the justice of God) with the measuring of human responsibility justly in the next. Classical theology was particularly concerned with balance as the specific measurement of one's actions, the good weighed against the bad. Obedience in the Ash'arī conception meant the accumulation of good deeds, discontinuous acts created by God and acquired by man. Thus in the eschatological manuals we find many stories of persons needing only one or two more good deeds to set the balance in their favor.

Kalām reached two opposing conclusions about the mixture of different kinds of deeds. For some, specifically the Khawārij and the Mu'tazila, the merit of an accumulation of good acts could be negated by even one grave sin. To commit a major sin, particularly *kufr* or *shirk*, is to deny faith and thus to destroy the positive effects of good works. The Ash'arīya disagreed, on the basis of such Qur'ān verses as S 99:7–8, which affirms that anyone who has done an atom's weight of good or evil shall see its results. No matter how numerous or serious one's sins, they said, whoever has an atom of faith will be taken from the Fire. Conversely, good actions will not automatically negate the ill effects of one's sins, for which punishment is merited. These two opinions represent quite different approaches. For the one, justice is an automatic process whereby good and bad are weighed equally and recompense is meted out in direct accord. For the other, that which came to be most representative of Islamic thought, the affair is finally God's decision. That of which we can be sure, said the Ash'arīya, is God's promise through His prophets that those who testify to the faith will sooner or later be rewarded.

Three elements came to be seen as bearing directly on the issue of the possible mitigation of the effects of sinful actions: God's mercy, human repentance, and intercession. The Islamic conception of God's compassion reflects an aspect of His power and authority more immediately than His love for humanity per se. He acts as He chooses; the Qur'ānic explication of God as merciful is in the context of His willing to be so. God is described not only as al-Raḥmān al-Raḥīm, the Merciful and Compassionate, but as the One Who forgives all sins except *shirk* (S 4:48, 110). This aspect of God as the forgiver of human waywardness is repeated throughout the Qur'ān. In the assurance that all who at the moment of death have faith [*īmān*] in their hearts will go eventually to the Garden, one finds clear expression of God's mercy as well as of the absolute importance of the act of faithful obedience.

The community generally agreed that the person of faith [*mu'min*] who has never committed a grave sin will go to the Garden, either immediately at death or after a sojourn of blissful existence during the *barzakh* period (see chapter two). Likewise anyone who rejects God's word [*kāfir*] was assigned by all the doctors of theology to eternal existence in the Fire. Some later traditions, however, extended God's mercy to these folk also, as we shall see. About two other categories of persons there was less agreement. One was the faithful sinner, or more precisely the sinning *mu'min*, and the other was one whose good and bad deeds balance evenly.

About the former there were several schools of opinion. The Khawārij said the sinning *mu'min* was eternally damned, the Murji'a felt that because every *mu'min* is saved so is the sinner, and the Mu'tazila relegated him to an intermediate position of *fisq* (literally depravity), indicating that if one in this position dies without repenting, he will be classed as a *kāfir* although punished less severely. The Ash'arīya rejected *fisq* as a category, maintaining only the possibility of *īmān* or *kufr*. God will be free to render judgment as He chooses, they said, but we know for certain that no *mu'min* will be eternally condemned to the Fire. The case of one whose good and bad deeds are equal received less attention in *kalām*. In the exegesis of S 7:46–50 what the verses call the companions of the heights [*aṣḥāb al-a'rāf*] are most often identified as persons of equal deeds, who remain in a kind of limbo until all others have entered the Garden. At that time, conclude most commentators, they will be washed in the River of Life and admitted to paradise.[50]

The Qur'ān makes frequent mention of repentance [*tawba*], referring both to the specific act of the sinner who repents of his action and to the turning of God toward one who offers his repentance, an acceptance of that response. S 4:18 clearly states that a last minute repentance made on one's deathbed is not efficacious and in fact earns one a severe punishment. Repentance, then, must be genuine. Because it is understood to entail a resolve not to repeat the same offense (and must not be offered merely out of ultimate terror), repentance must also come before one is about to die. As *kalām* came to accept God's power in obliterating the sins of those who have faith in Him (totally, according to the Ash'arīya, and with certain contingent forms of punishment in the opinion of some schools, such as the Māturīdīya), the obvious question was, To what extent is personal repentance necessary for one to be saved from the Fire? Islam in general recognized that *tawba* is obligatory for one who wrongs, but opinions again differed as to its absolute necessity for salvation. The Mu'tazila, who felt that God must accept the sincere *tawba* of the sinner, held to the necessity of repentance to free one from the intermediary position of *fisq*. The majority of the Sunnī community, however, felt that divine mercy and pardon are independent of human response, and that the only sin for which repentance is crucial for salvation is the ultimate major sin of *kufr* or *shirk*. Here again they relied absolutely on the assurance that if one is a *mu'min,* he will ultimately be afforded entrance to the Garden without condition.

Thus of the first two elements relating to the mitigation of sinful acts—divine mercy and human repentance—Islam placed far greater importance on the former, without which the latter would in any case be irrelevant. It is also important to recognize here, of course, that as significant as the stress on God's mercy itself was the absolute insistence on His freedom and omnipotent power to do as He chooses without reference to human action, as well as the confidence that His promise of final salvation for the *mu'min* will not be abrogated. A third and extremely important element also came to play in the hope for ultimate pardon: the issue of intercession, *shafā'a*. This possibility of intervention by an outside agent, as we shall see, has been a major theme in the eschatological expectations of the community at large and is detailed repeatedly in the stories accepted as part of the general descriptions of the events to take place at the day of resurrection.

The several forms of *shafā'a,* meaning "to intercede," "intercession," and "intercessor" occur twenty-nine times in the Qur'ān. On the whole, the notion of *shafā'a* in the Book is both general and clearly negative in regard to the last day: {Protect yourselves against a day when no soul will be able to recompense another in any way and no intercession will be accepted . . .} [S 2:48]; {Warn those who fear that they will be gathered to their Lord; there will be for them no friend and no intercessor aside from Him . . .} [S 6:51].[51] The basic argument of the Qur'ān is that God is sovereign in arranging the relationship between Himself and His creatures and that no human efforts at mediation can be valid and effective. Every individual is responsible for his or her own deeds and acts of faith, and will be called to full account for them. The Qur'ānic assertion of no intercession is intended to underline the fact that one has no hope that his wrongdoings will be ignored on the day of judgment and that there is no possibility that the "false gods" of the *mushrikūn* can intercede for him.[52]

Nonetheless certain passages of the Qur'ān have been interpreted as leaving room for the possibility of some kind of intercession. Specifically authorized with this function, aside from God Himself, are angels (S 53:26), true witnesses (S 43:86), and those who have made a covenant with God (S 19:87). Other verses, such as 20:107, 21:28, and 34:23, describe intercession for those who are acceptable. In the category of true witnesses room has been found for the inclusion of the Prophet Muḥammad as an intercessor for his community, although none of the twenty-nine occurrences of *shafā'a* refers to his name or person or specifically mentions the office of prophethood in this connection. God did call upon Muḥammad to ask forgiveness for living believers (S 47:19), and this has been taken by many to be the earthly precedent for intercession on the day of judgment.

Ḥadīth literature refers clearly to Muḥammad as intercessor for members of his community. Certain very popular traditions indicate a non-eschatological context, such as the story told by 'Ā'isha that the Prophet used to go occasionally to the cemetery to pray on behalf of the dead. In most cases, however, the intercession of Muḥammad has a specifically futuristic reference; in the later chapter on the events of the judgment we will detail some of the stories about the Prophet intervening on the day of resurrection for his community between the two soundings of the trumpet and at his pond [*ḥawd*].

This expansion of interpretation may well symbolize the transition from the earlier Qur'ānic stress on individual accountability to a recognition of the growing importance of communal affiliation and identity. For it is as a member of the *umma* of Islam that *kalām* as well as Muslim piety in general came to see that one could hope for the possibility of intercessory assistance on the day of resurrection.[53] Once again, the intercession possible is not generally understood to be for those classed as *mushrikūn* and *kāfirūn*, but for those who are in a condition of *īmān* even though they have committed transgressions. The issue of repentance arises again in this context; in general *tawba* has been seen to be a condition for intercession in both classical and contemporary Islamic interpretation.[54]

Critical to the legitimation of any understanding of intercession is the conviction that it can only be efficacious if carried out by and with divine permission. One of the most famous of the *ḥadīths* concerning this function is that in which Muḥammad is reported to have been offered by God the assurance that half of his community would automatically enter the Garden or else be given the privilege of intercession: the Prophet opted for the latter, symbolic of the general feeling that intercession would result in a more positive end for the Muslim *umma* as a whole.[55] Other *ḥadiths* also validate the notion that the *umma* will have very special privileges: "God told the Prophet, 'Cause your community to enter the Garden without judgment from the right gate'; The Prophet said, 'From my community 70,000 will enter without judgment.' "[56]

While some traditions attest to the fact that each prophet will have his own basin from which the members of his community will drink, *kalām* has generally held that intercession is primarily in the hands of the Prophet Muḥammad.[57] Al-Ghazālī in the *Iḥyā'*, however, affirms that if a group of believers is designated to go to the Fire, God will accept the intercession of all His prophets as well as of the truthful [*ṣiddiqūn*], the learned [*'ulamā'*], and the pious [*ṣāliḥūn*]. He also indicates that everyone who has good deeds to his credit can intercede with God for his friends and relatives.[58] Despite periodic attempts on the part of conservative orthodoxy to deny the efficacy of this kind of intervention,[59] the intercession of those considered to be part of the company of saints or friends of God [*awliyā'*] has played and continues to play a very important role in the lives of many Muslims.[60]

Contemporary Islamic thought in general is less concerned with the kinds of particulars debated by the early theologians and traditionists than with presenting a holistic picture of man's place and duty in God's overall plan for His creation. Modern theology places a heavy stress on the necessity of taking seriously the five constituent elements of *īmān:* faith in God, in His angels, in His messengers, in His books, and in the last day or day of judgment.[61] The last article is seen as man's ultimate end and goal, the guiding factor for his life.[62] Man's life is incomplete if considered from the perspective of this world only, where values are grounded in the transitory rather than the immutable and where the lack of accountability brings an inevitable slide into irresponsibility.[63] In the perspective of the relationship of this life to the next contemporary Muslim writers often find the role, function, and capabilities of humanity. As will be evident in the course of this study, there are some wide discrepancies in modern views of the various conditions of life after death and of the ways in which traditional material should be interpreted. In understanding man in light of these concerns of the hereafter, however, a number of elements are generally common to the modern perspective. They are neither unique to the overall Islamic understanding nor at odds with it, but stand out as peculiarly characteristic of present day thinking:

1. Man has a conscience and an inherent sense of justice but needs the awareness of the hereafter for the maintenance of high ethical standards. His conscience calls him to right action, but without constant sensitivity to the imminence of the day of judgment he easily falls into over-indulgence, which leads to injustice, a loss of ethical standards, and finally to corruption of the whole society. It is thus essential that man's participation in the world be by the principles of *dīn*, religion, and with the constant awareness of the reality of ultimate recompense.[64] For some the awakening of conscience and a sense of justice occur only as they become aware of the ultimate destiny and its relation to a life of vice or virtue. With a sense of the afterlife one sees the value of life in this world and experiences a pride in the possibilities for humankind.[65] All of this reasoning, of course, is in opposition to the humanistic perspective, which would credit man with the inherent ability to live a life of justice with no outside referents or standards.

2. Man is responsible and intellectually capable of understanding his responsibility. A purposeless existence for man is unimaginable. The Qur'ān has explained the importance of life after death and the necessity of faith in it in a manner which is acceptable to the intellect. This means that if one rejects the idea of living, it cannot be because of intellectual objections, but rather because man is fleeing from his own conscience and from the necessity of being responsible for his own actions, trying to cover the clear intellectual argument by ignoring or denying it.[66]

3. Man is essentially free, but he is not independent. In this argument one finds a kind of modern equivalent to classical discussions concerning the relationship of human freedom to the divine will. In discourses that often sound much like the reasonings of the ancient Mu'tazila, many contemporaries stress the basic freedom of man to make ethical decisions and to

choose a life of moral integrity. The value of the human being over the animal comes in his ability to free himself from slavery to his desires and sensual needs—those things characteristic of an animal-like existence—and to be liberated to those things that signify the higher life in awareness of God's commands. This is the human freedom worthy of the glory of God.[67] Despite this innate freedom of choice, however, it is an error to suppose that man is an independent creature fully capable of determining his own affairs. His status as vicegerent of God means that his use of the abilities and raw materials afforded him by God must be according to the plan and divine rules of conduct laid down for him. In most instances this seems to imply that a failure to recognize God's sovereignty in this way inevitably leads to defeat and destruction, a typically Qur'ānic point of view. Occasionally one finds reminiscences of earlier theological disputation in the insistence that past a certain point man simply cannot act outside of God's ordination. Man's freedom must be seen as falling within the compass of God's will.[68]

4. Man operates in his ethical life from inside the *umma* or community. As he is not independent from the divine will, neither is he independent from his fellows. The community of Islam is the only valid context from which individual Muslims can respond to the divine commands. One cannot be a Muslim outside of the *umma*; it is, in that understanding, the vehicle for or context of individual salvation. The Qur'ān is absolutely clear that no person is responsible for any other at the day of resurrection, but contemporary Islam is also extremely careful to underscore the importance of the collective life. All persons together are God's vicegerents, and in the common attempt to live according to the divine precepts each individual will find support and assistance. Thus in community, in the effective functioning of the social system, all persons are able to realize more fully the potential given them for movement towards lives of fuller ethical responsibility.[69]

5. Man is capable of continuing progress toward perfection.[70] This progress, carried on in the lower life, is immediately conditioned by faith in the last day and the possibility of eternal bliss in which perfection can be realized.[71] In this life man is tempted and tested; these temptations offer him immunization against further lack of awareness. He therefore learns to resist indulgence in the pleasures of the world and gradually through faith in the last day comes to the fuller realization of the purpose of life. Recompense will come both in this life and the next. God has breathed His spirit into man; He has raised him above the animals and given him nobility beyond anything else in His creation; in the fullness of the time to come human life will attain the perfection ordained for it.[72]

Chapter Two
From Death to Resurrection: Classical Islam

What happens to human beings after the process of death? It is possible that no single question has so engaged the imagination of mortals throughout the ages as has this one. The answers suggested have been various and many, comforting and frightening. In the case of Islam, because the Qur'ān is so explicit about the events of the eschaton and the particulars of the Garden and the Fire, little has remained to the imagination but the elaboration of detail in terms of eschatological expectations. However, if one thinks in terms of a continuous time sequence beginning with the death of the individual, there remains that period between death and the coming of the Hour for which Muslims from the earliest times have sought some kind of explanation.

Although little in the Qur'ān can be interpreted as descriptive of the state of the deceased before the resurrection and judgment, a few references are generally cited as bearing on overall questions of life and death. As has been mentioned above, several verses attest to God's knowledge of the hour of every person's death: we all live for a stated time [*ajal musammá*].[1] Two references also state that God causes us to die twice and to live twice [S 2:28; 40:11]. Commentators have proposed many possibilities for an interpretation of these lives and deaths, the most common being that the first death is before life in this world (i.e. before we are first born we are actually dead), the first life is given to us at the time of birth into earthly existence, the second death terminates life on earth, and the second birth is our revival on the day of resurrection. Some have understood the second life as referring to the revival in the grave, at which time the individual receives the first recompense for deeds and misdeeds done on earth.[2] All of this, however, still leaves untouched the question of the human condition between death and resurrection, that time/space often referred to as the *barzakh*.

Islamic tradition, as we shall see, has gone into great detail in describing the angel of death and the process by which death actually takes place. In the Qur'ān, however, the references to this process are actually very brief; in S 56:82 we are told that the soul of the dying person comes up to his throat, and in S 6:93 death is described as a kind of flooding-in process [*ghamarāt al-maut*] at which time angels stretch forth their hands and ask that the souls be given over to them. Exactly what happens after that the Qur'ān does not say, although the traditions describe the succeeding events elaborately. Again, the only clue in the Qur'ān as to whether or not the dead have any degree of consciousness is the indication in S 35:22 that the living and the dead are not alike, and that while God can accord hearing to whomever He wills, the living cannot make those in the graves hear them.[3] This distinction is supported by the commentary on the verses mentioning the *barzakh*, which stress the absolute separation between this world and the realm of the dead. Having passed into that realm, one can never return, either to right past wrongs or to communicate with the living.

It is apparent even to the casual reader of the Qur'ān that one of its most consistent emphases is the inerrant judgment of deeds and subsequent reward or punishment to come on the day of resurrection. The question of whether or not any punishment precedes that of the Hour, however, has long been debated. Consistent with the sketchiness of all of its commentary on the pre-eschatological period, the Qur'ān provides only brief and oblique references to what has been interpreted as the punishment of the grave. We do know that certain individuals, such as those martyred in the cause of Islam, are indeed living and not dead [S 2:154, 3:169], and that God will provide for them and they will rejoice in His bounty and blessing [S 22:58–59, 3:170–71]. It also seems that some persons are already in the Fire, although it is not certain whether such references are to past, present, or future punishment [S 40:46–49, 71:25]. Two verses speak of angels smiting the faces and backs of the *kāfirs* upon taking their souls at death, warning of the punishment of the Fire [S 8:50; 46:27]. Even contemporary Qur'ān commentators have taken this as a promise of literal punishment for those who deserve it, and many see in these verses proof-texts for the visitation of the questioning angels, of whom we shall speak shortly.[4]

Based on the evidence of the Qur'ān, then, it is difficult to say much with certainty about the period between death and resurrection, and next to impossible to construct anything like a coherent sequence of events. It is also true that the early centuries of Islam offered only limited speculation concerning this period and in fact felt little inclination to think of it as a period at all, as indicated by the general understanding expressed in the *ḥadīths* that this time will pass like the wink of an eye. Gradually, however, certain themes became more clearly articulated and details added, so that in the later manuals of eschatology one can find a great many particulars which, if strung together, provide a fascinating narrative of the sojourn of the individual after physical death.

This chapter will attempt an ordering of the various events suggested in these manuals and other materials so as to provide a general sequence of those things said to happen to the individual soul or spirit between death and the coming of the Hour.[5] By doing this, of course, one by necessity sacrifices another kind of chronology, that being the relative order in which Islamic theologians have dealt with certain questions as reflective of specific concerns.

The doctors of theology or *mutakallimūn* have generally been interested not in determining a sequence of events after death, but rather in using particular references to the *barzakh* state to illustrate specific points about the nature of God. Thus the creeds generally representative of orthodox Islam[6] make consistent mention of only two occurrences: the questioning of the angels Munkar and Nakīr, and the punishments of the grave [*'adhāb al-qabr*].[7] The extremely important concern for punishment in the context of theological discussion is part of the larger question of God's divine justice. As the details and particulars of the forms of this punishment came to be spelled out more clearly in the traditional materials, however, the general picture of events in the *barzakh* period was expanded, amplified, and enriched.

Constructing an outline of events believed to take place after the death of an individual, as these came increasingly to be part of the common belief of succeeding generations of Muslims, is a difficult and often frustrating task. The canonical collections of *ḥadīth* materials contain various references, but these are generally not in sequential order. Probably the easiest way to get an overview of what we are calling the narrative from death to the coming of the eschaton is to consider the ways in which the events have been ordered in the medieval eschatological manuals. These manuals represent a collation and ordering of the many traditions that came into circulation concerning life after death and resurrection. While descriptive in effect, their function as a whole was didactic and homiletic, implementing the divine injunction to command the good and prohibit the evil [*al-amr bi'l-ma'ruf wa-nahy 'an al-munkar*]. In this sense they both support the theological presuppositions of the *mutakallimūn* and provide a wealth of anecdotal material intended to instruct the faithful by means of stories and descriptions which fully explicate the ramifications of following or not following God's plan for humankind.

Of the various works that might be considered in this context, we have drawn much of the material for this section from five sources that have been particularly popular and which treat the general themes drawn in relation to this period: Abū Ḥāmid al-Ghazālī's *al-Durra al-fākhira* (eleventh century[8]); Ibn Qayyim al-Jawzīya's *Kitāb al-rūḥ* (fourteenth century, generally considered one of the most authoritative sources of orthodox views on the life of the spirit after the death of the body[9]); Jalāl al-Dīn Suyūṭī's *Bushrá al-ka'īb bi-liqā'i al-ḥabīb* (fifteenth century); Abū Layth al-Samarqandī's *Kitāb al-ḥaqā'iq wa'l-daqā'iq* (seventeenth century[10]); and the anonymous *Kitāb aḥwāl al-qiyāma*.[11] We have cited relevant *ḥadīths* from the traditional collections in support of general points; the reports concerning life after death in Islam are so numerous that only a sampling can be considered in an overview of this kind. The following narrative, while recognizing that there are somewhat different versions of most of the individual elements in the sequence, is an attempt to tell the story as it is most commonly relayed and in the order that is most generally accepted.

Often the manuals treat first the question of the nature of humankind in relation to the divine and the general significance of the creation. When they turn to issues concerning the fate of the individual after death, the first consideration is often of the angel of death. Usually called by the name 'Izrā'īl, this angel is pictured as immense and fearsome to behold. The following description from 'Abd al-Waḥḥāb Sha'rānī (sixteenth century) is typical of the various portraits one finds: He has a thousand wings, stretching from the heavens to the earth, from the farthest point of the east to the farthest point of the west, holding within his hands the entire earth with its mountains, plains, and jungles. For the faithful his wings spread wide in reception; for the disobedient they become like pincers. One should not be surprised to discover that the angel of death appears in different forms to different people, in his most terrible visage to the *kāfirūn*.[12]

The *Kitab aḥwāl al-qiyāma* (pp. 11–13) offers a detailed account of the creation of death and its relation to 'Izrā'īl. Authority and power over death are afforded to the angel, although ultimate responsibility for it belongs to God, its Creator. When God created death, He ordered the other angels to stand back and look at it. So awesome was the sight when death spread its wings and flew, that the angels fell into a swoon for a thousand years. Upon awakening, they assured God that He had created the mightiest thing of all creation, to which He replied, "I have created it and I am greater than it, and all creation will taste of it!" (p. 11). Recognizing that it must submit to 'Izrā'īl, death, in a wonderfully dramatic scene, for one last time cried out its own power:

> I am death who separates all loved ones! I am death who separates man and woman, husband and wife! I am death who separates daughters from mothers! I am death who separates sons from fathers! I am death who separates brother from his brother! I am death who subdues the power of the sons of Adam. I am death who inhabits the graves . . . . Not a creature will remain who does not taste me. . . . [13]

At the actual moment of the cessation of individual life, both death and the angel 'Izrā'īl appear to the one whose soul is to be taken. In fact, in many of the descriptions there is a blurring of identity between the angel and death personified. The dying person sees an awesome form approaching him, and he asks, "Who are you?" to which the answer is given, "I am (the angel of) death, who makes your children orphans and your wife a widow. . . ." No matter which direction the poor afflicted one turns, he sees death confronting him, telling him that his soul will be taken, for his term is up. The image is a grim one, in which man can find no escape from the inevitability of death. No compromise can be made, for God's decree is preordained and final.

It is clear in these eschatological materials that the angel of death himself, as God's instrument, has no responsibility for determining the moment of individual death. All is recorded in the heavenly register, and 'Izrā'īl only knows the time for taking a soul when God gives him a clear and specific sign. The angel who is responsible for recording the deeds of individuals informs the angel of death of the proper moment; the names of the blessed have lines of white light around them, while those of the wretched are surrounded by black lines. When exactly forty days of a person's life are left, say many reports, a leaf on which is written the name of the soul who is to die falls from the tree located beneath the Throne of God. By that sign 'Izrā'īl knows that the time of death has come.[14] A popular narrative records that whenever an individual is born, God instructs the angel entrusted to him to put into the semen in the mother's womb a speck of the soil of the territory in which he is destined to die; various stories are related about individuals apparently inexplicably desiring to go to one place or another, only to die upon arrival.

The question of the relationship of *nafs* and *rūḥ*, soul and spirit, is a complex and difficult one in Islamic usage.[15] Because the Qur'ān does not explicitly use the term *rūḥ* to refer to the spiritual aspect of human beings and because S 39:42 in comparing sleep and death talks about God's keeping the *anfus* of those who die, some writers have chosen to use the term *nafs* when describing what the angel of death is responsible for removing from the body. Others, however, explicitly suggest that the *rūḥ* is taken and the *nafs* remains with the body. To complicate the issue further, one finds in many collections of narratives such interchanging of usage that it is impossible to attempt to sort out a clear distinction between spirit and soul in this context. In the following discussion we will use the words spirit and soul reflecting the usages of *rūḥ* and *nafs* in the Arabic texts, ignoring what may appear as inconsistencies in these usages and noting that despite the Qur'ānic reference to *nafs*, the majority of commentators and traditionalists seem to prefer to speak of that which remains after death as spirit.

In describing the circumstances of death, several accounts suggest that the dying person is visited by four angels, who announce to him that they have been entrusted respectively with his provisions, his drink, his breath, and his term of life, and that these are all now expired. Then other angels called noble scribes come to his left and right. The following account from the *Kitāb aḥwāl al-qiyāma* describes the encounter of the soul with these scribes:

> The one on the right says, Peace be upon you. I am the angel entrusted with your good works. He takes out a white piece of paper, spreads it open and says, Look at your deeds. And at that he is joyful. And the angel on the left says, I am entrusted with your evil deeds. He takes out a piece of black paper and spreads it out, saying, Look! And at that the sweat pours from him and he looks right and left in fear of reading the page.[16]

The actual process of removal of the spirit/soul from the body has been greatly elaborated in some of the eschatological manuals. Al-Ghazālī, for example, in *al-Durra al-fākhira* (using both *nafs* and *rūḥ*) describes it thus:

> And when [one's] destiny approaches, that is, his earthly death, then four angels descend to him: the angel who pulls the soul from his right foot, the angel who pulls it from the left foot, the angel who pulls it from his right hand, and the angel who pulls it from his left hand. Some of the circumstances of the Malakūtī world may be unveiled to the dying person before he expires so that he sees those angels, not the way they actually appear in their own world, but according

> to the extent of his understanding. If his tongue is unhampered he may tell about their existence or the existence of others like him. . . . Then he is silent so that his tongue is tied, while they pull the soul from the tips of his fingers. The good soul slips out like the jetting of water from a waterskin, but the profligate's spirit squeaks out like a skewer from wet wool. (MS pp. 4–5)

In the *Kitāb al-ḥaqā'iq wa'l-daqā'iq* we find the narrative describing the various ploys man uses to avoid giving up his spirit to the angel of death. When 'Izrā'īl tries to take it from the mouth, the reluctant individual protests that only the *basmallah* (invocation of God's name) comes from his mouth; he proceeds to deter the angel from removing the spirit from other parts of his body by saying that God gave alms and smote unbelievers through his hand, his foot led him to the prayers and to visit the sick, his ear enabled him to hear the Qur'ān recitation, and his eye showed him the sacred books. Only when God orders the angel to write His name on the palm of the faithful one does the spirit depart his body.[17] The soul or spirit itself is described in the *Durra* as the size of a bee, but with human characteristics. When it finally streams out from the body, whatever its avenue of departure, it shudders like quicksilver in the hand of the angel (MS p. 7).

That death is considered a difficult and painful experience is quite apparent in Islamic tradition. Various statements offer assurance for the pious and faithful that things will go easily, as al-Ghazālī describes above, but on the whole the period from the first realization of impending death to the time when the departed spirit sees its body being washed and prepared for burial[18] is understood to be an agonizing one. One very famous report relates a conversation taking place between the prophet and his wife 'Ā'isha after she realizes that someday he, too, will have to depart this life. The Prophet describes for her the extreme difficulties encountered by the dying person in the process of leaving his home with his children crying for him, being put into the grave and covered with dirt, watching in the form of a disembodied spirit the washers preparing him for burial—'O washer, by God I swear to you, take off my clothes gently, for I have gone out from the devastating power of the angel of death''—having his body, which is suffering from the removal of the spirit, washed with water too hot or too cold, and in general agonizing over separation from his loved ones: "By God, O washer, do not make the winding around me tight, so that I can yet see the faces of my people and my children and my relatives; this is the last time I can look at them, for today I will be separated from them and will not see them until the Day of Resurrection. . . ."[19]

One of the particular trials of this sequence occurs when Satan comes to tempt the dying person to give up his faith. This is a popular subject for the manuals and often forms the matter of a chapter or sub-section. Again we see underscored the feeling of desolution and loneliness of the dying person, making him a prime target for a tempter. The person in this condition is generally described as suffering from an intense thirst and burning of the liver. Satan, not surprisingly, comes to the left side of the head and offers the agonized person a cup of cold water. The faithful believer cries out, "Give me some water!" not seeing who is offering it, to which Satan replies, "Say: The Prophet lied." As is the case in many such references in the eschatological literature, however, any real choice of response is only apparent. One already destined for the Fire succumbs to the temptation and drinks of the satanic water; the true *mu'min* refuses and, as the *Kitāb aḥwāl al-qiyāma* says, "ponders his future."[20] Al-Ghazālī offers a somewhat different version of this temptation in the *Durra* (MS pp. 8–9). He indicates that Iblīs may send one of his servants to the dying person, appearing in the image of a beloved member of his family. This relative will then tempt him to die as a Jew, "for it is the religion of the Messiah." Again, of course, God turns away all for whom He wills deviation, and to the faithful He sends Gabriel to drive off the demons. These fortunate souls actually smile with joy at the moment of death, secure in the knowledge that they are dying in the religion of the pious monotheists [*al-milla al-ḥanīfiya*] and the law of Muḥammad.

> When you look at the dying person and his mouth waters, his lips contract, his face turns black and his eyes become bluish, then know that he is miserable. The reality of his wretchedness in the hereafter has been unveiled to him. And when you see the dying person and his mouth is hollow as if he were laughing, his face beaming, his eyes cast down, then know that he has been told the good news of the joy that will come to him in the hereafter; the reality of his blessedness has been revealed to him. (MS pp. 10–11)

The theme of prefiguration of joys and torments is repeated in a variety of ways as one follows the sequence of death and after-death events, suggested already by the visit of the above-mentioned angels who record one's good and bad deeds. Many reports relate a welcome given by the grave to the one who has just died, and it is obvious that the form of this greeting is determined by the relative virtue of the deceased. In some instances the grave greets the faithful by promising an expansion of vision and a glimpse of the gates of the Garden. Far more narratives, however, describe the agony to be endured by the faithless, and the grave is said to warn him that it is a place of darkness, isolation, and loneliness, full of scorpions, snakes, and other such unpleasantnesses.[21] Descriptively this kind of imagery undoubtedly reflects the influence of pre-Islamic conceptions of the grave; didactically it becomes one of the series of instances whose elaborations are intended to warn the hearer about the results of a faithless and impious existence. One of the most frequently quoted narratives is cited in the *Durra* in this version:

> When the dead person is put into his grave and the earth is poured on him, the grave calls to him, "You used to enjoy yourself on my surface, but today you will grieve in my interior; you used to eat all kinds of delicacies on my surface, but today the worms will eat you while you are inside me."[22]

The *Kitāb aḥwāl al-qiyāma* (pp. 24–25) clearly develops this theme as a warning to the living: if they revel in the luxuries of life, they will experience quite the opposite in the grave. One must at all times be aware of both human finitude and the potential loneliness of the tomb; the sure way to elude this relentless retribution is the performance of specific deeds. One avoids the grave as the abode of isolation, darkness, earth, vipers, and the questioning of the angels by the respective duties of Qur'ān recitation, nightly prayer, right actions, saying the *basmallah* and the *shahāda* testifying to the oneness of God and to His Messenger Muḥammad.

Another way in which the soul immediately tastes the fruits of its religious duty or *'ibāda* is illustrated in the journey on which it is said to be taken by attending angels soon after death. Obviously based on the archetypical *mi'rāj* journey of the prophet Muḥammad, this trip is included in most accounts of afterdeath events, although the order of its occurrence differs from one commentary to another.[23] The most commonly cited details are included in the following composite narrative.

The soul of the faithful *mu'min*, as we have seen, slips quickly and easily from the body.[24] Angels (sometimes mentioned as two or four) clad in white with faces radiant as sunlight come carrying from the storehouses of the Garden winding-clothes and embalming fluid like sweet musk in which they envelope the newly-emerged soul.[25] Then they ascend with it up through the seven layers of the heavens, passing by previous communities "like swarms of locusts scattered about."[26] In some accounts Jibrīl is the specific guide for the ascending soul. At each successive heaven he knocks at the door, and when asked "Who are you?" replies with praises for the soul accompanying him. Each gate is opened, and they proceed until they reach the majestic pavilions and the Sidrat al-Muntahá,[27] signaling nearness to God Himself. The last stage of the journey is described by al-Ghazālī in this dramatic fashion:

. . . [Then] they pass respectively through oceans of fire, light, darkness, water, ice and hail. The length of each of these oceans is one thousand years. Then they penetrate the coverings affixed to the Throne of Mercy. There are eighty thousand pavilions of the Throne, each pavilion having eighty thousand balconies and each balcony having a moon radiant upon God, glorifying Him and venerating Him.[28]

Whether or not the ascending soul actually enters the presence of God seems a moot point. Some accounts suggest that it reaches the heaven where God Himself is to be found [*al-samā' al-latī fīhā Allāh*][29] and that God communicates the temporary fate of the soul to the accompanying angels, saying "Write his name in the uppermost heaven [*'iliyīn*] and return him to the earth,"[30] or "Return [the spirit] to his body, that it may see what will happen to his body."[31] Only the *Durra* indicates that God will actually speak to the deceased. There is a slight suggestion of playfulness in the narrative here, characteristic of many of the accounts in this work:

Then the Glorious One says, "Let him approach. Truly you are an excellent servant, O My servant." He stops him in front of Him, embarrassing him with some rebuke and reproof until the soul thinks that he is doomed. Then He pardons him, may He be glorified and exalted.[32]

Less frequently detailed is the parallel attempt of the unworthy soul to make this same ascent. In al-Ghazālī's account (*Durra*, MS pp. 17–18) 'Izrā'īl delivers the "evil soul of noxious body" to the guardians of hell, who wrap it in a hair shirt. The angel responsible for these guardians is Daqyā'īl, who attempts to lead the soul upward as did Jibrīl. But the gates of heaven are not opened to them (cf. S 7:40) and Daqyā'īl flings the soul from his hands. All of these events, whether involving the righteous or unrighteous, happen so quickly that when the soul is returned to the body, the washers are still busy taking care of the corpse.

The manuals pass over rather lightly the specifics of the process by which the soul is reunited with the body in the grave after this journey (or unsuccessful attempt), although they commonly attest to the belief that there is a joining of the spiritual and physical at this point.[33] The angels are said to place the good spirit in the center of the casket; apparently it is not yet joined to the body. From this position the deceased is able to see his relatives and friends grieving over him, although he of course cannot communicate with them. (There is a suggestion here that the departed has a very clear picture of who laments his passing and who does not!) After the funeral procession to the grave site, when the coffin it put into the earth, God commands the spirit to return to its body. As the *Kitāb aḥwāl al-qiyāma* states, there is no unanimity in these reports. Some say God puts the spirit into the body for the questioning of the grave, others that the spirit is questioned without the body, and others that the spirit somehow remains between its body and the winding-clothes.[34]

The events generally understood to come next in the after-death sequence are connected with the appearance of the interrogating angels. Attested to by the creeds and included in one or several narratives in all the collections of eschatological materials, these events are related according to a number of different narratives, and their recitation is sometimes confusing and even contradictory. Their frequent mention, however, suggests that on the level of popular piety a majority of Muslims is convinced of the validity of this cluster of events.

From the perspective of Islamic theology, the questioning in the grave is directly related to the issue of justice as an attribute of the divine. Both are inseparable from the whole issue of the punishment of the tomb, to which we will turn shortly. The sequence of events is often presented in one order in one collection of narratives and in a different order in another, so that one senses an inherent contradiction between the idea of questioning (in which presumably the deceased has the opportunity of determining his state in the grave by producing the correct responses) and the presentation of records by the visiting angels mentioned above (which would, of course, suggest that since the outcome has already been determined, such questioning is quite unnecessary). On one level there is clear justification for explaining such apparent contradictions as due merely to the layering of different materials from various sources. In a more profound sense, however, the entire eschatological study is constructed in such a way that one sees a variety of instances in which forms of reckoning and judgment are described didactically as means of affirming again that the opportunity for determining one's future state is in this life alone.[35]

The Qur'ān itself several times suggests, although certainly not in detail, the idea of some kind of punishment in the grave.[36] From this, and most probably borrowing from earlier Semitic traditions, generations of faithful believers developed the theory of two angels appearing to the deceased to ask him a series of specific questions concerning the content of his faith. Sometimes they are identified by the names Munkar and Nakīr, appellations which are non-Qur'ānic and appear rarely in the canonical traditions.[37] Their descriptions vary slightly from one account to another, but in general they are understood to be fearsome to behold, black in appearance with green eyes, having voices like thunder and eyes like lightening, and with long fangs rending the ground. It should be noted that some narratives omit these terrible details entirely, while others indicate that they appear in such a frightful image only to those who are destined for the Fire. This suggests again, of course, the logical inconsistency of their need to question one whose fate is already determined. The results of this questioning are not in themselves determinative of one's final state of bliss or punishment (which will be decided at the eschaton) but rather of one's intermediate condition while awaiting the day of resurrection. In this sense it can be seen as a preliminary judgment that both prefigures and predicts the final one.

There is some variation also in the suggestions of what questions the angels will ask of the deceased in the grave. The general version indicates that upon entering the grave, they order the dead person to sit up[38] and then ask him who or what is his Lord, his *dīn*, and his prophet. The correct answers, which the virtuous know immediately, are God, Islam, and Muḥammad. Some versions suggest other questions such as, Who is your religious leader [*imām*]?[39] What is this man who was sent to you and among you? and What knowledge do you have?[40] When the results of the questioning are in, the angels do one of several things. If the responses are correct, they open a window in the top of the grave (and/or a door to the right of the deceased) through which he can gaze at the Garden and feel sweet breezes wafting in. In some renditions the angels return with the spirit to the heavens, placing it in one of the lamps attached to the Throne.[41] Many of the collections include here a series of narratives about God's mercy and forgiveness. Most omit detail about the fate of the unfortunate, although they make occasional reference to a parallel door being opened to the Fire or frequently to the beating of the unfortunate with iron rods.

At this point in the general narrative a most interesting event occurs, seen as particularly so by those who have some familiarity with traditional Zoroastrian conceptions of the immediate after-death happenings. This is the visitation of a person described as having a beautiful face, lovely clothing, and (sometimes) a sweet fragrance, or as having an ugly countenance and exuding a noxious odor. Upon being asked to identify himself—"Who are you? I have never seen anyone more beautiful/ugly than you"—the person says either "I am your good deeds" or "I am your abominable deeds."[42] In Suyūṭī's version of this confrontation (*Bushrá,* p. 15) the person of beautiful countenance says to his fortunate progenitor, "Rejoice in that which gives you pleasure. This is your day which you have been provided." The deceased then responds, "Lord resurrect me now . . . so that I might return to my people."

This entire series of events, from the questioning in the grave to the intermediate rewards and punishments through the visit of one's good/bad deeds, is dealt with by al-Ghazālī in the *Durra* in predictably more complex fashion. He describes four categories of persons to whom the angels and the personification of deeds come, suggesting a somewhat different scenario in each instance. It should be mentioned that in his conceptualization another figure appears in the narrative, the angel Rūmān. The *Kitab aḥwāl al-qiyāma* (Chap. 15) also describes the visit of Rūmān, even saying that he arrives before Munkar and Nakīr, but gives this information in such a way as to suggest that it is a tradition not integral to the most commonly accepted sequence of events. In the *Durra* one reads that when the Prophet was asked, What is the first thing a person encounters when put into the tomb?, he replied that it is Rūmān, roaming about the graves (MS pp. 22–23). Described as having a face shining like the sun, he instructs the deceased to write down the good and evil deeds that he or she has done. Here we have yet another attempt to establish the credibility (or lack thereof) of each individual, or in other words to reaffirm in dramatic fashion the direct link between this-worldly responsibilities and ultimate recompense. The dead protests that he has no pen, ink, or paper, for which the angel orders him to substitute his own finger, saliva, and shroud. In a somewhat arbitrary attempt to ground this narrative in a Qur'ānic base, the tradition concludes with the deceased sealing the record and hanging it onto his neck until the day of resurrection.[43]

Returning to al-Ghazālī's four categories of deceased, we find that he deals first with those obviously considered the best in performance of *dīn*, referred to one time as the *'ulamā'*. The questioning angels according to this rendition are so fearsome that the soul leaps in fright back into the nostrils of the corpse (suggesting incidently a direct means by which the soul and body are resuscitated for the questioning). "Life is revived in his breast, and he then has a form such as he had at the time when the death agony came. He cannot move although he hears and sees." p. 23). The angels are rough and severe in their questioning, asking who or what is one's Lord, *dīn*, prophet, and prayer direction [*qibla*]. It is already understood by virtue of this category, of course, that the answers will be correct, but lest there be any question, al-Ghazālī insists (MS p. 24) that "God determines a sure and right response for those for whom He assures success . . ." (suggesting the classic difficulty of reconciling human actions and God's determinism in the context of a just judgment). The angels make the appropriate apertures in the grave for the temporary enjoyment of the successful respondent, and his good deeds in the form of the loveliest of creatures come to chat with him and put him at ease.

Al-Ghazālī's next category of those to be questioned is composed of people who did good works while on earth but were not sufficiently advanced to share in the secrets of the Malakūt.[44] Here, however, the personification of deeds enters before the angels and is described as having the best of forms with pleasant perfume and attractive clothing, suggesting a somewhat more materialistic orientation than was the case with the deeds of the *'ulamā'*. Then this congenial figure warns the deceased about the impending visit of Munkar and Nakīr, telling him not to be afraid. In a rather surprising development the personification of deeds actually instructs the soul in its own defense.[45] (Al-Ghazālī is obviously not oblivious to the contradiction suggested here, but rather includes this tradition as another way of underlining the consistent infusion of God's mercy into the rather sterile workings of mechanical justice.) When the angels enter the grave, the deceased is ready with his answers: God is my Lord, Muḥammad my Prophet, the Qur'ān my guide, Islam my *dīn*, the Ka'ba my *qibla*, and Abraham my father and his community my community (MS p. 25).

Al-Ghazālī then describes how the angels open a door on the left side of the dead person, showing him the terrors of the Fire. Again we see the suggestion that persons of this category, unlike the *'ulam*ā', are not automatically granted a reward for the good deeds they have done. Gazing at the serpents and scorpions and chains and boiling water and the Tree of Zaqqūm, the poor soul is quite naturally distraught. But have no fear, say the angels; that misfortune is not for you, for "God has exchanged your place in the Fire for a place in the Garden." Final disposition remains ultimately in the hands of God.

The third group described is those whose responses are obscure. This category includes the ones who cannot profess the Lordship of God or Islam as their *dīn* or the Qur'ān as their guide, and so on, because of temptations at death, insincerity, or waywardness. These persons suffer some kind of intermediate punishment such as beating or having their tombs set ablaze. In some cases the deeds are personified not as individuals but as dogs or pigs who then function as agents of punishment (MS p. 26). There is no indication in these instances that the specific judgment implicit is a prefiguration of one's final destiny.

The last and lowest category is the profligates. These persons do not merely find it difficult to answer the questions, as is true of the third group, but they simply do not know the answers. Their punishment takes a variety of forms, usually a series of beatings followed by the personification of their deeds in the shape of an animal particularly loathsome to them. Often the recompense is seen to be connected with a single misdemeanor rather than indicating the general outcome of a life of error:

> The story is told that someone who had died was seen in a dream and was asked, "How are you?" He replied, "I prayed one day without performing the ablutions, so God put a wolf in charge of me to frighten me in my grave. My situation with it is a most terrible one!" (MS p. 28)

What al-Ghazālī attempts in categorizing people in this kind of four-fold division is to suggest somewhat stylistically the obvious fact that human acts of omission and commission are infinitely diverse. That all persons are held accountable is clear; that there is some kind of ultimate division into the saved and the damned is also in the Qur'ānic message. But for al-Ghazālī, as for many other Islamic theologians, it is too simple merely to conclude that there will be a black and white division into those who are punished in this intermediate period in the grave and those who are not. He therefore suggests that with few exceptions each individual will undergo some kind of torment, slight or heavy, dependent upon the particular configuration of his or her *dīn* while on earth. (It has already been noted, but is worth repeating, that to take these descriptions too seriously as actual predictions of in-the-grave or eschatological events is to miss the point; they seem most clearly to be set forth as warnings and reminders to the living of the necessity of seeing their daily acts in an eternal framework.)

Many descriptions of the aftermath of the questioning of the grave portray the torments vividly and frighteningly. One commonly repeated report, for example, says that the camel of the Prophet was afraid while going through a graveyard at hearing, as only animals can, the shrieks of the damned suffering the torments of the grave.[46] Another suggests that the heat of the Fire is experienced in the grave itself: "The Prophet was walking with his friends by a graveyard when he realized that two people buried there were being tortured. So they cut off shoots from a tree and placed one on each grave to cool them off."[47]

As Al-Ghazālī suggested that there are many different shades of chastisement, so in another form the community came to accept that what is punishment for one individual might in fact be pleasure for another. In a very famous story 'Ā'isha tells the Prophet of her distress at hearing him describe how even the believer must undergo the questioning and the pressure of the tomb, to which the Prophet replies:

> O 'Ā'isha, the voice of Munkar and Nakīr in the hearing of the believer are like antimony in the eye and the pressure of the tomb to the believer is like the compassionate mother whose son complains to her of a headache and she strokes his head gently. But O 'Ā'isha, woe to those who doubt God—how they will be squeezed in their graves like the pressure of a boulder on an egg.[48]

Here we see the attempt to make palatable what orthodoxy came to accept as a fact, that the faithful and faithless alike will suffer the pressure [*ḍaght*] of the tomb, although only the *kāfir* also must undergo the *'ādhāb* or more strenuous forms of punishment. As is clear in this *ḥadīth,* the assumption that even the *mu'min* must undergo expiation for whatever small sins he has committed was soon balanced in the traditions by a more flexible interpretation and by an understanding of more positive forms of recompense granted to the faithful and just.

The earliest conceptions gave no suggestion of pleasures in the tomb; their concern was the questioning and subsequent punishment, the reality of which all Sunnī schools affirmed on the basis of numerous *ṣaḥīḥ* traditions. This emphasis was directly related to the understanding of the Qur'ānic verses discussing the two lives and the two deaths. As was mentioned above, many commentators interpreted the second life as that in the tomb and the second death as that coming after the brief period of reawakening to undergo the questioning and the punishment. The martyrs, on Qur'ānic assurance, go directly to the Garden and are thus not questioned or punished at all. As time passed, this category was enlarged to include others such as prophets and certain of the faithful (corresponding, it would seem, to al-Ghazālī's class of *'ulamā'*). On the whole it was felt that the period from the coming of the angels to the end of the punishment would be brief, some forty days for the *kāfir* or *mushrik* to only seven or eight for the *mu'min* who had committed a few sinful acts.[49] One of the first modifications of this reading, probably developing from outside influences, was an understanding that the just will enjoy in the union of the body and soul the reward of various pleasures in the tomb, such as having a window opened to paradise through which sweet breezes can waft, having the tomb greatly enlarged and filled with light, and the like.[50]

Most generally, because the Qur'ān has little to say about the period between death and resurrection, many scholars have looked for extra-Islamic influences to explain the rather elaborate mythology that grew up describing events to take place in the grave. No doubt some of these conceptions were holdovers from the beliefs of pre-Islamic Arabia, and others were brought into the Muslim community as it expanded in the first several centuries. Whether new or ancient, however, these ideas met with acceptance in popular Islam, and once part of the fabric of common belief they had to be dealt with by the theologians and if possible reconciled to Qur'ānic doctrine. As it developed in terms of a theological science, the understanding of what happens in the grave became known as *aḥwāl al-qubūr.* The specific treatment of the punishment in the tomb is called *'ādhāb al-qabr* and *fiṭn al-qabr.*

Many in the history of Islamic thought, of course, have denied any possbility of resuscitation of the body in the grave, its union with the soul, and the subsequent events described above. The idea of punishment in the tomb was generally refuted by the Mu'tazila[51] on the basis of such rational arguments as the following: one can see by looking at a corpse that it neither revives nor suffers; it is obvious that bodies are not eaten by lions or burned or subjected to other of the torments often suggested; no one has ever heard the dead reply to any such interrogation as that indicated in the narratives about Munkar and Nakīr. For such groups as the Ikhwān, al-Ṣafā', the vast majority of the philosophers, many Shī'a and others, the whole idea of punishment in the tomb is unacceptable, for it is predicated on the notion that the soul/spirit is reunited with the body and the total individual thus suffers (or is in some way rewarded). To these groups death means the release of the soul from the body; any idea of immediate reunion would be unthinkable. For the great majority of Muslims, however, the punishment of the grave has been a reality, affirmed in the creeds and writings of the *ahl al-sunna wa'l-jamā'a* (people of custom and the community), and specified in *ḥadīths* of strong and not-so-strong chains of transmission.

Ignoring for a moment the historical development or progression of ideas in the overall picture of the Islamic conception of the idea of suffering inflicted in the tomb, it may be useful to consider here some of the reasons why, in Islamic understanding, such punishment in fact is said to take place (or more precisely, how the idea of punishment in the grave supports the dominant Muslim ethical and theological understanding). From one perspective, of course, there can be only one answer to the question of why anything happens: because God wills it. Nonetheless there seem to be implicit in the arguments of the theologians, the flow of the *ḥadīth* narratives, and the ''morals'' suggested in the various stories related about how this suffering is manifested, certain suggestions of why God might will this punishment to happen:

1. To prefigure final destiny. In its simplest version the punishment narrative, subsequent to the questioning of the angels, says that those who can answer the questions (i.e. those who are able to make the ascension through the seven heavens) are in the long run to be the people of the Garden; those who cannot will be (temporarily or permanently) the people of the Fire.

2. To offer a form of expiation and purgation. From the perspective of God's merciful acceptance of even those who have erred, some mechanism seems necessary whereby they can in a sense be purified of the taint of those wrongdoings. Muslims have never been in complete agreement as to whether this means that only the sinful believers will eventually be taken to paradise, or whether with sufficient punishment (both in the grave and in the hereafter) all may be saved from eternal purgation.

3. To stress the understanding that despite all that the pious believer may have done according to the commandments of God while on earth, he still may have committed some transgressions, however slight, or failed to do certain things that he should have done. Many of the traditions suggest punishment for single sins of omission: ''Why are you punishing me when I carry out the prayer and pay alms and fast in Ramaḍān thus and thus? [The angel] replied, ''I am punishing you because you one day passed by an oppressed person who was calling for your help, but you did not help him. One day you prayed, but you had not cleaned yourself before urinating.''[52]

4. To change the mental attitude of the deceased who may be experiencing the sin of pride at having lived an exemplary life.

5. To warn the living. Here the focus changes completely, and we must see that for at least some of the compilers of *ḥadīths* and authors of texts the concern seems to have been not so much with a description of what happens to the dead as with urging a warning to the living to heed their ways. Many stories describe visits of the deceased to living relatives both to urge them to do justly and to chastise them for failing to perform some duty in regard to the dead (suggesting in many cases that the deceased suffer unduly for the irresponsibility of the living).[53]

6. To underscore the dominant Qur'ānic understanding that there is a direct continuity between this life and the next. In this sense *barzakh* might well be seen not so much a barrier as a bridge, linking our lives and actions on earth with the final dispensation of justice at the eschaton.

A great deal of Islamic tradition has assumed that after the period of the punishment of the grave most individuals will fall into a state of unconsciousness until the day of resurrection. The likening of sleep to death is a recurrent simile in many religious traditions, and one finds in Muslim commentaries frequent references to sleep as the small or lesser death.[54] This parallel has also been drawn in the reverse, in which death is seen as similar to or actually a form of sleep. In the *Kitāb al-ḥaqā'iq wa'l-daqā'iq*, for example, we read, "After the questioning of the angels say to the successful one, 'Sleep like a bride.' "[55] The *Bushrá* even suggests that there will be cushions in the grave on which the believer will "sleep the sleep of a bridegroom!" (p. 52). And in discussing the relation of body and spirit at death, al-Suyūṭī says that "the spirit is connected to its body in a way not like the connection of the earthly life, but resembling the condition of sleep" (p. 72). Many other references can be found throughout Islamic literature to this sleep state, such as the following related by Abū al-Qāsim al-Nisābūrī of the famous eight-century mystic Rābi'a al-Adawīya:

> Rābi'a used to pray all night, and when the day dawned she allowed herself a light sleep in her place of prayer . . . and I used to hear her say, when she sprang up in fear from that sleep, "Oh soul how long wilt thou sleep and how often wilt thou wake? Soon wilt thou sleep a sleep from which thou shalt not wake again until the trumpet call on the Day of Resurrection."[56]

There are, however, a great many exceptions to this theory. In some cases, such as al-Ghazālī's categorization of the souls of the deceased, the state of awareness is related to one's rank. Those in the second category, after initial awareness, fall into something resembling the sleep state, for after the angels show the soul the Fire and assure him that a better fate awaits," . . . they open for him the door to the Garden, and he is unaware of the passing of the months and years and ages" (MS pp. 25–26). Of one in his first or *'ulamā'* category, al-Ghazālī says, "He rejoices without ceasing and is full of bliss as long as he remains on the earth, until the Hour comes" (MS p. 24). Martyrs, of course, go immediately to the Garden (S 3:169–70) to reside in green birds,[57] and one finds references to suggest that others of the blessed will continue in some conscious state to enjoy the felicity of the grave.

With these speculations concerning the state of awareness of the soul/spirit after the questioning in the grave we move from the sequential narrative of after-death events to a general consideration of the conditions of the deceased awaiting the day of resurrection. While a variety of themes comes to bear on this question, most discussions of awareness, location, and the connection of the soul/spirit to the body are directly related to the issue of whether or not (and the means by which) the recompense of the tomb takes place.

The *Kitāb aḥwāl al-qiyāma* and the *Kitāb al-ḥaqā'iq wa'l-daqā'iq*[58] mention a particularly gruesome experience to be undergone by the spirit three days after its separation from the body. As these sources relate the narrative, it is not part of the more or less continuous series of events generally understood to take place immediately after death but seems rather to be part of a general group of traditions that stress the continuing efforts of the deceased to maintain some contact with the world of the living. According to this account, the spirit, having received permission from God to view its former body, returns to its grave and looks at the corpse from a distance. Blood (or water) has flowed from the nose and mouth of the corpse, and the spirit weeps for its condition, comparing life on earth with the present circumstance: ''O my body, my dear one, think of the days of your life. This place is a place of wretchedness and sorrow and pain and loneliness.''[59]

After five and then again after seven days this sequence is repeated, each time the spirit lamenting more loudly for the decaying state of its corpse and the afflictions—worms and scorpions eating the flesh—of the grave. It begs the body to recall the relatives and friends who are still on earth, grieving over its demise: ''Today they weep for me and for you (and will do so) until the Day of Resurrection.''[60]

An ever-recurring theme in the history of human religion is the belief that the dead in some way return to or ''haunt'' graves or places they once lived. For the most part Islamic tradition seems to have been satisfied to suggest that any actual intercourse between the living and the dead takes place through the medium of dreams.[61] In reports such as this one of the spirit lamenting over its body, as well as others related to the general theme of return, we see a strong reflection of the idea that it actually takes some time before the spirit can make a final break with its former surroundings:

> It is related from Abū Hurayra that when a *mu'min* dies his spirit circles around his house for a month, observing how his possessions are divided and his debts paid off. When the month has passed it returns to the grave, circling around until a year has gone by. It sees whoever prays for him and who grieves for him. After a year has passed his spirit ascends to [the place] where the spirits are gathered together for the day of resurrection, the day when the trumpet will be blown.[62]

A number of reports of this kind developed in an apparent attempt to answer such questions as, Where are the spirits of the deceased while they wait for the resurrection? Insofar as they remain in or near their graves, to what extent are they aware of the living? This particular narrative indicates that the dead have a high degree of consciousness of the activities and emotions of those still on earth, particularly as persons and events are related to the former life of the deceased. This is coordinate with those *ḥadīths* which suggest that at least for a brief period of time the dead are sensitive to the affairs of the living. According to al-Suyūṭī, "The dead person knows who washes him and carries him and who wraps him [in his winding clothes] and who lowers him in his grave" (*Bushrá*, p. 31). The dead immediately after burial are said to hear the footsteps of the living departing from the grave. Many reports relate that the Prophet urged the visiting of the dead in the graveyard, particularly on Fridays, as the dead will know and appreciate it: "From Abu Bakr: The dead person knows the visit of the living to him and gives greetings. . . . From 'Ā'isha from the Prophet: No man visits the grave of his brother and sits near him but that [the deceased] is sociable [*ista'nis bihi*] and greets him. . . ."[63]

Although the Qur'ān says specifically in S 27:82 that the dead will not be able to hear, a variety of stories, nonetheless, seem to contradict this, most indicating that the dead hear very well although they are unable to speak.[64] In the *Bushrá* (pp. 55–56) several *ḥadīths* indicate that they can both hear and speak: " 'Whoever does not have faith does not have permission to speak with the dead,' said the Prophet. Someone replied, 'O Messenger of God, do the dead speak?' 'Yes,' said the Prophet, 'and they visit each other.' " The *Durra* in its usual delightful narrative style relates a number of stories suggesting the general cognitive condition of the dead, clearly implying more than simply passive listening. For example, "The *Ṣaḥīḥ* [of Bukhārī] relates that the Messenger of God said, 'No one of you passes by the grave of his brother Muslim whom he knew on the earth and gives him peace but that the dead person recognizes him and returns peace to him.' " (MS p. 31)

As mentioned above, the usual medium for communicating this state of awareness, as well as subsequent instructions to the living, is through dreams, in which the living and the dead meet and interact. Again from al-Ghazālī, here is one of the numerous stories related in the *Durra* about dream communication:

> Someone has related this story: Our father engaged for us a teacher to teach us our lessons at home. Then the teacher died. After six days we went to this grave to visit him, and began to discuss with each other the matter of God's com-

> mand, may He be exalted. Someone passed by us selling a plate of figs, which we bought and ate, throwing the stems onto the grave. When night came, the Shaykh saw the dead man in a dream, and said to him, "How are you?" "Fine," he replied, "except that your children took my grave for a garbage pile and talked about me, with words that are nothing but infidelity!" The Shaykh reprimanded us, and we said [to each other], "Glory be to God! He continues to bother us in the hereafter just as he did on earth!" (MS pp. 31–32)

Such interaction of the dead and the living in sleep, again an idea corroborated by S 39:42, is affirmed very specifically by Ibn Qayyim: "The spirits of the living and the dead meet in sleep and they question one another." When the spirit of the living, upon awaking, returns to his body on earth for the remainder of his *ajal*, the spirit of the dead wishes to do the same but is prevented.[65]

Returning to the question of where the spirits dwell while awaiting the day of resurrection, it is immediately obvious that Islam provides no clear answer or even set of answers. The Qur'ān, as we have seen, is suggestive in a few cases only; to attempt to draw together in a logical fashion all of the traditions relating to this theme is an interesting but somewhat frustrating exercise. Some compilers of manuals are content to suggest several different kinds of answers without attempting to relate them to each other.[66] Others contain attempts by the authors to explain or categorize the various circumstances of spirits, drawing on the many traditions available. Thus al-Ghazālī again suggests four categories of "the people of the tombs," inverting the order this time from the least blessed to the most (MS pp. 32–34).

In his first group are those who remain lying on their sides "until their individuality fades away, their corpses become bloated and their bodies return to dust." The spirits of these, he says, wander around the realm below the earthly (or lowest) heaven. (Al-Ghazālī does not specifically say so, but this group would seem to correspond most closely to the general category of unhappy disembodied spirits often referred to as ghosts, common to the conceptions of many religious traditions.) The second group he calls "the ones God allows to slumber" so that they are in a general state of unconsciousness until the resurrection. Clearly for al-Ghazālī only certain persons are in the sleep state during this period. The third category, he says, is of those who remain in their graves for two or three months, after which they are flown up to the Garden on birds. In this group he includes both the martyrs and others remaining near where the trumpet is blown. He describes their ascent as happening "when their individuality fades away," suggesting the common notion that after a period of time the spirit of the deceased drops the ties which for awhile bind him to his former life on earth.

When he comes to the fourth category, that of the prophets [*anbiyā'*] and saints [*awliyā'*], al-Ghazālī suggests that the spirits have choice. Some prefer to remain on the earth, walking about it until the day of resurrection. Others, such as Abraham, choose to remain in the seventh or highest heaven, as he was seen by the Prophet in the *mi'rāj*, leaning against the Bayt al-Ma'mūr, surrounded by the children of Muslims.[67] Each of the seven heavens, says al-Ghazālī, is peopled by various prophets,[68] Jesus being in the fifth. These prophets and messengers remain in their respective heavens until the Hour. Five, however, are permitted to move at will: Abraham, Moses, Jesus, Adam, and Muḥammad.[69] Some of the saints "are stayed for the earthly resurrection," while others are to be found elsewhere (such as Abū Yazīd at the foot of the Throne eating at a table). The reference to saints remaining on the earth reflects long-standing and commonly held beliefs concerning the active intervention of "deceased" saints in the lives of those who come to their tombs with petitions. Al-Ghazālī concludes his categorical division by saying that "thus in these four conditions the people of the grave are given punishment, mercy, ease and honor respectively" (MS p. 34). Such are the conditions of the dead, he says; when their individuality disappears, some remain stationary, some move around, some are stricken, and others are punished (MS p. 36).

In Suyūṭī's *Bushrá* one also finds an extensive discussion of the conditions of the grave, but from a somewhat different perspective. The author first cites numerous traditions indicating some of the activities carried on by the dead. Several of the companions of the Prophet, according to one story, were sitting on a grave not realizing what it was. From inside it they heard someone reciting Surat al-Mulk until it was completed, whereupon the Prophet said, "This is an obstacle to and a salvation from the punishment of the grave." In another reference to Qur'ān recitation he tells of someone who, hearing these glorious sounds coming from a tomb, inquired of the Prophet about the sound. "Oh," said Muḥammad, "that is 'Abd Allāh [b. 'Umar b. Ḥarām]. Do you not know that God seizes the souls [of the dead] and puts them in lamps [*qanādīl*] of chrysolite and sapphire, then sets them in the middle of the Garden. And when night comes the souls are returned to them and they continue like that until dawn, when their souls are returned to the place where they were."[70] Citing other traditions as authority, Suyūṭī suggests that angels will stay in the grave of the *mu'min* until the day of resurrection, instructing him in any portions of the Qur'ān he may have failed to memorize (p. 50).

Many stories are related in Islamic tradition suggesting that the dead, upon arrival in the world of the tomb, are met by other departed souls, who welcome them. Some indicate that on the return trip through the heavens the angels deliver the newly deceased to the company of the souls of the faithful, who are happy to receive him and inquire about members of their families still on earth. Al-Ghazālī suggests *(Durra*, MS pp. 35–36) that if someone dies and does not meet any of his acquaintances, it may be that at the moment of death something causes him to become a Jew or a Christian, in which case he goes to join *them:*

> Then when someone else from the world arrives, his neighbors ask him, "What do you know about Fulān [the one who converted]?" He says to them, "He has died." They answer, "Truly we are God's and to Him we return. But he has been sent down to the community of the pit [*al-hāwiya*]."

Al-Suyūṭī cites a number of *ḥadīths* concerned with intercourse among the spirits of the departed, describing a variety of occasions in which they meet and visit each other. Probably meant more as a precautionary warning for the living than as an actual description of the activities of the dead, several reports from the Prophet tell of the importance of proper shrouding so that the deceased can visit each other in their graves without embarrassment. One delightful story describes a dream in which a man saw several (dead) women, but his own (dead) wife was not with them. He asked them where she was, and they replied that because he had been slipshod in wrapping her in the shroud, she was too shy to go out with them. So with the help of the Prophet the husband found a man of the Anṣār who was dying, and he wrapped two saffron cloths in his shroud. When night came, the husband again saw the women, and this time his wife was with them, wearing yellow garments (*Bushrá*, p. 55).

From these stories al-Suyūṭī leads into a more general discussion of the location and activities of the deceased. He begins by saying that the spirits are divided into two kinds, the blessed and the punished. The former are too busy with their punishments to be doing anything else, while the blessed are free to meet each other and visit and remind each other of what is in the world and what the people of the world are doing. Every spirit, he says, fits naturally into a company [*rafīq*] of like spirits, a companionship that continues from the earth through the *dār al-barzakh* and into the time of final recompense (pp. 56–57). He cites a great number of familiar traditions indicating the specific locations of souls: those of the martyrs are in green birds in paradise or in domes in the meadows of the Garden; the spirits of the believers are in *barzakh* going where they wish or in the Well of Zamzam or in birds perched on trees in the garden eating the heavenly fruit in the shadow of the Throne; the spirits of the *kāfirs* are in Sijjīn in the bellies of black birds or in the Wādī Barhūt in Ḥaḍramaut. What really interests al-Suyūṭī is not so much the specifics of these particular locations as providing some kind of logical structural explanation for how the spirit can be located in any far-flung place and yet still be connected in some fashion to the body in the grave.

He begins by saying that whether or not the body lives in the grave in the same manner it lived on earth is a matter for God's will and decision. Most obviously, he feels, its "aliveness" is related to intelligence and to its ability to hear, to which authoritative traditions attest. However, he says, if we look for example at all of the persons viewed in the various heavens by the Prophet on his night journey, it is clear that they were appearances without bodies as we know them; to be truly alive does not mean that they have bodies necessitating food and drink as on earth. Speaking more specifically about location, he says that the people of the Sunna agree that the spirits of the dead return sometimes (i.e. when God wishes) from 'Ilyīn or Sijjīn to their bodies in their graves, and that is particularly likely to occur on Friday eve. While in the grave, he says, the spirit and body are associated (pp. 57–58).

In a somewhat later section al-Suyūṭī goes into more detail about the meaning of this association between spirit and body. The mistake, he says, is in not being able to move in our thinking from the seen to the unseen. It is sheer error to think that because a spirit is connected to a body which is in one place, it cannot be in another place. On his night journey the Prophet saw Moses both standing in his grave and in the sixth heaven: "The spirit there is in the likeness of a body and is connected with the body so that it prays in its grave and returns peace. Yet the spirit returns [to the heavens] and is in the highest group [*rafīq*] and there is no contradiction between these two things; for the condition of the spirits is not the condition of the bodies" (p. 71). After all, mentions al-Suyūṭī, the Prophet said that he would hear whomever prayed near his grave or far from it; he is both in the grave and in 'Ilyīn in the highest *rafīq*. The spirit is connected with the body so that it can understand and hear and pray and recite. This seems strange to the earthly witness who knows nothing resembling that, but the affairs of the *barzakh* and the hereafter are of a different mode from those of the world.

All of the spirits are in different places and their abodes move, yet they are attached to their bodies in their graves, experiencing lasting bliss or punishment, as it is written (pp. 71–72).

Indispensable to a treatment of medieval considerations of the nature of continuing human existence after death is Ibn Qayyim al-Jawzīya's *Kitāb al-rūḥ*. In this comprehensive work the author has collected a great number of *ḥadīths* dealing with the activities and location of the spirits/souls of the dead and has offered his own interpretations, based on what he considers to be the prevailing opinion of the orthodox community, the *ahl al-sunna wa'l-jamāʿa*, of what conceptions are most tenable. His method of presentation is to ask a question, then attempt to answer it using what he considers to be the most authoritative traditions and opinions of the *ʿulamā'*. Of the many issues he raises, four are particularly relevant to our considerations here. (One finds in these discussions that Ibn Qayyim for the most part uses the terms *nafs* and *rūḥ* quite interchangeably.)

1. Does the spirit die or is death of the body only?[71] Opinions have differed on this question. Some say the spirit tastes death because it is a *nafs* and every soul tastes death [S 3:185]. Others say that the Qur'ānic reference to two lives and two deaths means that the first death is of the body and the second is of the spirit. Still others feel that spirits do not die, because they were created to remain, and only the bodies die; if the spirits died, they would not be able to experience bliss and suffering. Ibn Qayyim himself says that the correct answer is that the death of the souls refers to their separation from their bodies. If by the death of a soul is meant its destiny, then it tastes death. However, if by that is meant that it disintegrates and is annihilated, then it does not die: "The expression does not mean that it actually dies, rather that it remains after its creation in pleasure or in punishment . . . and it is like that until God returns it to its body" (p. 49).

2. How are the spirits distinguished from one another after their separation from their bodies so that they can become acquainted and meet? Are they shaped when they are removed in a form unlike that which they had before? (pp. 54–56). Unfortunately, he says, this is a question for which there has been no authoritative answer. Some would say that the soul is an accident of the body and as such is distinguished from other souls only on condition of its resurrection in the body; it is not distinguished from other souls after death when it has no existence in its own right. Ibn Qayyim feels that the soul *is* taken from its body in an image distinguished from others, "influenced and proceeding from its body as the body is influenced and proceeds from it." The body acquires goodness and wickedness from the good-

ness and wickedness of the soul, and the soul is in turn directly shaped by the attributes of the body (p. 55).

3. Does the punishment of the grave happen to the soul and the body, or to the soul without the body, or to the body without the soul? Do the body and soul share in the pleasure and punishment of the grave? (pp. 74 ff.). Here, he says, the *ahl al-sunna wa'l-jamā'a* agree that punishment and pleasure are for the soul and the body both. The soul enjoys pleasure and suffers punishment separate [*munfarida*] from the body as well as attached to it. Pleasure and punishment are for both body and spirit, just as they are for the spirit separated from the body. But does the body enjoy pleasure and suffer punishment without the spirit? This question has a variety of answers. The philosophers, for example, who deny the return of the bodies say that only the spirit will ever be recompensed. Some of the Mu'tazila agree that bodies will be returned, but not until the day of resurrection, necessitating that pleasure or punishment in *barzakh* is only for the spirits. Most of the people of *kalām and ḥadīth*, however, agree that the spirit will be returned to the body in the grave for punishment. Some of these say that punishment is of the spirit only, others that it is of the spirit and only indirectly of the body, and still others that it is of the body only. After a lengthy examination of the arguments, Ibn Qayyim concludes that the way of the *salaf* (pious ancestors) is to say that the dead person when he dies is in pleasure or punishment with the spirit and with the body.

4. Where are the spirits of the dead from death to the day of resurrection? (pp. 134–73). Ibn Qayyim discusses this question at length, listing a great number of responses from the most to the least acceptable according to the standpoint of orthodoxy. After an initial enumeration he discusses the pros and cons of each suggestion. For our purposes it is sufficient to indicate categorically the locales for the blessed and the damned of which he approves, and then to consider briefly the solutions he finds unacceptable. These listings are interesting not so much as the conclusions of a single writer, but as a rather complete catalog of the many Islamic opinions and traditions of the Middle Ages relevant to the circumstances of the deceased. (Many of these locations we have already seen suggested, although in less categorical a manner, by al-Suyūṭī in the *Bushrá*.) Some of these ideas are based loosely on the Qur'ān, but most are offered without such reference because of the paucity of concrete commentary in the Qur'ān on this subject.

In a few cases there seems to be no distinction made between the spirits of the *mu'minūn* and the *kāfirūn,* such as in those traditions that say spirits are in the vicinity of their graves (it is sometimes stipulated for seven days after burial only) or that they are in *barzakh* going where they please.[72] Ibn Ḥazm felt that the abode of the spirits is where they were before the creation of their bodies (p. 162). Most traditions, however, stipulate specific locations for the spirits of the faithful and faithless, often suggesting them in parallel form. Grouping these together, one gets an overall picture something like this:

Spirits of the *mu'minūn* are	Spirits of the *kāfirūn* are
a) with God in the Garden (along with those of prophets and martyrs)[73] unless they are guilty of a major sin.	a) in the Fire.
b) in 'Ilyīn in the seventh heaven (especially prophets).	b) in Sijjīn in the seventh ''hell'' under the army of Iblīs.
c) at the Sidrat al-Muntahá.[74]	c) in Sijjīn.
d) at the gates of the courtyard of the Garden, receiving its breezes and enjoying its fruits.	d) swimming in a river of blood.
e) on the right hand of Adam (S 56:8).	e) on the left hand of Adam.
f) by the pond [*jabīya*] or at the Well of Zamzam.	f) in Barhūt at the well of Ḥaḍramaut.[75]

Such, concludes Ibn Qayyim, are the possibilities that the *ahl al-sunna wa'l-jamā'a* have allowed for the location of spirits after death. Several other opinions have been put forth by others in the Islamic community at large, but these, he says, are beyond what can be considered acceptable. Some, for example, say that the conditions of the spirits can only be described as mere absence [*al-'adam al-maḥḍ*], a position held by those who consider that the *nafs* is one of the accidents of the body similar to its sensibilities and that like other accidents it is therefore annihilated at the death of the body (p. 137). He also mentions those who hold the opinion that every spirit goes to the body of an animal most similar to the particular characteristics acquired by that spirit or soul during its lifetime (the lion-like soul going to a lion's body, the dog-like soul to the body of a dog, and so on). These are the *mutanāsikha* (persons espousing transmigration) who deny the return [*ma'ād*] at the resurrection. This opinion, says Ibn Qayyim, is not even to be considered part of Islam (pp. 138, 166).

Keeping in mind these various opinions as to the relationship of the soul or spirit to the body after death and the implications for assuming its location, let us return to some general thoughts about the ways in which the living are seen directly to affect the circumstances of the deceased. References have already been made to this general area of responsibility. Not only are the dead usually understood to be cognizant of the degree to which they are missed and of the ways in which their personal affairs are being carried out, but the carelessness of the washers and those who prepare and wrap the body in its shroud has been seen by some to cause anguish to the departed. Many anecdotes indicate that disrespect for the area in which a body is buried (cf. the story of the figs above) as well as failure to care for the grave itself properly can cause extreme discomfort to its occupant.[76]

Besides these stories one also finds numerous *ḥadīths* in which specific instructions are given to the friends and relatives of the deceased about what they should do or not do to make the sojourn in the tomb more comfortable. These generally fall into one of two categories: those dealing with weeping for the dead and those discussing prayers and almsgiving on behalf of the dead. (Prayer in this context refers not to that done at the funeral itself, but to continued supplication on behalf of the deceased either at the grave site or elsewhere.) In neither category is it entirely clear that specific things are to be forbidden or advised on the basis of their direct ramifications for the condition of the deceased. In general one finds that praying and the giving of alms are good[77] and that lamentation is not,[78] but there seem to be many opinions concerning these matters.

In some cases we find that it is the degree of excess, particularly in regard to weeping, that makes the difference: "Loud lamenting is forbidden, but there is no harm in crying over the dead, although it is better to be patient."[79] Particularly objectionable is the practice of employing a female wailer,[80] a custom venerated in the Middle East since the ancient days in Egypt and Mesopotamia. A story several times related in the manuals is that in which the Prophet was found weeping for his dead son Ibrāhīm. When reminded that he had forbidden such crying, he replied that what is objectionable is loud lamenting, singing, the tearing of one's flesh, and ripping of clothes.[81] To the extent to which (excess) lamentation itself is forbidden, several reasons are suggested. One is clearly that it seems to imply that an injustice has been done in the taking of life, which of course cannot be the case, since every death is decreed by God. The following tradition from the *Kitāb al-ḥaqā'iq wa'l-daqā'iq* underscores this idea:

> It is related that when a man dies, the lamenters gather in his house, and the Angel of Death stands at the door of his house [and he says to these people], "What is this crying? By God, I have not reduced the life of any one of you. If your crying is on account of me, surely I am (only) a servant under orders. If it is on account of the dead man, surely he is under constraint. If it is on account of God Most High, then you are not believers in God Most High! By God, I shall return time and again among you!"[82]

Other *ḥadīths* suggest that it is simply a waste of time to lament the inevitable. The wife of one Ḥasan b. Ḥasan b.'Alī remained weeping on his grave for a year. At the end of that time, when she ran out of tears, a voice from the other side of the grave asked, "Have you found what you lost?"[83]

In other cases, however, it is made quite explicit that weeping actually worsens the condition of the dead.[84] In one narrative related from the *Ṣaḥīḥ* of Bukhārī the Messenger of God saw an orphan crying at his father's grave. Weeping himself out of compassion for the child, the Prophet nonetheless said, "Indeed the dead person is tormented by the tears of the living over him."[85] How many times one sees the dead in dreams, says al-Ghazālī, who tell you that their condition is poor because of certain persons who are weeping over them.[86]

In the *Durra* this affliction suffering by the departed because of the grieving of the living seems also to extend to having family and friends pray for them. Citing first a *ḥadīth* which says, "Do not pray among the graves, because that is an affliction that has no limit," al-Ghazālī in a somewhat lighter vein then relates a story about someone praying in the cemetery. In the intense heat he saw a figure resembling his father on the back of his grave, and crouching in fear heard the figure say, "The earth is too confined for you, so you had to come annoying us since some time with your prayers!" (MS p. 30). Other traditions, however, indicate that in fact prayers for the dead really are helpful. One of the most interesting of the traditions in this connection is that cited in the *Kitāb aḥwāl al-qiyāma* concerning the duty of a son to pray for his dead father as well as to give alms on his behalf:

> It is related from Abū Qalāba that he saw in a dream a cemetery, and it was as if the graves were split open and the dead came out of them. They sat on the edges of the graves and each one had before him a light. He saw among them one of

> his neighbors with no light in front of him and he asked him about it, saying, "Why do I not see any light in front of you?" The dead person said, "These others have children and friends to pray for them and give alms for them and their light is produced by that. I have only one son and he is no good. He does not pray for me and does not give alms on my behalf, therefore I have no light. And I am ashamed in front of my neighbors." When Abū Qalāba woke up he called the man's son and told him what he had seen. So the son said, "I will mend my ways and will no more do what I have been doing. And he was obedient and prayed for his father and gave alms on his behalf. And sometime later when Abū Qalāba saw the graveyard in his dream he saw the same man with a light brighter than the sun and greater than the light of his companions. And the man said, "O Abū Qalāba, may God reward you well for me. Because of what you said [to my son] I am saved from shame in front of my neighbors."[87]

In this story one can see not only a common sequence of successive dreams showing a situation before and after the event, but also the tremendous importance put on the role of community experience and the shame of having one's relatives and companions know that familial responsibilities have been shirked.

Such, then, are the various circumstances of the deceased in the period after death as understood by Muslim tradition. In the following chapter we will consider the next series of events in the Islamic eschatological story, those dealing with the resurrection and the final judgment of reunited bodies and souls.

Chapter Three

The Eschaton, the Judgment, and the Final Dispensation: Classical Islam

{Those who deny the meeting with God are losers, so that when the Hour comes suddenly upon them they will say, Woe to us that we took no note of it . . .} [S 6:31].

The promise, the guarantee, of the day at which all bodies will be resurrected and all persons called to account for their deeds and the measure of their faith is the dominant message of the Qur'ān as it is presented in the context of God's *tawḥīd*. One can find testimony of this assurance on almost every page of the Qur'ān. Volumes have been written by Western scholars of Islam analyzing the many verses that help weave the picture of what will occur at the resurrection, what the Prophet may have intended by various utterances, and how this all fits into God's supreme plan for humankind.

It is not the purpose of this chapter to review these analyses or even to represent the various structural outlines of Qur'ānic material. Rather it is to give a general overview of the sequence of events that Islamic tradition has documented for that day (with greater or lesser emphasis on relative events within the sequence), based not only on the many details suggested by the Qur'ān but also on the elaborations and additions provided as usual by the *ḥadīths*, the manuals, and the interpretations of theologians. With this outline as a backdrop we can better understand the ways in which contemporary writers repeat, reinterpret, and sometimes reject the particulars held dear by tradition, and put in focus the concerns that modern Islamic theologians consider vital in dealing with issues of resurrection and judgment.

Because the events seen to take place at the day of resurrection are numerous and presented in varying ways, we will follow the general pattern of the previous chapter and attempt to order these into a chronological sequence. This facilitation, however, is clearly intended neither to suggest that all treatments in the Qur'ān or the *ḥadīths* follow an unquestioned order, nor to cloud the real issues basic to the Qur'ānic/Islamic understanding of what the Hour means for the ways in which human beings live their lives. All of the events, from the signs of the coming of the Hour to the final assessment and determination, support two basic themes central to the understanding of Islamic eschatology: (1) bodies will be resurrected and joined with spirits in the reunion of whole, cognizant, and responsible persons, and (2) there will be a final judgment of the quality of lives lived on earth and a subsequent recompense carried out with absolute justice through the prerogative of God's merciful will. Upon these realities there is nothing in the Qur'ān or any other Islamic writings—scholastic or devotional—to cast the slighest shadow of doubt.

We have seen earlier that Islam actually espouses a belief in two judgments, the first to take place through and after the questioning of the grave and the second and ultimate judgment to be passed on the day of resurrection. As has already been observed, however, it is actually somewhat arbitrary to suggest that either an evaluation per se or a concomitant recompense is confined to either of these specific moments. The clear understanding of Islam, articulated with great insistence in contemporary writings, is the continuity of this world and the next. This continuity consistently implies a relationship between human responsibility and human accountability. Thus just as all of the events in the death process—the pain or ease of death itself, the reception of the grave, the journey through the heavens, the felicity of the sojourn in the tomb—suggest the relative merit of the deceased, so the cumulative events to occur at the day of resurrection also point to the final evaluation and thus the ultimate abode of every individual. By drawing such a connection, of course, these descriptions have served admirably as incentives to the living to improve the quality of their lives, for the pattern of one's faith and obedience, or lack thereof, is being woven every day, and the consequences of this pattern are both immediate and ultimate.

In terms of a precise order of events, however, no two presentations necessarily explain exactly the same sequence. Many, but not all, of the happenings accepted by orthodoxy are mentioned or suggested in the Qur'ān. Theologians have generally highlighted the particulars relevant to the points they see as dominant in the Qur'ānic understanding and have not been overly concerned with presenting a consistent narrative. To the extent to which details provided by the traditionists have caught the imagination and colored the expectations of centuries of pious Muslims, we will allude to them and attempt to summarize their content as well as intent. The continuous narrative can be subdivided in several possible ways; for purposes of ordering we will see it in four segments:

1. the signs of the Hour [*sā'a*] and events heralding the imminent end of the world;
2. the soundings of the trumpet, the resurrection [*qiyāma*], and the gathering together of all living beings [*ḥashr*];
3. the reckoning [*ḥisāb*];
4. the crossing of the bridge [*ṣirāṭ*], the possibility of intercession [*shafā'a*], and preparation for final consignment.

One of the issues that engaged theology in the young Muslim community was the question of whether the realities of the eschaton were to be interpreted literally or figuratively. The Mu'tazila are presented in the Ash'arī writings as having disavowed the reality of many of the specific elements traditionally included in the narratives of the day of resurrection, although the Mu'tazilī school embraced more than one opinion on this subject. In any case, the Ash'arī resolution affirmed that such things as the individual records of deeds (including the paper, pen, and ink with which they are inscribed), the bridge, the balance, and the pond are realities to be understood in a concrete and literal sense. These "realities" are enumerated and affirmed by the most popular of the creeds;[1] the exact nature of their reality is assigned to the knowledge of God alone.

Signs of the Hour [sā'a]

The adherents of religious traditions expressing millenial or eschatological expectations seem universally to experience difficulties in attempting to pinpoint the precise time at which such realities will occur.[2] Christians for twenty centuries have predicted the arrival of the parousia; Zoroastrians, while given a more precise timetable of events, have perhaps been doubly frustrated at having to reinterpret that schedule when it appears that the expected has not transpired. The Qur'ān itself gives no hint of when the eschaton is to arrive, and in fact insists that such knowledge is God's alone: {People will ask you about the Hour. Say, Knowledge of it is only with God . . .} [S 33:63].[3] Nonetheless it seems likely that the early Islamic community would be surprised to find that after fourteen centuries Muslims are still in expectation of those signs portending the cataclysmic conclusion of time.[4]

The signs by which we are to recognize the beginning of the end are known as *ishārāt al-sā'a* and are understood to be of several kinds. In the Qur'ān we hear primarily of the cataclysmic events (called the greater signs or *'alāmāt al-sā'a*) upsetting the rhythms of the natural world. Perhaps no portions of this scripture are more dramatic than these describing the events that will literally devastate the earth and reverse the natural processes, which throughout the Qur'ān are consistently cited as proof of God's ordinance and authority. See, for example, S 81:1–14 (Arberry translation):

> {When the sun shall be darkened, When the stars shall be thrown down,
> When the mountains shall be set moving, When the pregnant camels shall be neglected,
> When the savage beasts shall be mustered, When the seas shall be set boiling,
> When the souls shall be coupled, When the buried infant shall be asked for what sin she was slain,
> When the scrolls shall be unrolled, When heavens shall be stripped off,
> When Hell shall be set blazing, When Paradise shall be brought nigh,
> Then shall a soul know what it has produced.}

In the disruption of the natural order as portrayed in the Qur'ān one can see a reverse process of the creation. The heavens, understood as seven layers, are stripped away, rolled up, and destroyed. The stars, lamps set in the lowest part of the heavens, fall and are extinguished, while the sun and moon are covered. The earth itself shakes and rocks and is finally split apart and ground to dust, its mountains first put in motion and then leveled. Even the seas, divided from each other at the creation, mix together again in a primordial chaos.[5]

These natural disasters are paralleled, and in a sense prefigured, in much of the material of the traditions, which describe a corresponding decay in the moral order. In general one can see predicated a degeneration of the standards recognizable as crucial for the maintenance of Islamic society: piety will give way to pride and truth to lies, while licentious practices such as music, drinking of wine, usury, adultery, homosexuality, and the obedience of men to their wives over their parents will prevail. Sex will be performed in public places, cousin marriages will give way to extrafamilial unions, and there will be no Imam to lead the faithful in prayer. These and many other social aberrations are detailed in such works as Muḥammad ibn Rasūl al-Ḥusaynī al-Barzinjī's *al-Ishā'a li-ishrāṭ al-sā'a*,[6] which includes also the personal degradations of people eating like cows and hearts turning as hard as those of wolves. The *Mishkāt al-maṣābīḥ* confirms that ignorance and fornication will prevail, and the number of females will increase so that there will be fifty women for every man to look after.[7]

When the Hour is truly imminent, these general signs of moral disintegration will be joined by some very specific occurrences. Some scholars make the point not without justification, that it is difficult to separate eschatological predications from responses to actual political circumstances within the Muslim community.[8] Concerned from very early on with the fact of dissension in the ranks of the believers, the community often has associated the deep distress of this strife with the sense of imminence of the end and the proposition that the eschaton will be ushered in by major *fitan* or trials. It is in this context that descriptions of the antichrist al-Dajjāl, the creatures Yājūj and Mājūj (Gog and Magog), and the eschatological *mahdī* or savior are given. One finds, then, that two general characteristics are suggested of the period prefiguring the resurrection: the complete degradation of the community and the (temporary) success of the savior, who in some senses is seen to represent the ultimate victory of the *umma* of Islam. These characteristics are not necessarily contradictory because they are generally not synchronized but rather individually emphasized in order to make different points.

Let us look again at the way al-Barzinjī outlines the series of events heralding the end of the world. The signs of moral turpitude listed above he calls intermediate signs, or those of the second period before the resurrection (the first he describes as specific historical events). The third period, he says, includes signs of the closeness of the hour, the most important of which is the coming of the *mahdī*. The *mahdī* is cited as the one who will rid the world of *bid'a* (innovation), reestablish the *sunna*, and teach religion as did the Prophet:

> He will possess all the world, as did Alexander and Solomon. . . . He will return to Muslims their blessedness and well-being and will fill the world with justice. . . . He will accumulate extensive wealth and divide it equally among people in heaven and earth. Birds, beasts and all creatures will be pleased with him.[9]

Al-Barzinjī, as is traditional, understands this time of the *mahdī* to be when the low morality earlier displayed will be replaced with high standards and harmonious circumstances: the wolf and the ram will dwell together, children will play unharmed with scorpions and snakes, lives will be longer, and (perhaps causally) usury, plague, fornication, and the drinking of wine will disappear, evil ones will be destroyed, and none will remain who despise the people of Muḥammad.

In the context of the discussion of the *mahdī* al-Barzinjī takes up his descriptions of the Dajjāl, Yājūj, and Mājūj. This pattern is representative enough to serve as the basis for our understanding here. The Qur'ān makes mention of the beast of the earth (S 27:82), though without reference to name. The traditions refer frequently to the beast but never with a particularly lucid account of who or what it is. Sometimes called *al-masīḥ al-dajjāl*, the false messiah, this figure is treated either as a beast or monster or understood to be a human figure. Sometimes described quite graphically as blind in one eye, reddish in color, with the word *kāfir* written on his forehead,[10] his primary function is to lead the Muslim community away from the true way of God and to establish a kingdom with himself as the ruler. In this sense he seems to be identified both with the image of Satan commonly held by Christians in the medieval period, and with a false prophet whose reign will be for forty years (or perhaps no more than forty days). Again possibly reflecting some interaction with the Christian community, Muslims have generally suggested that the defeat of the Dajjāl will be at the hands of 'Īsá (Jesus). (Some eschatological manuals go into lengthy detail describing the demise of the fallen angel Iblīs [see S 7:11–18] in this context, although there is no clarity in the understanding of Iblīs' relationship to the Dajjāl. As the exemplar of disobedience to the commands of God, Iblīs is doomed to ultimate destruction as a kind of figurative first step in the unfolding of the drama of judgment.)

Before looking more specifically at the way in which Jesus in this context fits in with the theories of the *mahdī*, let us consider another constituent element in the picture of what al-Barzinjī calls the third period, the appearance of Yājūj and Mājūj. These two people are a recognized part of Middle Eastern mythology and are mentioned specifically in the Bible[11] and in the Qur'ān.[12] The Muslim tradition derives directly from the commentary provided in S 21:96–97, which is said to refer to the dam somewhere in the northeast corner of the earth built by Dhū al-Qarnayn to contain these creatures.[13] Placed in an eschatological framework, the verse suggests that one of the indications of the coming of the last days will be the breaking of the dam by these devastating creatures. Described as cannibals with varying degrees of height and breadth, Yājūj and Mājūj will be greatly multiplied at the eschaton and will sweep down as a scourge on the earth. The reports are replete with details of their conquest of humanity and subsequent railing against God Himself, Who will ultimately see to their demise by fire and a plague of worms, birds and/or other natural disasters.[14]

The exact relationship of Yājūj and Mājūj to the antichrist, Dajjāl, and to the coming of the *mahdī* is difficult to determine because of the multiple sources and the abundance of *ḥadīths* involved. Al-Barzinjī describes them as one of the major *fitan* by which the coming of the Hour is to be recognized,[15] along with the sun rising in the west (a commonly-mentioned phenomenon and one most clearly illustrative of the understanding that the eschaton signals a reversal of the natural order), a triple eclipse of the moon, and the appearance of 'Īsá. It is clear from the way al-Barzinjī orders his material that he sees the *mahdī* and Jesus as two distinct personages, not identical, both present in some way at the events ushering in the Hour. Others, however, understand the second coming of 'Īsá, suggested rather obscurely by S 43:61,[16] as the role and function of the *mahdī* (literally the divinely-guided one)—to kill the Dajjāl, to break the cross and decimate all Christians and their places of worship, and to inaugurate the aforementioned period of peace before the actual coming of the Hour, in which the *sharī'a* of the Prophet will prevail.[17] The particular place to which Jesus is predicted to descend for this messianic function is generally understood to be at the Great Mosque of Damascus or at Jerusalem; other local areas in various parts of the Arab world also lay claim to this honor by virtue of some particular tradition.[18]

Many scholars have looked at the association of 'Īsá b. Maryam with the *madhī* as being a clear indication of the influence of Judaism and Christianity on early Islam and the adaptation of the Christian savior to the figure of a just ruler who will reign over the millenial period of justice and peace.[19] Margoliouth suggests that the etymology of *madhī* might be from *mahd*, cradle, and thus refer to S 19:29, in which Jesus is said to have spoken in the cradle.[20] Despite these general associations, however, for most Muslims the coming of the *mahdī* and the return of Jesus are seen as two separate events. (The term *al-hādī*, guide, is mentioned twice in the Qur'ān, although the verbal form *madhī* does not appear.)

One of the clearest classical statements about the specific events of the eschaton is that of Ibn Khaldūn, introducing in his *Muqaddimah* a full and detailed discussion of the various theories regarding the *mahdī* and the traditions considered most authoritative in relation to it. For him *'Īsá* and the *mahdī* are definitely two distinct figures:

> It has been well known (and generally accepted) by all Muslims in every epoch, that at the end of time a man from the family (of the Prophet) will without fail make his appearance, one who will strengthen the religion and make justice triumph. The Muslims will follow him, and he will gain domination over the Muslim realm. He will be called the Mahdi. Following him, the Antichrist will appear, together with all the subsequent signs of the Hour (the Day of Judgment), as established in (the sound tradition of) the *Ṣaḥiḥ*. After (the Mahdi),

'Īsá (Jesus) will descend and kill the Antichrist; or, Jesus will descend together with the Mahdi, and help him kill (the Antichrist), and have him as the leader in his prayers.[21]

The political implications of the whole millenial idea in Islam, especially as related to the understanding of the *mahdī* and the rise of the 'Abbasids in the second Islamic century, are very difficult to separate from the eschatological ones, although a discussion of the former must remain outside the scope of this essay.[22] The hope of something better to come has informed both theology and socio-political expectations, and the translation of the promise of a time of universal peace and justice is easily made from this age to the next (and back again). Time calculations also tend to blur the lines between the literal and the symbolic. As there has been no consensus about when the end of the age is to come, so the estimates have varied greatly concerning the length of time both the *mahdī* and Jesus will reign and how long after their deaths (both are generally expected to die naturally) the actual Hour will arrive. Some predictions even indicate a series of descendents of the *mahdī*, who himself is said to rule five, seven, or nine years.

The descriptions of the savior differ as much as the chronological predictions, and offer as much specificity.[23] Of the house of the Prophet, he will be like him in character and in function, although a reformer rather than a prophet. While most of the traditions about the *mahdī* are credited to the Prophet Muḥammad, it is difficult to determine whether he actually anticipated the arrival of such an eschatological figure.[24] Clearly the passage of time solidified the belief in his coming. It is interesting to note, however, that none of the creeds selected for this study[25] mentions the *mahdī*, although both the *Fiqh Akbar II* and the *'Aqīda* of al-Ṭaḥāwī list the descent of 'Īsá among the indications of the Hour, along with the Dajjāl, Yājūj and Mājūj, and the rising of the sun from the west.

The Trumpet, the Resurrection [qiyāma], *and the Gathering* [ḥashr][26]

Know that Isrāfīl is the master of the horn [*al-qarn*]. God created the preserved tablet [*al-lawḥ al-maḥfuz*] of white pearl. Its length is seven times the distance between the heaven and the earth and it is connected to the Throne. All that exists until the day of resurrection is written on it. Isrāfīl has four wings—one in the East, one in the West, one covering his legs and one shielding his head and face in fear of God. His head is inclined toward the Throne. . . . No angel is nearer to the throne than Isrāfīl. Seven veils are between him and the Throne, each veil five hundred years distance from the next; seventy veils are between

> Jibrīl and Isrāfīl. While he is standing the trumpet [*ṣūr*] is placed on his right thigh and the head of the trumpet on his mouth. He awaits the command of God, and when He commands he will blow. And when the period of the world is completed, the trumpet will be brought near the face of Isrāfīl and he will fold his four wings and blow the trumpet.[27]

In this dramatic fashion much of Islamic tradition has portrayed in cosmic terms the angel who will sound the horn signaling the arrival of the Hour and will read from the guarded tablet that which is written concerning the lives of all who will then be brought to judgment. The sounding of the trumpet is mentioned several times in the Qur'ān[28] and it has been for the followers of the Prophet to determine for themselves the exact sequence of events after that. The Qur'ān mentions one blast of the trumpet in S 69:13 and two blasts in S 39:68, and some eschatological manuals expand this to three (a belief also expressed in some Jewish traditions).

Perhaps no single point in the entire sequence of eschatological events can match this period of the trumpet soundings for drama and excitement. The Qur'ānic imagery is at its best here, as in the description in S 69:13–16 (Arberry translation): {When the trumpet is blown with a single blast and the earth and the mountains are lifted up and crushed with a single blow, then, on that day, the terror shall come to pass, and heaven shall be split, for upon that day it shall be very frail. . . .} All of these events, coming at the first blast of the trumpet, are the expression in the physical world of the total disruption of the regular order of nature, by which God has made known to the world His continuing guidance. As human moral degeneracy has been seen to be one of the signs of the impending Hour, so now cosmic disintegration signals the end of the world and the imminence of the resurrection.

The second trumpet blast signals the dramatic final cataclysm, the great *fanā'* or extinction of all save God. Many traditional eschatological descriptions develop an elaborate vision of this ultimate desolation of the earth and all living creatures. The *Kitāb aḥwāl al-qiyāma* describes God as commanding the angel of death to annihilate the oceans, the mountains, the earth, and the heavens, despite their sad lamentations. He then asks the angel who of creation remains, and the reply is given, "O my God, you are the living who never dies. Only Jibrīl and Mikā'īl and Isrāfīl and the bearers of the throne and I, your weak servant, remain." And God says to him, "Seize their spirits!" Finally God commands that because of His word, all souls will taste death; even the angel of death himself must die, and so he does.[29]

With the extinction of all save the divine we have the final and perfect cosmic setting for the proclamation by God of His absolute and omnipotent oneness. This image of cosmic unity and the singleness of the divine is perhaps nowhere more powerfully portrayed than in al-Ghazālī's *Durra*. Paraphrasing the cataclysmic events of the Qur'ān and concluding with God's stripping away of the spheres themselves, he says that now in all the seven heavens and seven earths no living being will remain. The earth is empty of its inhabitants and the sky of its dwellers—even the sun, moon, and stars are destroyed—and in this scene of stark emptiness only God remains, alone as before creation:

> The God will manifest Himself in the clouds, seizing the seven heavens in His "O world, O Worldly one! Where are your masters? Where are your chiefs? You have beguiled them with your splendors and with your beauty you have kept them from concern for things of the hereafter." Then He extols His own praise as He so desires; He glorifies His eternal existence and His lasting power and never-ending dominion and victorious omnipotence and boundless wisdom. Three times He asks, "To whom belongs the Kingdom this day?" No one answers Him so He answers Himself, saying, "To God who is one alone, victorious!" (MS p. 39)

Expressed most graphically in such verses as S 28:88 and S 55:26–27, which say that everything perishes except His face, this understanding of *fanā'* underscores in the most striking way the meaning of God's oneness, *tawḥīd*, His self-subsistence apart from and independent of any living creature. From another perspective there must be a point at which all creatures are annihilated, because of the repeated Qur'ānic assurance that every soul will taste death. In order for God's *tawḥīd* to be manifested, there must be death; in order for His justice and mercy to be demonstrated, there must be life again, a re-investing of souls and bodies previously rendered lifeless with the living breath of God, by which they will be brought forth whole, cognizant, and responsible before the divine.[30]

As long as God wills, then, the universe remains empty of all save Him. Even the speculative traditions are generally loath to project a time limit for this period, which is, of course, by very definition beyond all human time constructs, although forty years seems to be the general estimate of many. When He so pleases, in any case, He will begin the process by which the resurrection will take place. Again the master of the dramatic, al-Ghazālī says that finally God will open one of the treasure houses of the Throne, and from it the sea of life will begin to rain upon the parched and barren ground, causing it to quiver with new life.[31] When all the earth is covered with four cubits of water, the actual re-growth of individual bodies will begin, starting with the coccyx.[32] Bodies will then grow in their graves, just as plants grow, until each has attained the form it had when death overtook it, the child a child's form and the adult an adult's form.

No doubt because the Qur'ān itself does not make explicit the chronology involved with the blowing(s) of the horn, the traditions do not present a consistent picture. The general understanding seems to be that Isrāfīl will be the first of creation to be resurrected and that from the Bayt al-Maqdis[33] he will give the blast by which all of the dead will be brought back to life. (We should recall from the previous chapter that among the places assigned by tradition to spirits awaiting the day of resurrection are the holes in the great trumpet of Isrāfīl. Part of this eschatological imagery, then, suggests the returning from the horn of all spirits to their newly regenerated bodies.) Qur'ān and reports alike leave no doubt, however, that God Himself resurrects the bodies, joins them with their spirits, and brings them forth for the final *ḥisāb* or reckoning. As He gave us life in the beginning, so will He give us life again at the end.

The fact of the resurrection of the body has been of continuing importance to Muslims and has raised very particular questions in certain circles of Islamic thought, such as those reflected in the later disputations between philosophy and theology.[34] It was not really a point of issue for early Islam, however, and bodily resurrection has never been seriously denied by orthodoxy. It is, as many have observed, basic to the message of God as proclaimed by the Prophet and articulated clearly by the Qur'ān,[35] especially in those passages in which the contemporaries of the Prophet are presented as having scoffed or raised doubts. It continues to be, as we shall observe shortly, a point of conviction for many of the contemporary interpreters of Islam to a world in which a rational and scientifically-infused populace continues to raise the same eyebrows of skepticism as did the compatriots of the Prophet.

There is, as has been indicated, no consistent understanding of the order in which resurrection is to take place. After Isrāfīl and the other archangels, the raising of mortals begins; the first to be resurrected is said to be Abraham, or Moses, or the Prophet Muḥammad.[36] The stress on the importance of Muḥammad's resurrection before the other believers is related not only to his recognized stature as the seal of the prophets, but also to the general understanding of his role as intercessor for his community, to be discussed below. The first of the animals to be revived is Burāq, the horse ridden by the Prophet on his *mi'rāj* journey. Typical of the almost mystical descriptions of these events it is presented by Abū Layth al-Samarqandī, in which Barāq is brought to life before his master:

> The first riding beast to be brought back to life by God is al-Burāq. God says to them, "Cover him." They cover him with a saddle of red gems; his bridle is of green topaz. . . . Then the tomb (of Muḥammad) splits open, and lo! Muḥammad sits in his tomb, shaking the earth from his head and beard. Jibrā'īl, peace be upon him, presents him with two vestments and al-Burāq, and Muḥammad says, "O Jibrā'īl—peace be upon him—what day is this?" Jibrā'īl says—peace be upon him—"This is the day of the Resurrection. This is the day of assembly and convocation. This is the day of promise and the day of threat. This is the day of separation. This is the day of meeting."[37]

Based on a number of scattered verses in the Qur'ān indicating the woeful condition of sinners on the day of resurrection, certain narratives suggest a classification of the revived into groups. According to an often-quoted saying of the Prophet, the first to arise will be the members of his community; even these are subdivided into categories based on their misdeameanors while on earth. As graphic here as anything from Dante's *Divine Comedy* are the metaphorical descriptions of punishments befitting the crime: those who were judgmental reappear as blind, the false *'ulamā'* are portrayed with pus running from their mouths and the curious as wearing tar vestments, the traitors resemble pigs, the vain are deaf and dumb, the self-serving have their feet tied to their forelocks, and on and on.[38] Al-Ghazālī (*Durra*, MS p. 46) suggests another symbol when he says, "At that moment everyone is equal, each sitting upon his grave; among them are the naked and the clothed, the black and the white." More common are the traditions which assert that "At the resurrection you will be assembled barefoot, naked and uncircumcised."[39] Al-Ghazālī says that while sharing the same condition of absolute powerlessness before their Creator, the resurrected are differentiated (as always on the basis of their past faith and works) by the relative strength or weakness of the lights they bear with them: "The lights of individuals at the resurrection are in direct proportion to their faith, and the speed of their steps in proportion to their good works."[40]

It is not difficult to imagine that the shock of finding themselves revivified, to say nothing of their concern for the outcome of the promised judgment, would put the newly resurrected into a state of intense fear. Islamic tradition has dramatized this fear into a circumstance in which the panic is prolonged and the time of waiting for the actual judgment understood as another mini-reckoning and recompense-cum-purification, in nature not unlike the circumstances of the deceased in their graves. (One can understand why theologians and exegetes have suggested several alternatives to the specific states alluded to in the Qur'ānic references to two lives and two deaths.) During the agonizing wait after the actual resurrection, the individual is said to be given ample opportunity to contemplate the imminent recompense for his past faults. The whole process culiminates in what is called the terror of the place of assembly [*al-maḥshar*], or the time of standing before God [*al-mawqūf*]. The Qur'ān alludes to this terror in such verses as S 21:103 (which speaks of *al-faza' al-akbar*) and S 37:20 ff., and the *ḥadīths* supply the particulars: at that moment the fear is so intense that persons will be standing in their own sweat up to their ankles, hips, or even necks. Only the prophets, saints, and most pious are said to be exempt from this agony, which is augmented by the seventy-fold increase of the heat of the sun.[41]

Before that final moment in which individuals will face their Creator (an idea familiar to Judeo-Christian tradition although less specifically stressed than in Islam), the traditions suggest a variety of specific circumstances in which those waiting may find themselves. They speculate on the actual time involved, as is true of the period between the trumpet blasts, but relegate it finally only to the knowledge of God. Some say the waiting will last 50,000 years, based on S 70:4; others read from S 32:4 that it will only be a thousand. As the time and chronology are less important than the ultimate significance of the event as a whole, so the details in the eschatological manuals are intended less for descriptive than for didactic purposes. Besides the light metaphor, al-Ghazālī mentions the creation of a camel on which people ride to judgment, the number loaded on one beast increasing according to the weakness of their faith and works. As usual, of course, the destination is assured to those of the community of Islam, despite the overload, and various verses of the Qur'ān are interpreted in elaborate detail to support the general theme that the pious will have a better time of it on the day of resurrection than the impious.[42]

After all the waiting and torment and desperate hopes of the resurrected that somehow their circumstances can be ameliorated comes the act interpreted by many to signal the moment of the judgment itself. Qur'ān S 68:42 mentions {. . . the day when the skin is exposed and they are called to fall down in prostration, but are not able to.}[43] Tradition has interpreted this uncovering to mean that God Himself exposes His leg as the signal for the beginning of the judgment process.[44] It can be seen as yet another sign that a felicitous end is assured for the faithful, for they in fact do prostrate themselves before Him, while the vertebrae of the impious become stiff so that they are unable to bend. At this point in the *ḥadīths* the progression of events becomes sufficiently complex that it is impossible even to suggest a common order. Each of the collections of traditions presents its own narratives about the variety of ways in which God reveals to the various categories of individuals what their fate is to be. These are all variations on a single theme, however, and that is the moment of reckoning—to which all of the preceeding events were but preliminaries and the reality of which the Qur'ān itself affirms with consistency.

The Reckoning [ḥisāb]

> {As for the one who is given his book in his right hand, he will say: Take and read my book. I knew that I would be called to account. And he will be in a blissful condition. . . . But as for him who is given his book in his left hand, he will say: Would that my book had not been given to me and that I did not know my reckoning! . . . [And it will be said] Seize him and bind him and expose him to the burning Fire! . . .} [S 9:19–31].

It is quite clear from these verses of the Qur'ān (see also 17:71) that each individual alone will be responsible for his or her past decisions, the cumulation of which is in some fashion recorded on high and presented as one's own book or pages [*ṣuḥuf*] on the day of resurrection.[45] (As we shall see below, when theologians began to interpret the implications of the possibility of intercession, the emphasis gradually shifted from individual responsibility to collective participation in a community.) Reports affirm that each day of an individual's life begins a new page, on which one or two angels inscribe his deeds,[46] that in some fashion these pages are assembled into a full scroll or record, and that, as attested to by S 17:13,[47] this completed book is fastened onto the neck of the deceased when his spirit departs his body at death. Sometimes each individual record is said to be part of a complete compendium of all human actions. Al-Ghazālī describes it as "a huge book . . . filling up the entire space between East and West, in which are recorded all the acts of the creatures" (MS p. 79). On the day of judgment the record will be revealed to each person individually, the results of the reckoning obviously predetermined by one's being ordered to take his book in either his right or left hand. For the heedless, this revealing of the record will come as a tremendous shock. Again, the circumstances of the presentation of one's record by the angels differ widely in the accounts, with variations incidental to the significance of the event itself.

(Beasts and birds are generally understood to be present at the day of judgment, although actual settlement is made only between animals that have harmed each other, specifically with their horns. After that all fade away into dust and do not participate in the final consignment to the Garden or Fire. Some traditions suggest that there are birds in the Garden for the pleasure of the blessed, as well as horses and camels on which they will be able to ride.)

The particular elements that make up the occasion of the reckoning have sometimes been categorized as the ''modalities of judgment.''[48] Although most of these modalities are based on scriptural references, the Qur'ān contains no ordering or even grouping of them, and to the extent to which the creeds affirm them, it is simply to say that they are realities. As has been illustrated in a variety of instances in the foregoing narratives, the judgment process, often referred to by the doctors of theology as the two judgments, is actually one continuous fact from beginning (individual acts of faith and deed) to end (ultimate dispensation). To isolate specific events or references or to attempt to find in these a natural progression is in one sense a misdirected effort, for the events function primarily to support from a variety of perspectives the basic fact of human responsibility. Thus while it seems logically unimportant on the one hand to assume the necessity of such particulars as the weighing of deeds or God's interrogation of each individual about his past life, the outcome already having been revealed continuously in the whole process of death and resurrection, such imagery enhances and provides one more dimension to the picture of what it means to a Muslim to be called fully and absolutely to account.

The Qur'ān refers numerous times to the *mīzān* (balance), one of the most important eschatological realities. In the singular it has been interpreted as the principle of justice and occasionally even the books through which the principles of justice are clarified.[49] As such it is also easily seen as the instrument of justice, the means by which human responsibility ordained in this world is assessed in relation to the next. In the Qur'ān the plural, *mawāzīn,* has the clearer eschatological reference of the scales by which deeds are weighed on the day of resurrection. The image of a specific weighing has thus been adopted as one of the modalities of judgment. It is sometimes said that Jibrīl and Mikhā'īl will operate the two pans of the balance, on which will be placed either the specific pages inscribed with the record of human actions or some sort of re-creation of the actions themselves. The *Kitāb aḥwāl al-qiyāma* (p. 81) quotes this description of the *mīzān*, citing Ibn 'Abbās as authority:

The *mīzān* will be set up on the day of resurrection with the length of each of its

> shafts the distance between the East and the West. The scale of the *mīzān* will be like the strata of the earth in length and breadth. One of the two scales will be on the right of the Throne, and it is the scale of good deeds, and the other on the left of the Throne, and it is the scale of wrong deeds. The scales will be piled up like mountains, weighted with good and evil deeds. That day will last for 50,000 years.

Vain is every protest of the individual that he has been dealt with unfairly or that there are mitigating circumstances by which judgment should be postponed or rendered lighter. In a very real sense the judgment is automatic, the foregone conclusion of one's own personal choices. As if to underscore again the hopelessness of any attempt at escaping the inevitable, the Qur'ān attests that {On that day We shall put a seal on their mouths, and their hands will speak to us and their feet will bear witness to what they have acquired} [S 36:65]. One's own limbs will testify to the truth and to the accuracy of the judgment rendered.

At this point in the cumulation of Qur'ānic narrative the judgment process itself is virtually concluded. The saved and the doomed are distinguished beyond any doubt, and only the graphic and detailed descriptions of the Garden and the Fire remain. This is not quite the end of the matter for tradition and theology, however. As the emphasis shifts from the individual to the community, the overwhelming imagery of God's justice as predominant in the process of judgment comes to be mitigated somewhat by the increasing stress on His enduring mercy, and into the bleak picture of the fate of the wrongdoer is injected some ray of hope. First, however, we need to note one more modality in the group accepted by Islamic tradition as operative on the day of resurrection, the bridge.

The Crossing of the Bridge [ṣirāṭ], *the Possibility of Intercession* [shafā'a], *and Preparation for the Final Consignment*

The Qur'ān contains numerous references to *sirāt* as meaning the path or way. Of these only two, S 36:66 and 37:23–24, have normally been cited to support the idea of a bridge to or over Hell, and both are rather indefinite. The latter refers to the *ṣirāṭ al-jaḥīm* and was adopted into Islamic tradition to signify the span over Gehenna, the top layer of the Fire.[50] The symbolic imagery of this term is especially rich: it is completely appropriate that the term used repeatedly in the Qur'ān to represent the proper and prescribed mode of action for all the faithful, the straight path, should be in a much more specific sense the last modality in the process that assesses the degree to which every individual has followed that path. Very probably reflecting an influence from Zoroastrian tradition in which the bridge plays a major role in the eschatological process,[51] the *ṣirāṭ* in Islamic thought seems to be yet another means of verifying rather than testing the relative merit of any given individual.

It is said that both the saved and the condemned must pass over the bridge, although the judgment process actually has been completed at the point at which the bridge is introduced in most narratives. Sometimes Jibrīl is said to be stationed at the beginning of the bridge and Mikhā'īl at the middle to question those who pass over it. The notion that this in any way tests the individual is further nullified by the commonly accepted understanding that God actually facilitates passage over the bridge for those already decreed to be just or pardoned. Here the complex categories of sin, as Islamic theology came to enumerate them, were brought to bear in concrete illustration; those judged guilty of sin but still considered to be *mu'minūn* fall from the bridge into the Fire, but only for a limited period of purgation. Those who have neither faith nor good deeds to their credit, however, find that the *ṣirāṭ* has become sharper than a sword and thinner than a hair,[57] and that their fall from it signifies an inescapable descent into the Fire of everlasting punishment. This inevitable fall is described in specific terms as having been caused not only by the narrowness of the passage but by increasing darkness. The faithful, on the contrary, move easily and swiftly across a broad path, led by the members of the Muslim community and first of all by the Prophet himself.[53]

In the imagery of the bridge one finds a useful focus for several of the themes that have occupied Muslim thinkers in the consideration of judgment and human responsibility. As has been the case in prophetic religions in general, Islam has suggested a variety of interpretations of the relationship of piety and works to salvation. In some of the descriptions of the bridge the degree of faith of the individual seems to determine safe passage. In others a concern for performance of the law bears the weight. (This is not to suggest, of course, that piety and concern for the law are in any way unrelated, but rather to point to the varying emphases on internal and external manifestations of one's *islām/īmān*.) In the *Kitāb aḥwāl al-qiyāma* (pp. 82–83), for instance, the bridge is described as having seven arches, each 3,000 years in length, which parallel the seven specific duties prescribed by the *sharī'a*. The servant will be questioned on each arch respectively about his *īmān*, his prayer [*ṣalāt*], his almsgiving [*zakāt*], his pilgrimage [*ḥajj*], his ritual washings [*wuḍū'*, *ghusl*], and his responsibility to his relatives.

Another and perhaps even more significant observation in relation to the *ṣirāṭ* is that here we see indicated a transition in emphasis from concern for the individual to concern for the community. The Islamic *umma* as a whole, with the Prophet at the head, leads the way across the bridge. Never is it suggested that human beings are not personally and individually responsible, but with this stress on the communal element comes the opportunity for Muslim theologians to reflect on the possibility that such affiliation might actually allow for some means of intercession.

Reference was made in Chapter One to the ways in which the general Qur'ānic denial of the possibility of intercession, *shafā'a*, was modified in the ensuing understanding of the community, and the Prophet Muḥammad was invested with the function of intervening on behalf of the Muslims on the day of judgment. The exact time of the intercession as it comes into the order of events seems to vary with the accounts. One of the most popular and often-cited of the stories validating Muḥammad as intercessory agent describes a long sequence generally placed somewhat earlier in the narratives, and put by al-Ghazālī in the *Durra* between the two soundings of the trumpet (MS pp. 59–65). According to this account Muslims waiting for the judgment for a thousand years seek restlessly for one of the prophets to intercede for them with God. They go from one to the next, but each has to refuse because of some particular problem or sin he has committed: Adam for eating the fruit of the tree, Noah for being too concerned for himself while his people were drowning, Abraham for disputing with his community about the *dīn* of God, Moses for killing a man, and Jesus because he and his mother are worshipped as gods. Finally they go to Muḥammad, and the Prophet says, "I am the right one! I am the right one [to intercede] insofar as God allows it for whomever He wills and chooses." Moving towards the pavilions of God, the Prophet asks for and is granted permission to intercede. The veils are raised, he falls in prostration for a thousand years, praising God, and the Throne itself trembles in tribute to him.

More generally the actual intercession is said to take place at the basin or pond [*ḥawḍ*] at which Muḥammad will meet the members of his community. Not referred to in the Qur'ān, the reports mention the *ḥawḍ* sometimes before but more often after the account of the *ṣirāṭ*. Its general location is somewhere near the balance and the bridge. By this time the judgment process itself is virtually concluded, and the symbolism of the basin seems to be, if anything, purificatory. It is said to contain delicious liquid as white as milk and as sweet as honey, which the faithful drink before entering the Garden. As usual the physical accounts are fabulous: huge in size, whiter than snow, smelling sweeter than musk, and containing numberless jars, the basin is filled by gold and silver spouts from the Garden itself.[54]

The question of the intercessory privileges of the other prophets has frequently been raised. Some narratives attest to each prophet having his own basin from which the members of his community will drink, but the general conclusion, as evidenced in the story above about the believers searching from one prophet to the next, has been negative. Al-Ghazālī in the *Iḥyā'* (IV, 377–78) outlines the uniqueness of Muḥammad's circumstance when he cites these words of the Prophet: Each prophet was sent to certain people but Muḥammad was sent to all people; on the day of resurrection he will be the *imām* and the preacher and the intercessor of the prophets; each prophet has a call [*da'wa*] to which he will respond, but Muḥammad's call is intercession for his people on the day of resurrection. Each prophet will have a pulpit or dais [*minbar*] of gold on the day, but the Prophet Muḥammad instead of sitting will stand before God because of his extreme concern for his community. The orthodox conclusion, expressed in the creeds of al-Ash'arī, al-Nasafī, al-Ṭahāwī, and Abū Ḥanīfa is that Muḥammad alone will have the right to speak on behalf of the faithful:

> Then the Prophet says to God, please hasten the judgment for my community. He continues to intercede until he is given a document for those who were sent to the Fire. The possessor of the place where the Fire is kept will say, O Muḥammad, you did not leave behind any fuel for the anger of your Lord [i.e. any more persons to be burned in the Fire of God's avenging justice].[55]

Thus popular belief chose to see that all but the most sinful will be saved by Muḥammad's intercession and God's mercy at the final time. The prevailing opinion is that all but the *mushrikūn*, those who have committed the worst sin of impugning the *tawḥīd* of God, have the possibility of being saved. Despite the emphasis put on Muḥammad as the agent of intercession, of course, only by the mercy of God can anyone be saved from the Fire: "God will take out of the Fire everyone who has said the testimony [*shahāda*]," says al-Subkī, "and none will remain save the *kāfirūn*."[56]

The Qur'ān leaves no question whatsoever that divine justice will prevail on the day of judgment, that retribution will correspond in direct proportion to the degree of one's faith [*īmān*] and the nature of one's acts of religious response [*'ibāda*]. Likewise every individual is responsible for himself alone and need not—in fact cannot—bear the burden of anyone else's actions. With the doctrine of intercession, however, one sees a softening of the formula of unrelenting retribution, so that justice is tempered with mercy; even the smallest deed registered to one's credit may in the long run be sufficient to bring him to salvation.[57]

The eschatological manuals delight in elaborating the stories about God's seemingly endless mercy for the wrongdoers who have been punished in the Fire. (One must, of course, again suspend any attempt to determine a time sequence; the question is not when such wrongdoers enter the Fire, but what God's saving of them says about Him as merciful Lord). In many accounts God orders His angels, prophets, and most faithful ones to rescue those who have done some good, then those who have done a little good, and finally those in whose hearts there is even an atom of good.[58] Some traditions even go so far as to say that when none in any of these categories remains in the Fire, then God will step in and bring forth even those to whom no good at all can be attributed. As the *Mishkāt al-maṣābīḥ* relates, "The inhabitants of paradise will say, 'Those are they who have been set free by the Compassionate One who has brought them into paradise without anything they have done or any good they have sent before them.' "[59] Thus one finds here a kind of purgatorial suggestion in the temporary chastisement of those who are *mu'mins* at heart, but whose wrong-doings necessitate some expiation before they can be allowed to enter the Garden. A graphic description of the bringing-forth of the faithful from the Fire is offered in the *Kitāb aḥwāl al-qiyāma*:

> [The Prophet Muḥammad] will come with the prophets and will bring out from the Fire all who used to say "There is no God but God and Muḥammad is the Messenger of God." Then the Prophet will hurry along to Jahannam. When [the angel] Mālik sees Muḥammad he will stand in honor to him. And Muḥammad will say to Mālik, "What is the condition of the miserable ones of my community?" Mālik will reply, "Their circumstance is calamitous and their place is straitened." The Prophet will say, "Open the door and lift the cover." So he will open it, and when the People of the Fire see Muḥammad they will call out together, saying, "O Muḥammad! The Fire has burned our skins and our flesh. You have left us in the Fire and Forgotten about us!" He will apologize to them, [saying], "I did not know of your condition." He will then bring them out all together, charred from the Fire having eaten at them. Then he will hurry with them to a river near the gate of the Garden, called [the river of] life. There they will bathe and emerge from it as beardless youths, with *kohl*ed eyes and faces like the moon. On their foreheads will be written: "These were in Jahannam, released by al-Raḥmān," and they will then enter the Garden . . . (pp. 101–02).

In several of the manuals one finds lengthy descriptions of those whose judgment has been positive and who will therefore immediately be led to the Garden in victory. Sometimes they are classified into various groups, each with a banner put into the hand of an appropriate messenger or prophet to lead them. The origin of the idea of eschatological banners is obscure,[60] but one can see clearly in the classifications of the righteous those qualities most prized at the day of reckoning as well as the affirmation that the lot of persons living in affliction while on earth is guaranteed to be better in the hereafter. Thus in the *Durra* (MS pp. 85–89) banners are given to the following persons, representative of categories of the saved: Shu'ayb (the blind), Job (the afflicted), Joseph (the righteous), Aaron (those who loved God), Noah (those who feared God), John (martyrs), Jesus (the poor), and Solomon (those of abundance).

With this long and complex series of events the judgment process is finally concluded, a story that runs technically from the signs of the Hour to the meeting of the community at the *ḥawḍ*, but which in reality begins with the first responsible act of the human individual as he begins to develop the pattern of his own *dīn* in response to the divine commandments and expectations. The recompense has been determined, and it remains now to see the ways in which Islamic tradition has understood, augmented, and amplified the promises of the Qur'ān expressed in its eloquent descriptions of the blessings of the Garden and the torments of the Fire.

The attempt to impose an order and a structured sequence on the events of the eschaton has been, as we have seen, a somewhat arbitrary one. To a limited extent Islam, or at least Islamic tradition, has found such an ordering to be necessary even though it is noticeably absent from the Qur'ān. From another perspective, however, it is clear that many of the issues around which the eschatological story has been woven do not necessarily relate to any given sequence of occurrences. God's justice and mercy can be illustrated through specific events but in themselves are apart from any ordered flow. Turning to the consideration of the abodes of the blessed and the damned, we find ourselves beyond time, beyond history, and beyond any need to see events and details in sequential order.

Because of the full and graphic descriptions of the abodes of the Garden and the Fire afforded by the Qur'ān, Islam has long labored under the charge that it holds a very materialistic conception of the afterlife. As was the case with the question of the modalities of the hour of judgment, the Islamic community has expressed a variety of interpretations as to whether or not the rewards and punishments of the life to come are to be understood in their most literal sense.[61] While the predominant understanding has been of the corporeal nature of the ultimate recompense, the positive affirmation of the reality of physical torment and pleasure, this view has generally not insisted that the realities of the next world will be identical with those of this world.[62] While definitely physical, recompense in the ultimate sense is generally understood to have a reality beyond what we are now able to comprehend. It is, in effect, another application of the Ash'arī principle of *bila kayf* (without being able to understand precisely how). Contemporary interpreters of the Qur'ān, as we shall see, are quite consistent in their understanding of the recompense of the hereafter as sentient yet in some way different from the experiences of this world.

Those within the Islamic community of a more philosophical or mystical orientation have, of course, demurred from a literal interpretation and insisted that the joys and torments of the saved and damned are rather to be understood metaphorically. Attempting to reconcile the various interpretations, some have posited several levels of understanding, each of which is relevant for an individual with the appropriate degree of perception. The vast majority of believers, however, has taken the Qur'ān in its exoteric meaning and understood the realities of the Garden and the Fire to be real and specific, anticipating them with terror or with joy. Before considering how modern Muslims see those particulars, let us look briefly at what the community has believed to await the errant and the righteous after the day of resurrection.

The Qur'ān leaves no doubt that the alternatives for each individual at the day of judgment are two: the bliss of the garden or the torment of the Fire. For the latter abode there are in the Book a variety of designations, seven of which have been seen as actual names or terms of specification: *hāwiya, jaḥīm, sa'īr, jahannam, laẓā, saqar,* and *ḥuṭāma*.[63] For our purposes it is sufficient to leave aside a detailed discussion of these names and their relative usage in the various portions of the Qur'ān. Even the most casual reader of the Book will immediately be impressed with the overwhelming understanding of the abode of the damned as Fire, *al-nār,* just as what might be called Heaven in other traditions is best rendered by its common Qur'ānic designation as the Garden(s). Many of the details of the Fire, as of the Garden, are reminiscent of the New Testament; others reflect on occasion the tone of early Arabian poetry. On the whole, however, the picture afforded by the Qur'ān is uniquely its own, articulated in a generally consistent and always awe-inspiring fashion.

Based on S 89:23, {And Jahannam will be brought near that day ... }, an elaborate mythology grew up around the image of the Fire as something moveable and specifically as a kind of beast. The *Durra*, for example, describes it as being summoned on the day of resurrection and arriving roaring and smoking, and walking on four legs bound each by 70,000 rings. When it is still 1000 years away, it escapes the myrmidons (denizens of the Fire) who hold it, but is recaptured and tamed by the Prophet Muḥammad (MS pp. 66–68). In a similar description the *Kitāb aḥwāl al-qiyāma* speaks of the Fire as having four legs (between each leg 1000 years), thirty heads with 30,000 mouths each, lips like 1000 mountains, and so on (p. 90). Despite this kind of personified image, however, the commonest understanding of the Fire has been of a structure organized in concentric circles.

The Qur'ān itself does not offer a detailed plan of the realms of the Fire, and it seems clear that the Prophet did not have such a plan in mind. S 15:43–44 describes Jahannam as having seven gates, each gate with its "appointed portion." Thus the idea developed that the Fire consists of seven layers, each descending one an abode of increased torment.[64] Gehenna [*jahannam*][65] is sometimes used to refer to the totality of the Fire and sometimes only to the top-most circle. An elaborate structure of relative punishments came to be worked out around the seven layers of the Fire, using the terminology suggested above to designate the realms of torture: the purgatorial fire [*jahannam*] for Muslims; the flaming fire [*laẓā*] for Christians; the raging fire [*ḥuṭāma*] for Jews; the blazing fire [*sa'īr*] for Sabaeans; the scorching fire [*saqar*] for the Magi; the fierce fire [*jaḥīm*] for idolaters; and the abyss [*hāwiya*] for hypocrites. Later traditions supplied each of the gates of the Fire with innumerable guardians who torture the damned. From the shallowest level the *mu'minun* will be pardoned and taken into paradise; that layer of the Fire will then be destroyed. Some accounts show Muḥammad as weeping when he realizes that members of his community will be in the Fire even for a short time.

Across the top of this structured layering of the Fire is the bridge of *ṣirāṭ* over which all must pass. At the opposite side, on the bottom of the pit of the Fire, grows the dreadful tree Zaqqūm (S 37:62–68) with the heads of devils for flowers, from which sinners must eat in mouthfuls that burn the belly like molten brass. The Qur'ān offers a number of rather specific indications of the tortures of the Fire: its flames crackle and roar (S 25:14); it has fierce, boiling waters (S 55:44), scorching wind, and black smoke (S 56:42–43); it roars and boils as if it would burst with rage (S 67:7–8). The people of the Fire are sighing and wailing, wretched (S 11:106), their scorched skins are constantly exchanged for new ones so that they can taste the torment anew (S 4:45), they drink festering water and though death appears on all sides they cannot die (S 14:16–17), people are linked together in chains of 70 cubits (S 69:30–32) wearing pitch for clothing and fire on their faces (S 14:50), boiling water will be poured over their heads, melting their insides as well as their skins, and hooks of iron will drag them back should they try to escape (S 22:19–21). To these terrifying details the *ḥadīths* could add only more elaboration and more specifics.[66]

The Qur'ān also makes very clear for which deeds persons are consigned to the Fire: lying, corruption, failure to have faith in the message of the prophets and in God's revelations, scorning God, denying the coming of the Hour and the reality of the Fire, failing to feed the poor, enjoying too much luxury in this life and thinking wealth will make them immortal; the *jinn* are doomed because of their efforts to seduce humankind.

Some see the descriptions of the Fire, particularly as they become elaborated in the reports, as directly paralleling the descriptions of the Garden: heat vs. the coolness of paradise, the division into layers (though the Garden is often understood to have eight instead of seven), the Zaqqūm tree opposite the lote tree of paradise,[67] the presence of rivers, and the like. While the tree of the pit has heads like devils, it should be noted that in reality angels [*al-zabānīya*][68] guard the gates of the Fire rather than satans [*shayāṭīn*], and there is no reigning devil who is lord of the lost because Iblīs, the fallen angel, was defeated and destroyed at the hands of the Mahdī. While the Qur'ānic descriptions of the Garden do not specifically mention God, they clearly promise that the faithful will gaze upon His face, a joy of which the inhabitants of the Fire are deprived for the duration of their stay.[69] The Qur'ān nowhere states however, that this loss contributed to the agony they are undergoing (although the reports do have references to this effect). Torment, in other words, is portrayed in physical rather than spiritual or psychological terms in the Qur'ān, and regret, if expressed, is for the consequences of one's deeds rather than for the actual commission of them.[70]

As has been the case in later Islamic conceptions of life in the Gardens, traditions reflect some rather extreme imaginings in the attempt to characterize the nature of the agonies awaiting the damned.[71] Scorpions as big as mules and snakes like camels torment them; stinking rivers full of vile creatures entrap them; the damned have black charred skins, huge long tongues, mouths vomiting pus and blood, entrails filled with fire; their bodies will be greatly enlarged so that they can more adequately experience the torture. All suffer by fire, although the degree of punishment differs according to one's sins. The damned attempt to escape, but each time the guardians of the Fire seize them and throw them down again. Such descriptions are, of course, not exclusive to Islamic mythology; they are rivaled if not exceeded in much of the eschatological literature of other traditions (one can look, for example, at the fantastic descriptions of the multitudes of hells afforded in Mahayana Buddhist literature).

Turning to the abode of reward, we find in the Qur'ān some very specific categories of people for whom eternal habitation in felicity is assured: those who refrain from doing evil, keep their duty, have faith in God's revelations, do good works, are truthful, penitent, heedful, and contrite of heart, those who feed the needy and orphans and who are prisoners for God's sake. These form, again, a close parallel to the acts of ommission and commission that afford one a place in the Fire. There are also very detailed descriptions of the nature of the reward and of the habitations to be enjoyed by the virtuous.

Paradise in the Qur'ān is generally referred to as the Garden [*janna*], although its descriptions are usually of Gardens in the plural. There are two references to the name Firdaws (S 18:107, 23:11) as the abode of the blessed. As was true of Qur'ānic descriptions of the Fire, nowhere does the Book offer an ordered picture of the structure of the Garden. On the basis of several scriptural suggestions, however, a very detailed structure was later posited, which roughly parallels the divisions of the Fire. In S 23:17 God says, {We created above you seven paths [*ṭarā'iq*] . . .}, which supports the conception of a seven-tiered heaven, a structure familiar to Middle Eastern cosmogony since the early Babylonian days. Another view held that there are actually eight layers or realms of paradise, for which Qur'ānic sanction is found in eight different names given for the abode of the blessed.[72] Some feel that the addition of another realm beyond the seven paralleled in the Fire is to accommodate the elect, who are greater in number than the damned.[73]

Certain descriptions of the Garden indicate that Firdaws is actually the most spacious and highest part of the Garden, directly under the Throne, from which the four rivers of paradise flow. Others say that it is the second level from the top and that the uppermost portion is either the Garden of Eden[74] or 'Iliyīn. Further possibility for speculation is afforded by S 55, which talks about two Gardens: {As for him who fears standing before his Lord there are two Gardens [*jannatān*]} [S 55:46]. All descriptions following this verse are of things in pairs—two fountains flowing, fruit of every kind in pairs, beside these two other gardens with two springs (S 55:62,66). On the basis of this Sura some commentators have distinguished four separate realms of the blessed, of which either Firdaws or Eden is the uppermost.[75] Still others understand that the seven levels suggested by the Qur'ān are the seven heavens, above which is the Garden or final abode of felicity, while many see paradise as only one entity with many names.

Representative of the medieval conceptualization of the layers of the Garden is this description from the *Kitāb aḥwāl al-qiyāma* (pp. 105–06):

> There are seven gardens. The first of them is the abode of the garden [*dār al-jinān*] and it is of white pearl. The second is the abode of peace [*dār al-salām*] and it is of red sapphire. The third is the garden of refuge [*jannat al-ma'wan*] and it is of green chrysolite. The fourth of them is the garden of eternity [*jannat al-khuld*] and it is of yellow coral. The fifth is the garden of bliss [*jannat al-na'īm*] and it is of white silver. The sixth is the *jannat al-firdaws* and it is of red gold. And the seventh of the gardens is Eden [*jannāt 'adn*] and is of white pearl. This is the capital [*qaṣāba*] of the Garden and it is elevated over all the gardens. . . .

Within the Garden(s), regardless of structure, we do know of certain identifiable features through specific Qur'ānic references. Many verses speak of the rivers flowing underneath. On the basis of S 47:15, which describes rivers of water, milk, wine, and honey, tradition has said that four rivers run through paradise, issuing from the highest realm. These have been identified as Kawthar, Kāfūr, Tasnīm, and Salsabīl.[76] There is neither too much heat in the Gardens, says the Qur'ān, nor bitter cold, and there is plenteous shade from spreading branches dark green with foliage. S 53:14–16 describes the lote tree of the upper boundary, the Sidrat al-Muntahá, which tradition soon located specifically at the top of the realm of the Gardens as a parallel to the tree of Zaqqūm at the pit of the Fire. S 39:73 says that people will be driven into the Garden in troops until they reach it, whereupon the gates will be opened and they will be welcomed. Again later writers have elaborated this into a detailed description of the eight doors giving access to paradise.[77] Some structure is suggested in the Qur'ānic promise that {. . . for those who are faithful to their Lord there are rooms [*ghuraf*], and above them rooms built over them . . .}; it was an easy step to supply this description with a multitude of particulars.

Qur'ānic illustrations of the joys awaiting the dwellers in the Garden are sufficiently rich that tradition had done little but amplify and elaborate on them. The graphic scenes portrayed in the Book are full of the kind of detail so noticeably absent in relation to the immediate after-death period. Thus from the Qur'ān we learn that the faithful are content, peaceful, and secure;

they hear no idle talk and experience only peace; they do not taste death; they enjoy gentle speech, pleasant shade, and fruits neither forbidden nor out of reach, as well as cool drink and meat as they desire; they drink from a shining stream of delicious wine, from which they will suffer no aftereffects (S 37:45–47); they sit on couches facing each other as brothers, wearing armlets of gold and pearls, green and gold robes of the finest silk and embroidery, waited upon by menservants [*ghulmān*] (S 52:24, 56:17, 74:19).[78]

One of the joys afforded to the inhabitans of the Garden, specifically to males, is the companionship of young virgins with eyes like guarded pearls. These creatures, called in the Qur'ān the *ḥūr,* have been the subject of a great deal of discussion on the part of traditionists and commentators, and not surprisingly their presence in the Qur'ānic descriptions has occasioned spectacular elaborations in later Islamic eschatological writing. They have also been the subject of some derision by insensitive Western observers and critics of Islam, on the basis of which Muslim apologists sometimes have attempted to identify them with the faithful Muslim women who are promised a place in the Garden with their husbands. (For a fuller description of the *ḥūr* see Appendix B on the role of women in Islamic discussions of the afterlife.)

We observed above that the torments of the damned are described in the Qur'ān as physical rather than spiritual; we should note here, however, that despite the graphic terms in which the physical pleasures of the inhabitants of the Garden are portrayed, there are clear references to a greater joy that exceeds the pleasures of the flesh. Thus we read in S 9:72: {God promises to the faithful men and women Gardens with rivers flowing below in which are delightful habitations in the Gardens of Eden. And [there is] acceptance [*riḍwān*][79] from God, which is greater than [the pleasure of the Gardens]. . . .} Space does not permit more than a brief sampling of the elaborations Islamic tradition provided of the basic descriptions of the Qur'ān. Detailed pictures have been presented of what life will be like for those who earn God's reward. Choirs of angels will sing in Arabic (the only language used in paradise), the streets will be as familiar as those of the dwellers' own countries, inhabitants will eat and drink 100 times more than earthly bodies could hold and will enjoy it 100 times more, their rooms will have thick carpets and brocade sofas, on Fridays they will go to a market to receive new clothing to enhance their beauty, they will not suffer bodily ailments or be subject to functions such as sleeping, spitting, or excreting; they will be forever young.[80] While the Qur'ān insists that no aftereffects will occur from imbibing the wines of the Garden's rivers, the possibilities of heavenly intoxication have afforded the type of fanciful description found in Abū Layth al-Samarqandī, reportedly from the Prophet:

> On Saturday God Most High will provide drink [from the water of the Garden]. On Sunday they will drink its honey, on Monday they will drink its milk, on Tuesday they will drink its wine. When they have drunk, they will become intoxicated; when they become intoxicated, they will fly for a thousand years till they reach a great mountain of fine musk, from beneath which emanates Salsabīl. They will drink [of it] and that will be Wednesday. Then they will fly for a thousand years till they reach a place overtopping a mountain. On it are thrones raised and cups set out—[as in] the text: Every one of them will sit on a couch. Ginger wine will be brought down to them and they shall drink. That will be on Thursday. Then He will rain down upon them vestments from a white cloud, for a thousand years, and jewels for a thousand years. Attached to every jewel will be a black-eyed maiden. Then they will fly for a thousand years till they reach a perfect level spot. That will be on Friday. They will be seated on the plateau of eternity. The finest wine will be brought to them, sealed with musk. They will drink (it).[81]

We have spoken thus of the two obvious alternatives according to which the fate of the resurrected is determined: the Fire of punishment and the Garden(s) of reward. With one possible exception, these are the only options afforded by the Qur'ān, and tradition has found no reason to amend this (other than in relation to the question of whether or not punishment in the Fire is never-ending). In the Qur'ān, however, one verse has led to a great deal of speculation concerning the possibility of a third place where persons who have completed their judgment process may go, at least temporarily. This is S 7:46: {And between the two is a partition [*ḥijāb*], and on the heights [*al-aʿrāf*] are men who know them all by their signs. And they call to the inhabitants of the Garden, 'Peace be upon you.' They do not enter it, though they wish to}. The exegesis of this verse has developed what some have called the "limbo" theory of Islam, or the supposition that there is an intermediate class of people who do not automatically enter the Garden or the Fire.

The Qur'ān contains no other reference to the *aʿrāf*, although it does mention a wall [*sūr*] of separation in S 57:13 (with no specification of its location), which many commentators have equated with the *ḥijāb*, whose uppermost portions are the *aʿrāf*. It is clear from the Qur'ān that this partition separates the inhabitants of the Garden from those of the Fire, and that the men on the heights can view persons in both circumstances. It seems very doubtful that the Qur'ānic intention was of an abode for those understood to be in an intermediate category, but this has come to be the most commonly held interpretation.[82]

The verse has elicited wide speculation, and early commentators suggested a great variety of possibilities in explanation of it. Both al-Ṭabarī and al-Rāzī in their expositions on the passage list various theories that have been posited about the inhabitants of the *a'rāf*, among which are the following:[83] (1) they are the most excellent of the pious people, such as the righteous [*ṣāliḥūn*], the legists [*fuqahā'*], the learned doctors [*'ulamā'*], and the martyrs; (2) they are not humans at all, but angels who distinguish between the blessed and the damned before taking them to the Garden or the Fire; (3) they are the prophets; (4) they are persons killed fighting in the way of God, but who disobeyed their parents in so doing; (5) they are persons whose good deeds keep them from the Fire and whose evil deeds keep them from the Garden, i.e. those whose actions balance in terms of merit and demerit, and who are therefore the last to enter the Garden, at the mercy of their Lord.[84]

The majority of exegetes have supported the last possibility for both negative and positive reasons. Citing the last phrase of the verse, which says the men of the *a'rāf* do not enter the Garden, they insist that this rules out the most virtuous of the Islamic community, who would automatically be granted such entrance. They therefore posit an intermediate position, the highest place on the partition separating the Garden from the Fire, from which the dwellers on the *a'rāf* gaze down at the inhabitants of the two abodes and recognize them by their distinguishing signs. (These signs are most often said to be the smiling, glad faces of those in the Garden and the black faces and blue eyes of those in the Fire!)[85] Their good and bad deeds equal, they must wait until all the rest of humanity has been assigned its just destiny. The people of the heights call out to God, asking Him that they not be consigned to the Fire, the agony of whose inhabitants they witness, and express their hope of joining the dwellers in the Garden. The majority of exegetes use this verse as another occasion to extol the mercy of God, saying that the dwellers on the *a'rāf* will, in fact, finally be granted admission into the Garden through His good will and pleasure.[86] Many include the particulars of the entrance into paradise, such as the initial bathing in the river of life [*nahr al-ḥayāt*] so that they can go into the Garden refreshed and purified.[87]

For the most part Islamic theology has not concerned itself with questions about the location and structure of the Garden and the Fire on the understanding that only God knows these particulars. (The traditionists, as we have seen, have been much more ready to speculate in this realm). Likewise *kalām* has been less interested than the transmitters of *ḥadīths* in the precise form of the bliss or torment of the hereafter. It has, however, been especially concerned with two questions regarding the future life. The first of these is the existence of the Garden and the Fire, in particular the issue of whether or not they have already been created, as well as whether or not the abodes of both punishment and reward are eternal. The second matter of great interest to theology has been the matter of the *ru'yā Allāh*, the vision of God.

The creation of the two final abodes was one of the issues most sharply defined in the debates involving the Mu'tazila and their theological opponents. The majority of the Mu'tazila rejected categorically the notion that the Garden and the Fire have already been created on the grounds that the physical universe does not allow for their existence yet. They also argued that because of the Qur'ānic assertion that between the trumpet blasts all will be destroyed but God, it is more reasonable to assume that these abodes will be created after the great *fanā'*. The Ash'arīya countered by saying that location is not the issue, and that it is not impossible to imagine another world or level of existence unattainable by our present faculties. As for the *fanā'*, they argued, it is true that all will be destroyed, but that creation and recreation are in any case a constant process. The Qur'ān states that Adam and his wife were in the Garden of Eden; thus it must already be in existence, and numerous *ḥadīths* attesting to the night journey of the Prophet indicate clearly that he was given a vision by God of both the Fire and the Garden. We read in the orthodox creeds the clear statement that the Garden and the Fire are a reality and that they are already created and in existence.[88]

The affirmation that the abodes of recompense have already been brought into being is usually paralleled by the insistence that they will continue to exist, that neither they nor their inhabitants will pass away. This is not inconsistent, they say, with the reality of the *fanā'*.[89] The intention of the Qur'ān itself is not entirely clear in this context. Forms of the verb *kh-l-d* are used numerous times in relation to statements about the afterlife, as in S 50:34: {Enter [the Garden] in peace; that is the day of eternity [*yawm al-khulūd*]}. This is the only use of the form *khulūd* in the Qur'ān; *khuld,* however, is used six times, four of which apply to states of recompense: 10:52 speaks of the torment of eternity, 32:14 talks of the punishment of eternity, 41:28 calls the Fire the *dār al-khuld*, and 25:15 promises the *jannat al-khuld* to the pious. The form *khālidūn* is used numerous times to describe the stay of the wicked in the Fire, as in 43:74: {The guilty ones are in the punishment of

Jahannam khālidūn}.[90] On the other hand, some verses seem to leave open the possibility that punishment will not necessarily be forever. S 78:23, for example, states that {They will remain in [the Fire] for a long time [*aḥqāban*]}; the even more suggestive 10:107 says {*khalidūn fīhā* [eternally in it] as long as the heavens [*al-samawāt*] and the earth endure . . .}; and 6:128 makes clear that eternally means only for as long as God wills. Concerning the Garden in the Qur'ān we find eternality assured in such verses as 3:198, 4:57, and 57:12, which says that the righteous will be *khālidūn fīhā,* and 35:35, which describes the reward of the abode of everlastingness [*dār al-maqāma*].

On the basis of the Qur'ānic assurances in descriptions of the Gardens as well as a firm faith in God's justice in addition to His mercy, neither the theologians nor the traditionalists have questioned the eternal nature of the Garden and the residence of the faithful in it.[91] The question becomes more problematic in relation to the Fire, however. As we have seen, trust in God's mercy as tempering the harsh realities of absolute justice led in the final analysis to the growth of the doctrine of intercession in the face of numerous Qur'ānic denials of such a possibility. With the several verses actually suggesting ways in which "eternally" might be mitigated or reinterpreted, it is not surprising that the conviction grew that at least for some, punishment may not necessarily be everlasting. The upper level of the Fire, as was noted above, was interpreted by many as abiding only as long as necessary for Muslims there to have their sins purged. Some orientalists have suggested that Gehenna in this sense is roughly parallel to the Christian idea of purgatory,[92] as was suggested in the commentary above on intercession. Others feel that such an analogy has only a very limited application and that real differences are to be found; punishment in Gehenna, for example, is different from that of other sinners in degree only and not kind, and while Christian purgatory is for the soul alone, Muslim Gehenna is a place of torment for the resurrected body in its totality.[93]

Two questions are at issue here. On the one hand is whether or not certain sinners, specifically Muslims who have testified to faith in God and His Messenger but who are guilty of wrongdoing, will have only a temporal punishment. On the other hand is the question concerning the possible salvation of all sinners from the Fire at some unspecified time when total purgation has been accomplished. As to the first point, whether or not one wants to press the analogy of purgatory, there is no question that the majority have held to the view that the faithful will not have to suffer eternally for the errors they have made.[94] The second point has been more controversial. The creeds do not suggest the final passing away of the Fire—". . . neither they [the Garden and the Fire] nor their inhabitants will vanish";[95] ". . . they will never cease to exist"[96]—and the vast majority of reports support the understanding of the eternality of the Fire. But on the basis of such Qur'ān verses as 11:107 ("as long as the heavens and the earth endure") many have held that it is not only possible but likely that at some future time all sinners will be pardoned and the Fires of punishment will be extinguished forever.[97]

Ibn Qayyim al-Jawzīya in his *Ḥādī al-arwāḥ* (p. 250 ff.) provides a summary of the arguments generally given for and against the ultimate cessation of the Fire. He cites first the report (from Muslim and Bukhārī) according to which a spotted ram is placed between the Garden and the Fire and the inhabitants of both locales asked if they recognize it. They do, with terror and joy respectively, and announce that it is Death. The ram is slaughtered, and the word is given that all will exist eternally without dying. This authentic *ḥadīth*, says Ibn Qayyim, has been used by exegetes to affirm the eternity of both abodes. Among the arguments of those who say the Fire will never cease, he gives the following: the explicitness of the Qur'ān that torments are eternal, the consensus of tradition that only monotheist Muslims can escape the Fire through intercession, the word of the Prophet that the Fire is eternal, and the appeal to reason which says that a just God would not offer the same reward to the evil as to the good.

Ibn Qayyim's own predilection is toward divine leniency in the long run and thus the eventual dissolution of the Fire. He provides a lengthy list of arguments in support of this view, among which the following are suggestive of the thinking on this issue: (1) the Qur'ān affirms that the inhabitants of the Fire will suffer as long as the Fire endures, but if the Fire is annihilated, then suffering will cease; (2) if God so pleases to pardon and free the wrongdoers, He can and will do so; (3) it is innovation [*bid'a*] to say that both the Fire and the Garden will be annihilated, but not to say that only the Fire will be; (4) three passages in the Qur'ān indicate that the Fire is not eternal (6:128, 11:107, and 78:23, all of which are referred to above); (5) it is not possible to equate divine anger with divine mercy; (6) the Fire is a means of purification, while the Garden as reward is an end; (7) given its purificatory function, it would be senseless if the Fire continued after the purification has taken place; (8) even torment is an expression of God's mercy and not His vengeance, so it is impossible to suppose eternal torment; (9) God keeps His promises but is not obligated to keep His threats (of eternal punishment), and the remission of those threats is part of His mercy. Ibn Qayyim then gives as the ultimate rationale for his conclusion in favor of mercy the saying of Alī b. Abī Ṭālib regarding the entry of the pious into the Garden and the sinners into the Fire, "God will do then as He pleases." In general it can be said that the non-eternity of the Fire has prevailed as the understanding of the Muslim community, supported by al-Ash'arī's opinion that punishment is not of unlimited duration.[98] We will see in the section on contemporary Muslim understanding of the afterlife some of the ways in which this question of the eternality of punishment is now viewed.

The other matter of concern to Muslim theology in this context has been the question of the beatific vision of God. S 75:23 provides what many have felt to be positive affirmation of that vision: {On that day faces will be radiant, looking toward their Lord}. The Qur'ān also speaks of the *wajh Allāh*, the face of God (2:110, 30:38–9, 76:9), and the face of the Lord (13:22, 55:27, 92:20). The *ḥadīths* have affirmed that such a view of the divine is to be part of the reward of the faithful. The Prophet is reported to have given such positive assurance as the following:

> When the inhabitants of paradise enter it God most high will ask, "Do you wish me to give you anything more?" and they will reply, "Hast Thou not whitened our faces, hast Thou not brought us into paradise and saved us from hell?" The veil will then be removed, they will look at God's face, and will not have been given anything dearer to them than looking at their Lord.[99]

Many in the early Islamic community, however, denied that such a vision is to be understood as a direct view of the actual face of the Lord. The Jahmīyah, whose opinions on the non-eternality of both the Garden and the Fire failed to gain general acceptance, felt strongly that neither in this world nor the next will anyone actually be able to see God. Sharing this view were the Mu'tazila, who argued that since, in their understanding, God is an immaterial substance devoid of accidents, He is by definition not visible. To admit that He can be seen would be to imply corporeality and therefore limitation. The issue, of course, was that of *tashbīh*, anthropomorphism, to which the Mu'tazila and others in the Muslim community were rigidly opposed.[100] They sought support not only in rational arguments but in such Qur'ān verses as 6:103, {Vision cannot attain to him . . .}.

The majority opinion, however, rejected the Mu'tazilī opposition to the possibility of the *ru'yā Allāh*, following the conclusions of the school of al-Ash'arī that the vision of God in the next world is indeed a reality. This was not, however, a complete concession to *tashbīh*. Applying once again the *bilā kayf* principle, they held that while the promise of the vision of God will be kept for the faithful, the precise means of that vision as well as its content must for now be unexplainable. This vision, then, came to be seen as a second reward for the faithful in paradise beyond the pleasures of the Garden, and was attested to as the ultimate joy beyond anything that can be expressed either in this world or by the physical senses in the next. Thus we read in the creeds such affirmations as the following: "The Beatific Vision (*al-ru'yā*) is a Reality for the People of the Garden without there being any encompassing or modality (*kayfīya*)";[101] "Allah will be seen in the world to come. The Faithful will see Him, being in Paradise, with their bodily eyes, without comparison or modality. And there will be no distance between Him and His creatures."[102]

If theology was content to affirm the vision in general while refraining from any attempt to suppose the particulars, the *ḥadīths* as usual abound with detail about the encounter of the faithful with their Lord. While the Qur'ān in describing the Garden does not discuss such a meeting, one finds assurance in the reports that reward will include some activity in the presence of God. According to one set of narratives the elect upon first entering the Garden will gather around a table to enjoy a feast of a huge fish and an enormous roasted bull, which has been prepared for them since the beginning of creation. God Himself is present to offer to His faithful ones delicacies kneaded into a kind of pancake.[103] Each Friday, according to another series of narratives, God will personally invite the men and women of the Garden to visit with Him. The men follow the Prophet and the women his daughter Fatima, approaching the Throne, which is described as a huge esplanade of musk. The veil of light before the Throne lifts, God appears with the radiance of the full moon, and His voice can be heard saying, "Peace be upon you." Such joy, it is affirmed, far exceeds the pleasures of the Garden.[104] And from Ibn Māja as reported in the *Mishkāt al-maṣābīḥ* (II, 1208–09):

> Jābir reported the Prophet as saying: "While the inhabitants of paradise are in their bliss a light will shine out to them, and raising their heads they will see that their Lord has looked down on them from above. He will then say, 'Peace be to you, inhabitants of paradise,' the proof of that being the words of God most high, 'Peace, a word from a merciful Lord.' He will then look at them and they will look at Him, and they will not turn aside to any of their bliss as long as they are looking at Him till He veils Himself from them and His light remains."

Thus has classical Islam understood the divine promises concerning death and resurrection, residence in the temporary world of the *barzakh* and final habitation in the abodes of recompense and reward. In the two succeeding chapters we will consider ways in which modern Muslims have accepted, rejected, or reinterpreted this classical material in light of their concern for articulating what it means to be Muslim in the contemporary world.

Chapter Four
From Death to Resurrection: Modern Islam

Contemporary Muslims, theologians and others as well, treat Islam and Islamic topics as a whole in a wide variety of ways, clearly reflected in the different approaches they take to questions of life after death. Some of this variety, no doubt, is because only recently in the Islamic world have there been sustained attempts at consultation [*shūra*] and consensus [*ijmāʿ*] in articulating the elements of the faith, such as the annual conferences at Azhar, Mecca and elsewhere, and the establishment of international bodies like the Muslim World League and the Islamic Conference. It is also the case that those writing on Islamic subjects in this century have not necessarily been trained in Islamic centers or well versed in the traditional Islamic sciences. Much of the cause of the defense of Islam has been taken over by persons who have studied Islamic subjects in the West and have been influenced by Western thought, as well as by many who are "professionals" in other disciplines such as medicine, law, engineering and the like. These persons are writing out of personal devotion and concern that Islam not be seen as irrelevant to the modern world in a time when Western ideologies, customs, patterns of thought, and grounds of validation are appropriated and utilized by Muslims. The variety is thus a factor in the different perspectives that modern writers represent; it is justified in the Islamic understanding because of the pervasive nature of Islam as the totality of life with no bifurcation between secular and sacred.

All of the modern writers, in one way or another, address the Western ideas to which Islam has been exposed, and all respond in some form to what they see as the heavy emphasis on rationalism that has characterized so much of Western thinking. The nature of this response, however, differs rather widely. The great majority of contemporary Muslim writers, in fact, choose not to discuss the afterlife at all. They are satisfied with simply affirming the reality of the day of judgment and human accountability without providing any details or interpretive discussion. There are several reasons for this. One is a kind of embarrassment with the elaborate traditional detail concerning life in the grave and in the abodes of recompense, called into question by modern rationalists. Another explanation is that up to the nineteenth century Islam had strongly emphasized the hereafter, largely under Sufi influence, and had turned its attention away from life in this world. Many of the modern thinkers are thus anxious to reinstate what they understand to be the true Islamic emphasis on the importance of *dunyá* as well as of *ākhira* and on the strength and potential of the community in this life. It is not that the afterlife for them is ultimately of less importance, but rather that they have conceived their task as emphasizing that which has somehow become devalued, stressing in particular the work ethic that will help achieve material and technological parity with the West.

Among those who treat questions of the afterlife in a more specific way are again several very distinct approaches. One is general reiteration of the traditional materials as they were outlined in Chapters Two and Three, an affirmation of the classical teachings as continuingly valid. Those writing from this perspective, for purposes of general classification, we are here calling "traditionists." These writers appear to have accepted the idea of the termination of individual interpretation [*ijtihād*] and are therefore anxious not to add in any way to the corpus of interpretation; rather they affirm the writings of the earlier scholars as definitive and valid for all time. Their contribution, they feel, comes in presenting the material in modern Arabic, which makes it accessible to the average reader, occasionally rearranging the narratives so as to make them more chronological.

A second group is concerned with more interpretive analyses of life after death. Such analysts we refer to as "modernists," which is intended to reflect their approach as distinct from the traditionists rather than to identify any tendencies of what might in other reviews of modern Islam be called conservative or liberal. In the present chapter we will view ways in which they understand the *barzakh* in light of contemporary concerns with such issues as science and the immediate life after death, the possibility of continuing human development, and the reaffirmation of the Qur'ānic stress on ethical responsibility. While it is not always possible to distinguish in approach between Arab and Indo-Pakistani writers, in general the latter sometimes seem to place greater emphasis on a kind of Darwinian evolutionism presented as a vindication of Islamic ideas. One sees in much of their writing strong influence of Sufism as well as a response, either negative or positive, to elements coming out of the Indian milieu as a whole.

A third classification of those who specifically treat questions of life after death is particularly relevant to the consideration of the *barzakh*. This group articulates the findings of nineteenth- and twentieth-century Western spiritualism and adapts these notions to traditional Islamic ideas concerning communication with the world of the spirits and the general state of affairs of the deceased. The advocates of such a position we refer to as "spiritualists." For the most part they flourished at the time of British colonial rule and were therefore exposed to much of the popular European and American spiritualist writing. They were also, however, responding to Western orientalists and missionaries, who accused Muslims of having a sensual and material conception of the hereafter. In articulating the details of the life of the spirit after the death of the body these writers were not only providing a specifically spiritual interpretation of Islamic conceptions, but also grounding these ideas in the findings of Western "scientific" experimentation, thus in effect vindicating both the Qur'ān and many of the details provided in the *ḥadīths*. Spiritualism also provided a justification of certain Sufi ideas of the spirit which had come under attack by the secularist followers of Muḥammad 'Abdu.

Recognizing that these three categories of traditionists, modernists, and spiritualists are fluid and certainly not always mutually exclusive, let us look at what some contemporary Islamic writers have said about life after death, considering first the material relevant to what we are calling the period of the *barzakh*.

The Traditionists

In general these authors order their material in a chronological sequence from death to the events of the day of resurrection. For the most part, as was indicated above, they reiterate the *ḥadīths* with little or no commentary or interpretation. Occasionally, however, they suggest or refer to contemporary developments that reveal the fact that they, too, are writing from the perspective of the twentieth century.

For example, one of the most complete collections of traditional material about the afterlife to be found among the modern writings is that of Aḥmad Fā'iz, entitled *al-Yawm al-ākhir fī ẓilāl al-Qur'ān*. Borrowing his material from al-Ghazālī's *Iḥyā' 'ulūm al-dīn,* he describes in rather gruesome detail the pain of the *nizā'* or death struggle permeating the entire body to every vein, every joint, and the root of every hair.[1] Death, he says, is worse than the stroke of the sword, the cutting of the saw, or the twisting of the pincers, because it attacks both the body and the spirit. The final intensity of the pain comes from the extreme sadness experienced by the one who is to die. It is interesting to note, however, that while clearly accepting the conclusions of tradition on this matter, he nevertheless takes pains to describe death as "a period of progression in the development of men (p. 61), the final stage of which will be reached at the resurrection. This idea of progress and development, not antithetical to some of the traditional materials, is particularly characteristic of modern understanding.[2]

Modern writers most frequently mention the specifics of the related occurrences of the questioning in the grave and the subsequent punishment (or reward) for the same reason that they were accepted as credal statements in the orthodox formulas. Sometimes they include the *mi'rāj*-like ascension of the soul in this narrative, as well as the appearance of the personification of one's good or reprehensible deeds.[3] The focus of the questioning concerns one's God, prophet, and *dīn*.[4] Sometimes the punishment is simply mentioned; elsewhere the questioning angels are identified as Munkar and Nakīr, whose response to incorrect answers is to hit the misguided one with an iron rod.[5] Their general understanding is that the torments of the faithless are balanced by benefits to the pious, such as having their graves widened or getting breezes from the Garden through the top of the tomb. Almost all of these details, offered in very traditional fashion, are included in Shaykh al-Islām Ibrāhīm al-Bayjūrī's *Sharḥ al-Bayjūrī 'alá'l-jawhara*,[6] which has been part of the syllabus of al-Azhar High School in Cairo.

Traditionists see the idea of punishment as an integral part of the understanding that the entire afterlife process from death to the final consignment to the Fire is one continuing sequence.[7] They clearly view punishment in the grave as an initial step in the whole system of retribution.[8] Again it must be emphasized that the real point is not so much description as admonition. Citing another story about a conversation between 'Umar b. 'Abd al-'Azīz and the grave, Fā'iz warns the reader not to be tempted by attachments to this world when one knows that it will pass away. Remember, he says, that the grave warned 'Umar that the world will only continue for a short time and that the dearest is he who has been humiliated, the richest is he who has been poor, the youngest is he who has been old, and the living is the one who is dead. Where are the earth's people who built its cities and planted its trees, admonishes Fā'iz, and yet only lived on it for a few days? (p. 93).

In general, contemporary Islamic writers are less concerned than their medieval counterparts with musing about the possible location of the spirits of the dead. References to their going to such places as the crops of birds in the Garden or to the well of Zamzam[9] are generally in the context of discussion of the nature of the spirit and its relation to the soul and the body, reminiscent of Ibn Qayyim's *Kitāb al-rūḥ*. We have already observed that neither ancients nor contemporaries among the Muslim theologians have been successful in determining a consistent distinction between *nafs* and *rūḥ*. On the whole, unless a particular point is being made, modern writers use the term *rūḥ* to refer to the continuing human element after death.

Mustafá al-Ṭayr in his *Hādī al-arwāḥ* comments on Ibn Qayyim's opinion that each spirit will take the image of the body it inhabited so as to distinguish it from other spirits. Such identification is unnecessary, says al-Ṭayr. While spirits need not actually resemble their former bodies, however, he feels that it is nonetheless correct to assume that spirits will in some way be differentiated from one another (p. 24). Also following closely the pattern of the discussion set by Ibn Qayyim, Khalīfa says that spirits do not cease to exist after death and thus escape punishment; that punishment is not of spirits alone, for bodies and souls are reunited; and that after death the spirit does not go into the body of an animal, bird, insect, or other creature appropriate to its nature.[10] In this kind of discussion, as is often the case, one sees the applicability of arguments outlined by medieval scholars to the types of questions being raised by secularists, rationalists, and others today. Khalīfa does affirm that, based on the proofs of the *sunna* and authoritative writings, one can know that the spirits are in different locales—the more "spiritual" on higher levels and the more worldly not rising above the earth (p. 267). Agreeing with many of the classical commentators that God permits a freedom of movement to the spirits, he says that "The spirit goes out into the wide spaces and floats in the creation of God wherever God wants it to go and it is predestined to go. The body is like a cage and the spirit is incarcerated in it. In the *barzakh* the spirit is free to go and socialize with others, experiencing both pleasure and pain." (p. 8). Despite this freedom of movement, however, according to Khalīfa there is some sort of communication between the spirit and all or part of the body, which he calls a "*barzakh*ian" communication; in this way the spirit experiences directly the bliss or punishment applicable to that body.[11]

Carrying the traditionalist understanding of the continuing relationship of spirit and body to its logical conclusion, some have argued against performing autopsies. Given the fact that the traditions indicate clearly that the dead can feel and do suffer, these writers suggest that it is the gravest of sins to leave one's body for the experimentations of medical science.[12] These traditionist writers are in agreement with their predecessors that in some senses the dead are aware of the living. Khalīfa provides a lengthy discussion of the deceased observing who is washing him and what is going on during the funeral preparations,[13] and describes how the living should read Suras al-Raʿd (13) and Ya Sin (36) to assist in the process of the spirit leaving the body, according to the instruction of the Prophet.[14] Al-Ṭayr says that the dead indeed hear and respond to the greetings of those who pass by their graves, although there is nothing in the *sunna* to prove that the deceased is influenced by the wishes of the living or that any kind of necromancy is possible through bringing forth the spirit and asking it questions.[15]

One finds in these writers, for whom tradition provides a reliable base of information about the realities of the circumstance between individual death and resurrection, a general affirmation of the agony of death and the role of ʿIzrāʾīl, the journey of the spirit to the presence of God, the questioning in the grave by Munkar and Nakīr, punishment (and reward) in the tomb, the continuing relationship of body and spirit in the realm of the *barzakh*, and some indication of the awareness on the part of the dead of the continuing ministrations of the living to them. In the genre of modern writing termed modernist, writers either ignore or reinterpret these traditional concepts in light of different perspectives on the continuing existence of the individual after death.[16]

The Modernists

Modernist Islamic writers and theologians, attempting to elucidate the basic Qurʾānic theme of continuity between this life and the next, are generally more interested in discussing the nature of human responsibility and accountability than in articulating details of the life after death. Their approach to the material is homiletic rather than didactic; they are concerned less with the teaching of particulars than with preaching the message of the meaning of death and resurrection for the living of an ethical life. As part of the constituent elements of *īmān* as indicated in the Islamic creed, faith in the afterlife is essential to being Muslim. It is the incentive for acting responsibly in this life—for growing, developing, and improving—and through these efforts, for striving to establish the true Islamic order in the world.

Thus most of these works fail to present anything like the general sequence of events between death and resurrection given (though with variations in detail) in the classical manuals of eschatology or even in many of the traditionist writings. In general the modernist interest is to illustrate the continuum of human life from birth in this world to the final birth or resurrection, suggesting in the course of these discussions ways in which to understand the particulars of the Qur'ānic promises of recompense. Implicit in much of the traditional material—that descriptions are less a portrayal of what is actually to come than a directive on how to live one's life now—contemporary writers state this directive clearly and explicitly. It is not at all surprising, given this orientation, that the modernist works speculate hardly at all about the immediate after-death events or about life in the *barzakh*. To the extent to which the implications of their approach are relevant to our present consideration, it seems most efficient to attempt to outline some of the general characteristics they seem to share. One can glean through these the specific purposes for which they have intended their writing.

In a much more explicit way than may have been the case in earlier works, modernists attempt to help people deal with the question of death, which in most societies today is a phenomenon increasingly isolated from our everyday lives. We tend to think very seldom about eschatological concerns, says Abū'l-A'lá al-Mawdūdī, but in dealing with the death of a loved one, each of us comes face to face with his own mortality.[17] Sometimes modernists discuss the Qur'ānic analogy between sleep and death, not now with the attempt to consider the nature of the soul, but rather to help us understand that death is as natural as what we experience every day in sleep and that we can understand something of the after-death condition by considering what occurs during sleep.

Rather than restating the traditional affirmations that death is a fearsome and agonizing ordeal, these writers assure us that it is merely a transitional stage in a continuous and flowing process: "The spirit is always in a condition of nowness—death is merely a transition from one place or condition to another."[18] And, "Up to a point, the soul and the body together constitute a unit and are indissoluble; then dissolution comes and that is the end of life upon earth, but that it is not the end of life itself."[19] One should rest easy with the idea of death, say the modernists, because although each moment is a gift of life from God and a borrowing from Him, life itself is truly God's and not ours, as in the *ḥadīth qudsī*: "Live however you like, for thou art dead. . . ."[20] Death is, in fact, a rest from the troubles of life. Thinking about death should bring calmness to the soul because it is merely a journey to another life, a change in the order of life, and a single step on the road to eternity. Do not fear death, says Sa'īd Ṭah al-Kurdī in his work *al-Maut fī khidmat al-ḥayāt*, for truly it is in the service of life.[21]

Closely connected with these concerns, and clearly the basic understanding of all Islamic thinking on death, is the affirmation that life does continue after the death of the body. Faced with the threat of spreading atheism and the often attendant claim that our life on earth is final unto itself, Islamic writers are united in their attempts to affirm that the Qur'ānic message of continuing life is true, if subject to varying interpretations: "Islam insists on belief in the life after death. There are several matters of belief which Islam regards as essential, but belief in the life after death is concomitant with belief in the Existence of God (5:70). Failing belief in the life after death there is no faith at all." The Cairo journalist and physician Muṣṭafá Maḥmūd, self-styled interpreter of eschatological realities in numerous widely-read books, insists that the soul does not disintegrate at death but is characterized by continuity and awareness. The brain cells will die and disintegrate, he says, but the memory will continue, remaining alive and constantly reminding us in our second spiritual life of every deed we have done.[23] (One sees here a suggestion, to be elaborated below, of the way many modern writers understand the question of retribution and punishment.) Ḥasan 'Izz al-Dīn al-Jamāl, a medical doctor also expressing concern for the proper understanding of death, makes this analogy, borrowing his terminology from the scientific achievements of the space age:

> Death is the missile which we ride to take us to this planet, and this body we have is nothing but a space suit in which we appear on the stage of life. . . . This game we play is measured to us and our motives are recorded in intervals that are short or long depending on the length of our lives. Thus we ride death to return from whence we came to the house of decision, leaving behind us this costume or clothing which we call the body.[24]

These writings explicitly affirm that the link between ethical responsibility in this world and accountability in the next is both the means for and the guarantee of human immortality. One feels in reading these modernists a real sense in which eschatology is *now* in the immediateness of human ethical responsibility.[25] The emphasis on human accountability implies, of course, a fulfillment of this-worldly endeavors in the world to come, with the understanding of Islam as the religion of the middle position [*wasaṭ*] linking *dīn* and *dunyá*, the activities of this world and the next.[26] Here no distinction is made between the immediate after-death period and the eschaton; the point is to see all of life, from the present to eternity, as one continuum.

This emphasis on accountability is very much part of the modernist concern for affirmation of individuality and individual free will. Pointing to scientific proof of the uniqueness of each person (fingerprints, voice analysis, and the like), 'Abd al-Razzāq Nawfal says that no matter how many millions of people have lived, each is an individual unlike any other. In the same way each person's deeds are his own, the consequences of which one cannot escape.[27] A predominant theme in modernist writing, sounding much like a basic tenet of the Mu'tazila, is that God in His absolute justice has given man complete freedom. Misuse of this freedom leads to many of the problems of today's society. We know by our divinely-endowed instincts that justice and order are the laws of existence; thus our responsibility lies in the intuitive knowledge that injustice equals disorder, and if not punished for this disruption by human laws, we will be called to account by divine law.

Looking at the traditional accounts of life in the *barzakh* as considered in Chapter Two, one can see that every attempt was made to view the grave as a continuation of the kinds of activities in which an individual engaged while on earth. Clothing and comfort are important, the spirits carry on general forms of social intercourse, and life continues much as it does for those still on earth. While in one sense the modernist writers put great emphasis on continuity, it is markedly different from that suggested in these traditions. As indicated above, the continuity is of life itself, and of the entire birth and death process, and also of Islam as the *dīn* of accountability tying together this world and the next. For the writers in this group, however, it is clearly not continuity of life *as we know it* on earth. They in fact affirm quite the opposite, as in this statement in the *Majallat al-Azhar* that "the conditions of life in the hereafter are of an intricate nature and different from those of this life . . . the very ideas of time and space as relating to the next world are different from those here, and therefore we cannot conceive of the real nature of that world in terms of this world."[28]

While the conditions of life after death must be described, if at all, in human terminology, the limitations of this terminology are to be recognized and the life to come understood as of a character different from life on earth. The experiences of the next life are seen to be far more intense than is true here, and our minds and emotions here can only hope to glean some proximate and intuitive understanding of them. We see this idea articulated even more clearly in discussions of the life eternal, i.e. the life to come after the day of resurrection. Some of the modern writers of this group often draw no distinction between the immediate life after death and the ultimate life everlasting; others, like Maulana Muhammad 'Ali, make it extremely clear that the *barzakh* is only a prelude to the coming resurrection and that both are beyond human comprehension:

> All questions connected with the life of the other world are of an intricate nature, inasmuch as they are not things that can be perceived by these senses . . . the very ideas of time and space as relating to the next world are different from those here, and therefore we cannot conceive of the duration of *barzakh* in terms of this world. Moreover, the full awakening to the higher life will take place in the Resurrection. . . .[29]

We have seen in Chapter Two that much of the concern of early and medieval Islamic theology was the question of what constituent element of the human person will be punished in the grave: Will it be the soul alone, the body alone, or some combination of these? General consensus until the modern period has agreed on the last of these alternatives, that both the physical body and the spirit or soul will share in the torments or the bliss of the tomb. Contemporary Islamic thinkers of this modernist group, however, agree that the physical body plays no role in the immediate life of an individual after death. "The *barzakh* concerns the *rūḥ* and not the *badan,*" says Khalaf al-Sayyid 'Alī, "and there is no punishment of the body in the immediate after-death period, but punishment of the spirit only. God alone knows the particulars. *Kayf al-na'īm? Ya'rifu Allāh. Kayf al-'adhāb? Ya'rifu Allāh.*"[39]

In many cases denial of the physical body in the *barzakh* is only part of the general denial of any role for the physical body in the afterlife. Muhammad Zafrullah Khan, in contrast to protestations against autopsy and leaving one's body to science articulated by the traditionalist al-Adhamī, says that aside from decency and respect for the dead it makes no difference whatever how the body is disposed of. The soul in its rebirth into the new life after death acquires a new frame in which to experience what is to come.[31] Describing the nature of these experiences, he condenses what the traditionalists have described as the agony of the death process and the punishment of the grave into one process by which the soul undergoes certain trials or joys dependent on the state in which it comes to the new life: "A diseased soul will react painfully, very painfully, to the conditions of the life after death. It may suffer indescribable tortures, according to the degree to which its faculties have become diseased during its life on earth. A healthy soul will react joyfully to all the conditions of the life to come." (pp. 189–90).

There is no question that most of these modern writers understand some kind of punishment or reward to take place in the grave. Like their ancient counterparts, they make it quite clear that the nature of this retribution results directly from the quality of one's life on earth. But here we have no questioning angels, no iron rods, and no straightening of the tomb, at least not literally. In the *Mashāhid al-qiyāma fi'l-Qur'ān* Sayyid Quṭb argues that suffering in the grave in fact may best be understood as a psychological condition, physical punishment being a clear impossibility after the death of the physical body. From a psychological perspective, he says, the fear and awesomeness of the event of death itself and the aloneness experienced provide in themselves a kind of suffering (pp. 57–61). Stressing that the rewards and punishments generally understood to be future events really begin right in this life, some have turned the entire interpretation of the punishment of the grave to a this-worldly context. M. Sadeddin Evrin of the Institute of Advanced Islamic Studies in Istanbul goes so far as to say that the reference to "those who are in the tombs" in S 19:20 is to those on earth who are heartless, selfish, rude, and immoral, and he goes into a lengthy discussion of psychic capacities with the implication that punishment is self-administered at every moment.[32]

Despite the stress on continuity between this world and the next, however, most modern writers do not go as far as Evrin in interpreting the retribution of the grave in purely psychological terms. Nonetheless they emphasize that *now* is the time to begin to work out one's destiny. It is a very difficult process to realize the nature of sin and attempt to rectify one's own mistakes, says Syed Abdul Latif. But it is easier to do it in this life than to do it in the *barzakh*, the state of transition, where "one will have to realize the hideousness of sin and burn out all impurities attached to one's soul on its account."[33]

Even these writers who come closest to the traditional understanding of the specific after-death events often add an allegorical interpretation. It is interesting to note that the two-volume work by Aḥmad Galwash entitled *The Religion of Islam* (1973), adopted by the Islamic World League of Mecca as approved Islamic literature for promoting the preaching of Islam, in giving both the traditional and the modern perspectives on this question suggests a reconciliation of the two. In the first volume Galwaṣh attests to the words of the Prophet that the dead person will sit in the grave and be questioned by the angels called "tempters," that sinners will suffer the torment of the grave, and that God is able to restore life to the deceased so that he may understand any question asked of him.[34] But in the next volume he offers this interpretation of the punishment of the grave:

> The Messenger of God warned that sinners, after death, will be tormented by so many snakes; some simple-minded men have examined the graves of the sinners and wondered at failing to see these snakes. They do not understand that the tormenting snakes have their abode within the unbeliever's spirit, and that they existed in him even before he died, for they were but his own evil qualities symbolized. . . .[35]

Given the above-mentioned general characteristics of this genre of writing, how do modern interpreters define and understand the nature of *barzakh* and the life experienced therein? Simply put, they see it as a period of separation, purification, preparation, and progress, using their discussions in this context again to affirm the absolute reality of human freedom and responsibility. Particularly in the Indo-Pakistani writers we find suggestion of a steady movement toward perfection, beginning in this life and culminating in the eschatological hereafter.

Again based on the two Qur'ānic references to *barzakh*, many writers reaffirm its meaning as a barrier or a separation of the dead from the living. *Barzakh* in this sense refers not to a special place for the dead, in which they are kept from the land of the living, but rather, as Muṣṭafá Maḥmūd suggests, refers to the laws that prevent mixing. All references to *barzakh* are to physical forces that preserve everything in its place, he says, for the world of the spirit operates under different laws, and communication between the two realms is impossible.[36] In many instances the life of the *barzakh* is seen as a particular stage in the development of human life. The three levels of physical development—dust, embryo, and birth—are compared to the three stages of spiritual development. The first is this life, the third is the resurrection, and the second is the stage which intervenes between two, called *barzakh*. This is the stage of higher spiritual life.[37] Those who compare the immediate life after death with life in the womb here refer to the often-quoted Qur'ānic verses about two lives and two deaths, seeing the next birth as coming at the resurrection.[38]

The *barzakh* is a state of moving [*intiqāl*] from one place to another according to Khalaf al-Sayyid 'Alī. Instead of stressing the sort of random movement suggested in the traditions, however, where at least some classes of spirits were understood to have the freedom to transport themselves at will from one locale to another, these modernists tend to see the possibility of movement as inherently related to the idea of progress and a steady upward movement toward perfection (sometimes seen as having its culmination at the eschaton). Again they cannot emphasize too strongly that, despite recognition of the barrier-like nature of the *barzakh*, this movement and progress is a continuous process beginning in this world: "All that is in the world bears witness that everything is changing and progressing upward," says al-Mawdūdī. "The law of progress inheres in the whole universe, so that the order in which we now live is moving toward a better order."[39]

This moral evolutionism sees each stage as a preparation for the next. Thus life on earth is merely the time for preparing us for all subsequent levels of existence. Referring to the Qur'ānic reference to God's having formed human beings by successive stages [S 84:19], Syed Abdul Latif applies this idea to the crossing of the barrier into the *barzakh*. To be sure, he says, a biological evolutionism is implicit here, but the Qur'ānic reference to this movement is essentially ethical: "It is to emphasize that even as from a lower stage to a higher stage man's development has been marked in the process of his making, even so thenceforward the movement upward has to continue."[40] In his earlier comments about *barzakh* as a place where one burns out the traces of sin, we see the notion of a state of purification; implicit in his discussion is the attendant idea of progress to a purer state.

Elaborating his metaphor of life after death as another womb-existence, Muhammad Zafrullah Khan compares the soul at death to a sperm drop. In the succeeding womb stage it develops certain faculties that will better equip it for the peculiar conditions of the hereafter. The birth of the soul into a new life "after passing through the process of developing its faculties to a certain degree" is the resurrection. Moving to a rationalist argument, he indicates that the grave cannot refer to the specific place of burial, because not all bodies are in tombs (some being cremated, or devoured or otherwise disposed of); therefore what is to be understood by the grave is "the phase through which the soul passes after death, and in which it continues till resurrection, which corresponds to the phrase through which the embryo passes in the womb while it develops the organs and faculties appropriate to its life upon earth."[41]

This idea of progressive moral development through the life in the *barzakh* implies a state of conscious awareness in this period, although the modernists generally do not state it in quite that way. Protected by recognition that the quality of existence is beyond our powers of description or comprehension, they are not forced to deal directly with the idea suggested in some of the traditions that this is a period of sleep or unconsciousness. A few, like Maulana Muhammad 'Ali, say that, in comparison with the complete spiritual awareness that will characterize the time of the resurrection, the *barzakh* is a state of semiconsciousness or sleep. He goes on to affirm, however, that those who have experienced an awakening of the spiritual life on earth will enjoy a much more vivid consciousness in the *barzakh*.[42]

We should note in this connection that some contemporary writers have gone to great lengths to stress that despite the notion of progress and preparation, Islam in no sense espouses any idea of the possibility of transmigration from one physical body to another. Agreeing with Ibn Qayyim that this is quite beyond anything that the Qur'ān can support, they may be particularly insistent on this negation both as a counter to the possible incursion of traditional Indian thought into Islam[43] and as a clear affirmation in the face of a growing international fascination with the doctrines of karma and rebirth.[44] One of the most articulate opponents of transmigration is al-Mawdūdī,[45] whose Indo-Pakistani background undoubtedly gave him early exposure to this doctrine. He bases his explanation of why transmigration is untenable sometimes on pure logic and other times on a priori Islamic tenets: (a) the cycle of transmigration is said to be eternal; (b) this implies eternality of matter as well as of spirits, which science has proven cannot be true; (c) one would have to admit that all characteristics of human and animal life are properties of the body and not the soul, for the soul that formerly possessed the power of the brain while in man becomes irrational when put into an animal and is totally dormant in a vegetable (d) moral elevation is appropriate for a human being but not for a plant or animal; how could an unthinking plant or animal transmigrate upwards?; (e) transmigration leads to non-violence, which is destructive for a nation; people decline both in physical strength and in the power of the intellect, and the nation becomes susceptible to attack; (f) belief in transmigration is anti-social, leading to monkery and escape from the world; how could a nation aspire to civilization with such a suggestion that the world is evil? Thus, he says, we see that transmigration is against the understanding of science and the human intellect and an obstacle in the way of civilization and progress.[46]

Finally, it is necessary to note the modernist tendency to verify Qur'ānic revelation by scientific research, proving its authenticity, accuracy, and validity as a text relevant for modern life. This trend reached its apex several decades ago in the works of such persons at Ṭanṭāwī Jawharī and M. Farīd Wajdī,[47] who among others attempted to validate Qur'ānic insights through "rational" and scientific findings. By the Qur'ān we are able to discern what is true in science, insist such writers, and established scientific facts act as a proof for faith and the truth of the Islamic message.[48] They therefore see science and the verses of the Qur'ān as coming to the same conclusion about life after death and the features of eschatology.[49]

This emphasis on science is even more characteristic of the group that holds to and expounds the tenets of nineteenth- and twentieth-century spiritualism. For these thinkers, the scientifically verifiable fact that spirits of the dead can be seen and communicated with is the focus of their often extremely elaborate descriptions of the immediate life beyond the grave. Let us consider this group, then, as a third general classification of Muslim writings dealing with the period between death and resurrection, recognizing that of the three general categories of writers they are the most specifically concerned about the immediate life after death.

The Spiritualists

As we shall see, many of the themes of contemporary Islamic spiritualist writings are a direct outgrowth of, and quite compatible with, much that Islamic tradition has affirmed. This kind of Muslim interpretation, however, has also leaned heavily on writings of the spiritualist movement that arose in Europe and the United States in the mid-nineteenth century, both as a response to naturalist attacks on religion and as an attempt to counter the rising influence of scientific materialism. Like their Western counterparts, the Muslims have stressed the rational and scientific (i.e. based on empirical data) nature of their findings, and have in this way attempted to bridge the growing gap between the inherited "dogmatic" approach and that represented by modern science.

Egypt has been the recognized center of Islamic spiritualist writing for somewhat over a century. In the beginning attention was drawn to this viewpoint primarily by those who wanted to ridicule or attack it.[50] Gradually more sympathetic writings appeared, attempting to make available to the Arabic-speaking world some of the Western research into spiritualist phenomena and to justify the validity of these findings in terms of modern science as well as traditional Islamic doctrines. Ra'ūf 'Ubayd, author of *al-Insān rūḥ lā jasad* (1964), provides a useful summary of the ideas of some of the most important Muslim spiritualist writers up to the middle of this century (pp. 202–12). This review can serve as a brief but helpful introduction to our present consideration of the ways in which Islamic spiritualists understand the life of the *barzakh*.

One of the first prominent Egyptian writers to defend the research of spiritualism and to show how its findings correlate with the findings of modern research was Ṭanṭāwī Jawharī[51] in his *Kitāb al-arwāḥ* (published in 1918) as well as the *Jawāhir fī tafsīr al-Qur'ān al-karīm*. In the *Kitāb al-arwāḥ* he translated in its entirety an essay on spiritualism by the Englishman Sir Oliver Lodge, a practice frequently adopted by these Muslim writers. Defending this translation in his exegesis [*tafsīr*] of S 2:154 (that those who are slain in the way of God are still living),[52] he says that Lodge proved that our spirits are eternal after death, that there are worlds above us and surrounding us in relation to which we are only tiny ants, and that the inhabitants of those worlds (i.e. the spirits of the dead) help us and think about us. Jawharī equates these spirits with the supporting angels discussed in the Qur'ān, saying that science has proved that the universe is orderly and that there is not one but many worlds, about which we know very little. It is popular in Egypt, he comments, to say that we men of science know more than the ignorant men of religion and thus should imitate Europe and deny all foolish talk of angels and heavens. The real point, however, is to know the sciences and to see how they help us to understand religion.

The first journal dealing positively with spiritualism, *al-Ḥayāt*, was edited by Muḥammad Farīd Wajdī. As the publisher of the *Majallat al-Azhar* from 1934 to 1952, Wajdī wrote numerous articles on spiritualism, as well as the four-volume work *'Alá aṭlāl al-madhhab al-māddī,* arguing that because modern science has destroyed materialistic interpretations, spiritualism provides the natural completion for the development of modern thought. Another well-known Egyptian, Aḥmad Faḥmī Abū'l-Khayr, devoted himself to making the writings of western spiritualists known to the Islamic world.[53] Publisher of a monthly journal entitled *'Ālam al-rūḥ* (1947–60), he also authored a number of other works on spiritualism. In the introduction to *Ẓawāhir ḥijrat taḥḍīr al-arwāḥ*, which is a translation of a work by Edwin Frederick Powers, he writes,

> Those who oppose spiritualism—most of whom are atheists or religious imbeciles—attempt to gain strength for their opposition by saing that the spirit is "*min amr rabbī*" and that we have no right to discuss it. . . . This is a foolish argument from both the religious and the scientific points of view. Who has claimed that the spirit is not of the domain of God? But just so are matter, energy and the exchange between matter and energy the domain of God, as well as light and electricity and rays, some of which are discovered and about some of which we as yet know nothing at all.[54]

Ra'ūf 'Ubayd attempts in his summary of the works of these Egyptian spiritualists to establish the credentials of the spiritualist movement as legitimate by underlining the prominence of the persons who have been involved in it. Most of the men he selects for reference are well recognized in the Islamic and governmental circles. Others whose works he cites specifically are 'Alī 'Abd al-Jalīl Rāḍī, professor at the Kulliyat al-'Ulūm,[55] Shaykh Muḥammad Ḥasanayn Makhlūf of the Majlis al-Shu'ūn al-Islāmīya at al-Azhar, former Shaykh al-Azhar Muḥammad Muṣṭafá al-Maraghī, and the well-known rector of the Azhar, Maḥmūd Shaltūt. These writers have attempted to work from two directions in authorizing spiritualist findings. On the one hand they draw on some of the general understanding of the activity of the spirit in the intermediate world as developed in medieval literature, implying that new research is supportive of traditional Islamic understanding.[56] From the other direction they emphasize that the spiritualist interpretation goes hand in hand with new scientific research into the nature of matter and its transformation into energy waves.[57] Finally, of course, they claim that all one finds in the Qur'ān concerning the spirit and life after death, recompense and punishment, has been proven by modern European and American spiritualism by respected mediums and scientists; ample proof is provided by the results of scientific experimentation.

This concerted effort to draw together the conclusions of classical Islam and modern science has drawn attacks from both sides—the *'ulamā'* and the scientifically educated—accusing spiritualism of being both non-Qur'ānic and non-scientific. Opponents levy the charge that spiritualism is nothing but charlatanism, trading on the grief of the newly bereaved, supporting their claims with pseudo-scientific verbiage, and tricking their victims by quoting scripture and talking about the universal values of humanity, freedom, and equality. Lulling the gullible victim into comfortable agreement, say these opponents, the medium then moves him into the supernatural realm and, with attempts at scientific explanations and scriptural support, suggests that mediums are essential vehicles for God's guidance. The spiritualist movement they see not only as responsible for a serious misinterpretation of religious literature, but as a plaything in the hands of those who have only partial and incomplete knowledge of what modern science is beginning to unveil.[58]

On a different level, some who are reluctant to recognize categorically the ability to communicate with spirits of the dead for fear that it might upset traditional beliefs have urged caution. Muṣṭafá Muḥammad al-Ṭayr in *Hādī al-arwāḥ* raises these questions:

> Some of the spirits that have been brought have said that they are in the Garden and at rest. But their owners were not Muslims, and how could God allow that?

> Is it not taken for granted that he who does not believe in the oneness of God and the Prophethood of Muḥammad and the truth of the *sharī'a* is a *kāfir*? How could he be free in God's kingdom so that he could be reached and communicated with when we know from the *sunna* that he is imprisoned in the Fire? (pp. 34–35).

Al-Ṭayr goes on to say that while spiritual healing is real and useful in many cases, particularly for otherwise incurable diseases, there is a danger in too quickly assuming that it tells us anything about the spirits of humans who have died. It is possible that assistance comes from the spirits of *jinn* who have taken on the form and characteristics of the person whose healing help was sought.[59]

The proponents of spiritualism marshal a variety of arguments to support their claim of both religious and scientific validity. In an attempt to strengthen the bastion of Islam against contemporary anti-religious forces, they see spiritualism as one of the strongest weapons in destroying prevailing materialist philosophies. Building on the idea of moral progress, discussed above as one of the major themes of the modernists, they claim that a proper understanding of spiritualism helps motivate people toward social service, service of others in the material or ethereal world being the only way for spiritual advancement.[60]

One of the most widely-read of the modern Egyptian commentators on spiritualism (and in general on matters having to do with death and resurrection in the Islamic understanding) is 'Abd al-Razzāq Nawfal. A prolific writer,[61] Nawfal writes with a strong conviction of the realities affirmed by the Qur'ān. In every instance he insists not only that the conclusions of philosophy and science are alike on matters having to do with the continuing life of the spirit, but that Islam has preceded everything in this knowledge and affirmation of its truth. Well acquainted with Western scientific/spiritualist research, he makes constant reference to the kinds of experimentation that he feels "proves" the contentions of spiritualism. Centers for the study of parapsychology in Europe and the United States, he says, have proven through photography and hundreds of thousands of experiments that the spirit of man is existent in itself, that it departs the body at death and starts another life.[62] Not only have cameras caught the image of the spirit, but the measurement of a specific loss of body weight at death proves that something (the spirit) has departed.[63] Citing the various attempts at scientific communication with the dead (including the efforts of one Western researcher to reach them by telegraph), he again affirms that this possibility of communication has been acknowledged by Islam from the beginning.[64] Taking seriously the attempts of spiritualist researchers to validate their findings, he sees such means as hypnosis, fingerprinting of materialized spirits, and experimentation with mediums as offering supportive proof.

Several references have been made to the relationship of spiritualism and materialism, one's perception of that relationship naturally colored by the stance one wishes to take in regard to the spiritualist endeavors. Nawfal spends a great deal of time, with limited success, attempting to explain how a better understanding of the nature of the material world sheds light on the nature of the spiritual world. His key term is vibration [*ihtizāz*], that by which a material substance changes from one form to another, and from a visible material shape to an invisible, non-material shape, which process he identifies as the changing of the vibrations inside the atom.[65] The electronic vibrations of the brain also permit communication over long stretches of space. This used to be considered the domain of the spiritual, he says, but now science has proved that these vibrations are actually a kind of electricity (informed by the physical but not restricted by it). This electricity, he contends, is inolved in the life after death and is the means by which the dead are continuingly aware of the activities of the living.[66] ('Ubayd, incidently, says that this principle of *ihtizāz* helps explain the puzzle of sleep. The science of the spirit has proved that sleep is merely the extreme slowing down of the vibrations of the ethereal body, contrary to its nature and forced upon it by the fact that the material body is dormant.)[67]

One of the proofs of the spirit with which we are all familiar, Nawfal says, is the smile of the new-born baby. It knows as yet nothing of this world but is still responding to the sensations of the other world. The connection with this other world fades during life on earth but is resumed after death. Here again he points to the importance of the smile, this time on the face of the dying person, who has recognized the spirits of his loved ones conducting him into the new life. Taking these "proofs" into account, Nawfal elaborates his understanding of the relationship of body and spirit as well as of the pre-existence of the spirit in another and different realm, to which it returns to death: "Whereas the body is certainly and categorically not existent more than one time in this world, the life that one feels he has experienced before is the spiritual life in another world."[68] In a variety of places Nawfal reiterates the theme that before life on earth man had a previous spiritual life, which in some cases we are even able to remember. This recognition adds credence to the conviction that we will live spiritually after this life.[69] Nawfal consistently maintains that this pre-existent spiritual life is in no way to be confused with reincarnation or metempsychosis, which he feels in any case is disproved by the fact that the number of living beings is constantly increasing.[70]

One of the prime contentions of spirituality, particularly as it has developed in the West, is that, by the execution of certain procedures, the spirits of the dead can be materialized and communicated with. Interestingly, while Islamic writers do not ignore this aspect of the spiritualist science, they do not give it the greatest emphasis. True to the outline above of the general approaches of modernist Islamic writers to questions of life after death, spiritualist writers seem most concerned with proving the existence of the spirit, harmonzing (or proving the inherent consistency of) the results of research with the understanding of the Qur'ān, and describing in some detail the life of the spirit in the *barzakh*. Nonetheless they generally understand that in the spirit world are some who by God's permission are available for assisting those of us still in this material world. As long as the seekers are sincere in their requests, these spirits are ready to help us in knowing what will improve our lives.

Some Muslim writers have gone into specific detail about the particulars of the materialization process. Muḥammad Shahīn Ḥamza says that modern spiritualism has shown clearly that God created certain people to have the special physiological condition by which they can see and communicate with spirits, and that this ability is not related to the quality of one's religious or spiritual life. (Even some animals, he says, have it.) In order for a spirit to materialize it must have ectoplasm, which Ḥamza likens to water vapor. It emanates from a living person who is in front of the spirit that is to materialize (the actual materialization only occurring if the spirit is willing). Every living being possesses some amount of ectoplasm, which is what scientists are able to photograph. Relying on the same "proofs" that Nawfal finds so convincing, Ḥamza says that one of the miracles of God is that the materialization of a spirit has the fingerprints of the spirit possessing the body; the voice of the dead speaks through the living medium.[71]

Ḥamza puts forth a warning about endeavors to communicate with the spirit world, saying that there are three kinds of spirits with whom one might come into contact. These are the angels, the *jinn* and devils, and human beings who have preceded us to the spiritual world. He does not elaborate on the angels but indicates that the *jinn* and satans, who are older in relation to the world than man, exist in order to communicate with us and to bring harm to our religious endeavors. These spirits are the first to try to take advantage of attempts to open communication between this and the spiritual world. Even among the spirits of humans, he says, are many who are as bad as the *jinn* in their intention to bring harm to the living. In the *barzakh* world they make every effort to communicate with human beings, to lead them into error, and to tempt them with seductive words: "If there is any session in which there is communication with the spirits, spirits of the evil ones of both men and satans or *jinn* are the first to come to deliver their message of evil in which they rejoice."[72] In the spirit world, however, are some (human beings) who are pious and elevated, guiding us to fulfill the commandments of God. They are available to answer any requests sent to them from our world and are ready to guide to a better life any who sincerely seek the good. Ḥamza indicates that the serious and sincere spirits are annoyed with the stupid questions that grow out of overly materialistic concerns; their aim is also not to answer questions which are part of the world of the unknown [*'ālam al-ghayb*], but only to provide true religious guidance.[73]

The sleep image, as we have seen, is a recurring one for Muslim writers in describing the death state. More than an analogy because of the Qur'ānic references to God's holding the soul during sleep as during death, the image has been greatly amplified in traditional literature to show that sleep is actually a time of intercourse between the spirits of the living and the dead. Not surprisingly, modern Muslim spiritualists have made much of this as another possibility (the first being seance communication) for coming into contact with the spirit world.[74] They describe sleep as a temporary departure and soaring of the spirit in preparation for the permanent departure to come at death. During this process the soul or spirit meets other spirits both of the living and the dead, learning some of the secrets otherwise veiled from it: "The traveling spirit may meet with the spirits of relatives and friends in the land of the *barzakh*; they will inform him about the future . . . some of the learned say that dreams that inform about the future tell what will happen to the sleeper after his death."[75] The dream events, or travels in the spiritual realm, are generally seen as a preparation for the events of the *barzakh* so that one will not be too surprised upon his arrival after death. Even if the conscious mind forgets the dream experience, it is stored in the unconscious to aid the spirit through the death process. This, in fact, spiritualists see as the greatest benefit to accrue from their science: that when spiritualist truths are disseminated, they will allay the general fears of people concerning death.[76]

Quoting extensively from the writings of Western physicians, metaphysicians, and spiritualists, Nawfal offers a variety of illustrations to prove that the death process itself is not painful and that we have nothing to fear in death.[77] The results of all studies prove, he says, that the moment of transition is a sweet moment when all pain eases. In light of the descriptions of death suggested in medieval manuals, it is interesting to consider here a rather lengthy passage in which Nawfal presents the modern spiritualist understanding of this process:

> The dying person starts losing the feeling of pain as his senses enter a state of coma . . . therefore we cannot claim that a dying person has any feeling that could be described. The soul starts to slip away from the lower limbs so that the person is unable to move his legs, or even feel them. Next the soul slips away from his hands and he stops feeling them and loses the ability to move them. At such a time a quick thought of what awaits him passes through his mind as he sees the ghost of death. His body therefore trembles strongly and he feels thirsty. This is only a result of his anxiety about something for which he is not well prepared. His throat therefore becomes dry and he feels something like a tremor. The soul then slips away from another part, and only his heart, beating faintly and automatically, and his brain which is still communicating fully with his soul, remain in their original state. But his awareness is no more the same since the quantity of blood in his brain has been reduced and consequently his intellectual level has been lowered in relation to the life which he does not feel or apprehend except through the senses of his body. The soul starts to overcome the body completely and knows that it will last after death. At this point, the believer in life after death differs from the non-believer. The first follows a road that he is sure of and believes in through religion. As for the second, he fears this path because he is not prepared for it, not believing in it beforehand. The soul sees other souls but thinks they are living because it is actually still seeing living people. . . . The clarity of both worlds depends on the degree of the soul's exit from his body. If the soul has slipped away to more than half of its strength, it sees other souls more clearly than the living people. If the opposite is true, it sees the living more clearly. Therefore, a dying person often talks to the dead, calls them, or smiles at them. Talking, calling and smiling are nothing more than an expression of the degree of communication between the soul and the body or their separation. In the case of smiling, the vision of souls is not fully clear; in calling it is clearer though from a distance, and in talking it is clear and close and therefore the moment of transition is at hand. The soul then slips away from the areas of understanding, memory, and then the whole brain. It rushes to the wider and broader world—to the other world. The transition has been fulfilled.[78]

Mention was made above of Ra'ūf 'Ubayd's citing of Shaykh Muḥammad Ḥasanayn Makhlūf as an exponent of spiritualism in Islam. As the Muftī of Egypt in the 1940s, Makhlūf is a valuable, supportive authority for those seeking to justify the spiritualist endeavor in light of its critics. In 1947 Makhlūf articulated a particularly explicit statement of many of the doctrines that the spiritualist movement holds most dear, quoted at length or referred to in many if not most of the modern works we have considered in this section.[79] In fact Makhlūf expresses a conception of the immediate after-death circumstance of the spirits quite in harmony with the ideas developed by medieval Islamic writers, which in itself indicates how congenial these basic themes generally are to the understanding of spiritualism. In this statement he expresses the particulars of a description of the life of the spirit in the *barzakh*; as such it serves as a convenient framework of ideas that are taken and greatly elaborated by writers such as Nawfal, 'Ubayd, Ḥamza, Rāḍī and others. Accordingly to Makhlūf the spirit (a) is alive, comprehending, hearing, and seeing during its life in the *barzakh*; (b) communicates with other spirits of the dead and of the living; (c) feels bliss or punishment, pleasure or pain, according to its condition and the deeds it did while in the earthly life; (d) is not bound by space or any other restriction; and (e) is permitted by God to communicate with all or part of its former body in a "*barzakh*ian" communication (through which process the body feels bliss or punishment).

Taking these points as a general outline, we can see that the spiritualist descriptions of what life is like for the spirit in the *barzakh* can be arranged quite conveniently into these categories. In order best to understand the significance of what these writers intend by saying that the spirit is alive, hearing, seeing and the like, we should first consider the other points in his sequence; otherwise Makhlūf's general order is a very useful one for seeing the development of ideas.

The spirit communicates with other spirits of the dead and of the living. In the *ḥadīths* we saw repeated the idea that when a soul has separated from its body, it will be met both by angels and by the spirits of relatives and friends whom it knew on earth. This is strongly affirmed by the spiritualists, who say that the first thing the soul sees on transition is crowds of angels accompanied by friends and relatives who preceded him to the second world. These help him overcome any confusion he might feel in his new circumstances. Sometimes this process takes a long time, depending on one's degree of preparation in life, but the familiar spirits stay with the new arrival as long as necessary.[80] Great stress is put on the comfort provided both through the efforts of one's relatives and by the very joy afforded to the dying when he first glimpses his loved ones. This is the reason, Nawfal indicates, that the dying person often has a smile on his face. Ḥamza (*al-Rūḥīya*, p. 169) cites a number of little narratives passed on by those who have died, such as: "When I opened my eyes after death I first saw my mother and father who had preceded me in the land of the spirits. . . ."

This idea of communication becomes greatly expanded when these writers begin to report the nature of familiar relationships in the *barzakh*. The Qur'ānic promise that families will be together in the hereafter (S 13:23) traditionally has been interpreted as applying to the final resting-place in the Garden. Here, however, we have the affirmation that the family is gathered anew even in the *barzakh*, but with the stipulation that marital relationships that were unhappy on earth are severed at death.[81] The operating principle in the *barzakh* is love, and that which does not reflect love is inappropriate; those who have not found love on earth will indeed find it in the next world. This principle of harmony seems to be behind the idea expressed by the spiritualist writers that communication is by telepathy rather than by means of verbal language,[82] that there is no hypocrisy either personal or social, and that the main responsibility of the spirits in the *barzakh* is to "sow the seeds of love among men of all religions."[83]

The spirit feels bliss or punishment, pleasure or pain, according to its condition and the deeds it did in the earthly life. Makhlūf himself elaborates this idea somewhat in his *Ḥukm al-Islām* (pp. 33–34) in saying that the only exception to the dead being aware of the visits of the living to their graves is that some are too occupied with their punishment to enjoy this sociability. They are "imprisoned" until their suffering ends or until God gives them permission to visit, meet, and be aware of others. For the spiritualist understanding, joy and bliss are the norm of the *barzakh*, and punishment for those whose lives on earth necessitate it is a stage through which they must go before entering the "normal" condition of the life there. Ḥamza draws the relationship between the above points when he describes the activities of the spirit in this new world: "It will meet with spirits of similar mind, it will stretch out its hand to others and they shall do good together either to those still living on earth or those on their way to heaven. As for the sinner, punishment is incumbent on him. He passes through a difficult time of pain. . . ."[84]

True to general Islamic conclusions about the inevitability of some kind of punishment in the grave, all of the spiritualist writers affirm this reality. Aside from communication with the body expressed by Makhlūf in his last point (which we will consider shortly), the understanding not surprisingly is of a recompense of the spirit rather than of the body. Both the negative and positive aspects of this recompense are understood to be mental conditions; for the "good" the spiritual world is seen as a beautiful place and for the "evil" as a thick, dark, tomb-like atmosphere in which spirits are unable to communicate with others. Far greater than the torture of the fire is the punishment of one's own conscience. The exact form of this punishment seems to be based not only on the degree of one's *kufr* while on earth, but on the particular way in which one expires. Ḥamza says that the disobedient one who dies from a painful disease or an accident continues to feel the agony in an augmented way until he is released by the mercy of God.[85] 'Ubayd suggests that suffering is due to one of three causes: attachment to the things of the world and pain at their loss, shame at the exposure of all of one's deeds done on earth, and regret that one's past actions prevent it from as yet attaining the higher levels of existence it sees other spirits reaching.[86]

The spirit is not bound by space or any other restriction. Before stating the positive dimensions of that affirmation, let us see how it is expressed negatively. The descriptions of punishment often suggest that the very lack of both movement and sociability are characteristics of a kind of chastisement. On the one hand the spirit may desire to return to the earth but cannot, causing it pain. It is also unable to move freely in the spiritual realm and enjoy intercourse with other spirits (one is reminded here of al-Ghazālī's four categories of spirits in the *barzakh* as outlined in the *Durra*). Most spirits, however, gradually are released from this circumstance and are able to move freely in the spirit world (again as affirmed by Ibn Qayyim, al-Suyūṭī and others). Whether one states this as an easing of punishment or as a gradual awakening to the realities of the new life is immaterial (quite literally), for these are but different ways of expressing the same reality for the spiritualist.

In the spiritual world, for those who are able to enjoy it, time is nonexistent and space uninhibiting. Motion is easy; each spirit is able to move from one place to another faster than the speed of light whenever it so desires. Because there is no restriction on movement, spirits from higher levels are free to come down and communicate with those on lower levels. This access, however, is not reversible. Because of the constantly repeated notion that the spiritual world is one of levels and stages, those as yet spiritually unadvanced cannot (rather than may not) attain to the higher reaches even temporarily. Although the suggestion is sometimes made that *barzakh* is comprised of seven basic levels (in line with the Qur'ānic suggestion of seven levels of reality) like an inverted pyramid, with the narrowest at the bottom and the broadest at the top, these are not to be understood as posing anything like the geographical, social or political barriers encountered on earth. They are rather the areas of "spiritual space" appropriate to the degree of readiness of each spirit.

Upon separation from the body the spirit is said to go to the stage coordinate with its degree of spiritual and moral understanding while on earth. One of the reasons that we have differing descriptions of the *barzakh* is that each spirit sees and knows what is on his own particular level and may communicate that to those remaining on earth. Upward mobility is certainly possible, based on an increase in knowledge on the part of the spirit and the degree to which this enables him to love and assist other spirits. According to Nawfal this knowledge is gained through the same senses that man uses on earth, except that it comes at a faster rate.[89] As the spirit ascends from one rank to the next, it becomes increasingly luminescent, as in S 66:8, {Their light will go before them, by their right hands, and they will say, Our Lord! perfect for us our light . . .}. With every elevation, differences among the spirits will decrease so that in the highest regions all distinctions will disappear. "Only the good spirits of all nations and religions will be there," says 'Ubayd, "and there will be mutual understanding and love."[88]

We should note one more thing in relation to the idea of movement and progression in the *barzakh*; this has to do with the understanding of age. The idea that progression implies a freeing of all that attached the soul to the body and a purifying from all diseases and defects in the other world, combined with the notion that upward movement is linked directly to intellectual growth, leads to the general conviction that both childhood and old age are conditions in some way inappropriate to the full spiritual life of the *barzakh*. While it is held that spiritual bodies will have the same outward appearance and shape as material bodies on earth (and thus will be recognizable to others), these bodies and their attendant intellectual capacities will be as of persons in the full bloom of maturity. One arrives in the *barzakh* in the same shape as when he died—a child, a youth or an old person—but gradually "recovers" from that condition.[89] The child will grow in the company and with the assistance of friends and relatives, and the aged will slowly become younger, for the ethereal world does not know old age.

God permits the spirit to communicate with all or part of its former body.

> When I left my body I found that for a long time it was very difficult to free myself from earthly bonds. It is hard for me now to describe the geography of the *barzakh*. I was surprised to find out that I was very tied to the place where I was born in the world and had grown up. . . .[90]

This brief narrative of a communication related by Ḥamza suggests what we have already noted above, that it can be quite difficult for the departed spirit to sever its relationship to this world and particularly to the body to which it had so long been attached. Those who die believing that the abode of the spirit after death is the grave may remain, because of this faulty belief, more than normally attached to their physical bodies for awhile.[91] While there is some understanding that the hopeless desire to return can be seen as part of the punishment of the grave, it also is clear that it is not only the souls of the recalcitrant to whom this desire applies. Based on what they feel is evidence from the beyond, Makhlūf and others indicate that even while the friends and relatives of the deceased may be helping him in the spirit world to overcome this attraction, there are occasions whereby, with God's permission, some final kinds of communication do take place.

In some instances the soul may try to cooperate with the living in preparing his body for burial. (Nawfal suggests that this may be because the body is an obstruction to one's honest desire for release from worldly ties, and a hastening of the burial process facilitates this emotional severance.[92] Assistance may take the form of helping to move the body along in its casket during the funeral procession, in some cases making it appear that the body is almost flying. This has led to the spread of tales about the dead flying away with their coffins, pursued by the attendants of the funeral. 'Abd al-Jalīl Rāḍī says that he knows personally of an instance in which the body of a dead man in his coffin kept flying from one place to another so that it would not have to be buried in a place that did not suit him; the burial party finally succumbed to the wishes of the spirit and buried his body in a location of his own choosing.[93]

Regardless of whether or not one gives credence to these kinds of stories, it is important to recognize the firm belief of the spiritualists that the soul/spirit/mind alone lives on after death in the *barzakh* and that any communication permitted by God between the spirit and its body is solely for the purpose of aiding the spirit to realize its ultimate release in the realm of the *barzakh*.

The spirit is alive, comprehending, hearing, and seeing during its life in the barzakh. This understanding, for which one can find abundant support in the traditions, is of course the basic tenet of all spiritualists and the point at which Makhlūf begins his statement. We have elected to discuss it last as a general category in which to consider some of the various kinds of activities in which these writers suggest the spirits are engaged.

We should perhaps add a word about the nature of the spiritual being that resides in the *barzakh*. According to the spiritualists, that which survives is the ethereal body, composed of minute atoms assembled in a form corresponding to the physical body.[94] This body, enlivened and empowered by the intellect, is what is meant by the term "spirit" [*rūḥ*].[95] Intellects are clearer and more productive in the *barzakh*; in fact all the apparently "physical" surroundings are actually the result of thought-projection. The general environment in which one finds himself is in this way the creation of one's own mind, and commonality of experience is caused by the like-mindedness of all of those inhabiting any one plane or level.[96]

Beginning with the frequently-cited *ḥadīth* that the dead will be reciting the Qur'ān in their graves, these writers go on to say that other spirits will instruct in the memorization of the Qur'ān any who have not yet achieved that accomplishment. In like manner spirits from higher levels will come down to give general kinds of instruction to those on lower levels; some even say that the *barzakh* has the equivalents of institutions of higher learning, with lectures on an intellectual plane far beyond anything we on earth can imagine. Spirits will be more energetic in the next life than on earth, and there will be no sloth or inactivity. In fact the *barzakh* is characterized as a place of great activity, all directed toward the loving service of others and the joy of work itself.[97]

The spirits enjoy a high level of civilization, with opportunities for reading and research, music, art appreciation, and advanced kinds of entertainment. They talk, walk, eat, drink, marry, and—according to some—even procreate.[98] They sleep when they wish rather than out of necessity, and eat and drink from habit or for pleasure. Food is enjoyed through spiritual taste rather than ingestion, as the spirits have no digestive apparatus. In short, life is good in the *barzakh* and gets better and better as one proceeds up the spiritual ladder. The *raison d'être* for existence as well as the means of advancement is the love and service of one's fellows, both those living on earth and those living in the spiritual realm; through this service one is understood to express and experience the true meaning of the worship of God.[99]

Chapter Five
The Eschaton, the Judgment, and the Final Dispensation: Modern Islam

In the materials of classical Islam it is fairly easy to distinguish between commentaries relating to the period between death and the eschaton, and those dealing more specifically with the last day and judgment. The Qur'ān, as we have seen, confines itself by and large to the latter, the traditions order their narratives so as to make the sequence of events quite recognizable, and the creeds and treatises of theology for the most part categorize their statements so that their applicability to the several segments of the eschatological story is obvious.

When we turn to modern Islamic thought and writing about life after death, however, such a distinction becomes less easy to determine. While in the classical materials a kind of subdivision is possible even between the events of resurrection and the details of the final abodes of recompense, the modern writers make no such easy distinction. As will be quite evident in the succeeding analysis, even the attempt to separate commentary relating to the eschaton from that pertinent to the immediate period of life after death is easily frustrated. In fact, it is perhaps not too extreme to say that the distinction between *dīn* and *dunyá* itself is sometimes hazy for the very reason that modern Muslims put such emphasis on the continuity of life in this world and the next and on the direct cause and effect between actions now and circumstances to come.

Thus we will see that many of the themes laid forth in Chapter Four apply equally to the commentary under consideration here. It is also true, however, that certain of the emphases of contemporary thought are most appropriately analyzed in the context of reflections on the nature of the eschaton, judgment, and final consignment. In this chapter, then, we will consider some of the ways in which these themes are drawn in relation to the particulars of the great eschatological guarantee of the Qur'ān that bodies will be resurrected, judgment accorded, and rewards and punishments meted out to all persons according to their due.

As we saw in the previous chapter, tradition has assigned to the last days before the eschatological cataclysm a series of happenings based to a very limited extent on the suggestions of the Qur'ān. Some contemporary Muslims continue to espouse these in the same manner as the classical manuals have described them, giving a specific and literal interpretation. Sometimes these are listed as the ten major signs that will herald the coming of the resurrection, as in al-Bayjūrī's *Sharḥ*, used in the syllabus of al-Azhar High School.[1] Other writers present a somewhat shortened set of occurrences, still accepting in general the traditional understanding of these events. The five most commonly cited as major signs of the coming of the resurrection are (1) the appearance of the false messiah or Dajjāl, who will last on earth for forty days; (2) the coming of 'Īsá, who will kill the Dajjāl, destroy the cross, and establish the tax [*jizya*], after which will come a period of abundance characterized by adherence to the law [*sharī'a*] of Muḥammad; (3) the appearance of Yājūj and Mājūj, accompanied by drought, famine, and corruption; (4) the coming of the beast of the earth;[2] (5) the rising of the sun in the west.[3] The appearance of the Mahdī is generally mentioned, but again there is no consistency of opinion as to whether or not he is to be identified with Jesus.

The understanding of the signs of the Hour lends itself to several concerns particularly characteristic of contemporary thought. One is the tendency to attempt to reconcile the Qur'ān with modern scientific findings. In this case the specific natural phenomena mentioned in the Qur'ān as signaling the arrival of the eschaton are cited in light of Western scientific findings about gases, rifts in the atmosphere, magnetic forces and the like.[4] One finds in this kind of analysis attempts to justify the Qur'ān in terms of science, to validate the findings of modern science by what are seen as Qur'ānic antecedents, and to validate Islamic precedence in understanding scientific truths realized by the West only centuries later.

Another way in which the interpretation of the signs serves the interests of modern writers is in reference to the moral degradation said to occur in conjunction with the physical catastrophes of the time. Many of these interpretations, even those with a strongly traditional flavor, reflect ways in which these writers have chosen to express their particular concerns about the state of affairs, and especially of Islam, in the world today. Sometimes this takes the form of a general concern, as in 'Abd al-Rahman Azzām:

> It is a cause of grief that we should behold in the world today a foreshadowing of God's pending judgment. There is no evidence that much piety exists either among Muslim nations, considered regressive, or among the Christians and Jews, who are regarded as progressive. Beliefs seem to have deteriorated and beneficence to have departed; love of this world's goods has prevailed, and ingratitude has arisen everywhere. Has the promise of God approached?[5]

In other instances specific characteristics of our time are cited as indications that the end is near. Thus Khalīfa, in describing the minor signs said to presage the coming of the Hour, mentions the tendency of men to dress like women and says that this has already come to pass; women are either indistinguishable from men or go to the other extreme and expose parts that should never be seen in public. We have also gone overboard in constructing elaborate buildings, he says, with undue pride in our human accomplishments. All of this signals the imminence of the Hour *(Dār*, pp. 330–31). In describing the activities of Jesus in the coming age Khalīfa reveals a contemporary Arab response to political circumstances when he underlines the suggestion of the *ḥadīth* that "God will send all the Jews fleeing, and there will be nothing that God will leave that a Jew can hide behind" (p. 332).

Even more specific in his analysis of current circumstances as fitting the predictions of the signs of the Hour is Muḥammad Māḍī Abū'l-'Azā'im.[6] The *fitan* predicated by traditionists like Tirmidhī and others, he says, we have already witnessed with our own eyes in such events as the coming of Ghulām Aḥmad in India, who has claimed to be the Christ and has interpreted the Qur'ān according to his own inclinations.[7] He also cites the arrival of the self-proclaimed Mahdī of the Sudan as an indication that "these *fitan* have spread and are signs that the resurrection is near." The rising of the sun in the west is understood as unnatural not only for cosmological reasons, but (reflecting the anti-Western bias of many Arab Muslims) because all good things have come originally from the east, the breeding place of God's revelations. "These lights have been covered and these things have disappeared," says Abū'l-'Azā'im, "and the West has become the Ka'ba of the deceived ones and the center that emantes darkness, perfidy, evil and immorality . . ." (*Tafṣīl*, p. 40).

This attempt to see the traditional signs of the Hour realized in events and characteristics of the present day is common to much contemporary interpretation. In general the signs are seen as negative, true to the traditional understanding of the *fitan* that will destroy the moral order as well as of the cosmic disruption of the natural order. The relation between these two is expressed in the interpretation of Ibrāhīm 'Awaḍayn, for example, who says that the cosmic changes preceding the resurrection will begin in man himself, affecting his nervous system and making his senses disfunctional. Since man is by nature perfectly attuned to the rhythm of life, when the rhythm malfunctions he will immediately reflect the disturbance within his psyche, a circumstance of which we can see indications even now.[8] At other times, however, the end of the age seems to be understood in a more positive light as the natural consequence of human progress in the social and material orders. 'Abd al-Razzāq Nawfal, who in general disregards the specifics traditionally cited as signaling the Hour,[9] feels that one of the signs of the coming of the eschaton is the fact of increased civilization, advancement, and building. Unlike Khalīfa, who disparages this emphasis on construction, Nawfal applauds human achievement and feels that in the present generation man has reached the highest peak of civilization.[10] "What more can man do?" he asks. "Is this not a sign that the resurrection is coming and its signs have appeared?"[11]

Some writers, then, attempt to emphasize the relationship of Qur'ānic predictions to scientific knowledge and to use the traditional categories as a means of offering a critique on the state of affairs in the world today. Others take the occasion of a discussion of the signs of the Hour rather to express their understanding of the power and wisdom of God. One of the most detailed descriptions of the signs of the Hour, a complete cataloguing of all Qur'ānic and *ḥadīth* material on the subject, is found in Aḥmad Fā'iz, *al-Yawm al-ākhir fī ẓilāl al-Qur'ān* (esp. pp. 105–76). The presentation of detail, however, makes it clear that Fā'iz is doing more than providing a mere list of particulars. Writing in a homiletical style, he uses the material as a means of illustrating God's greatness contrasted with man's finitude, underlining the inevitable nature of human accountability. All of these signs, he indicates, point to the fact that the universe will disintegrate, the laws holding together this beautifully ordered system will malfunction, and after its separation from the control of the law, its parts will be scattered. Implicit in this explanation is the recognition of a symbolic relation of the natural universe to the role of the individual and the *umma* in response to God. The whole is maintained, in unity and obedience to the law; when the world ceases to obey God's law, the whole malfunctions and all beauty and order become chaos. While man may imagine that the punishment of the Day is far off, in truth it is very close. Man will find no place to hide and no protection; there is no running from the might of God.

Many of the contemporary writings also insist that it is better not to speculate on what the Qur'ān does not designate specifically and clearly. Thus for many writers the classical events of the Hour remain part of God's knowledge, to be understood in limited ways only. The *sā'a* is the highest of the unknowns, says Muṣṭafá Maḥmūd, and God has not revealed it to anyone, including His prophets. When all the signs of the Hour come, there will be no more doubt in anyone's heart—but then it will be too late. For now it is best to believe in the unknown without need of proof or specifics. God alone has the key to open all of these symbols and signs.[12]

> Then God will order Isrāfīl to blow the trumpet. He will blow it twice, and with the third blowing all things will be stunned [*yus'iq*] except those whom God wills (the exception being Mūsá and those who bear the Throne, the Throne itself, the Garden, the Fire, the human tail-bone, the spirits [*arwāḥ*], the Tablet and the Pen. Then God will restore the bodies as they were constituted of the original parts, after they have been dispersed. . . .[13]

This statement by Muḥammad 'Awwād describing the day of resurrection is typical of twentieth-century Muslim writers who relate events according to the classical understanding. 'Awwād accepts the modifications made by later traditionalists to the Qur'ānic descriptions of the *fanā'*, in which all perishes but the face of God.[14] He also expresses the opinion of many contemporary Muslims that the resurrection means the reassembling of the same elements of the body that constitute the human frame in its earthly existence.[15] ('Awwād continues this narrative with a classic description of the spirits coming from the holes of Isrāfīl's trumpet to join with the bodies that rise out of the graves.)

As this study has observed more than once, the question of the physical resurrection has concerned interpreters of the Qur'ān since the earliest passages describing it were recited by the Prophet. No less than did the listening community at Mecca, skeptics today continue to question the plausibility of resuscitation of the earthly physical body. Thus, much of the defense of bodily resurrection is in direct response to questions raised by rationalists and others about such a possibility. One finds this response articulated in a variety of ways. The point most often made is that He Who created the first time can and will create again (see S 36:78–79). Some even argue that re-creation may be easier to accept because the component parts or elements, though completely dispersed, are nonetheless part of creation.[16] All of life is a process of creation and re-creation; bringing forth life out of death at the resurrection is simply another, though more dramatic, way of expressing the naturalness of all of life's cycle of death and rebirth.[17]

Some contemporary writers, such as 'Awwād in the above-quoted description of the events of the Day, testify to the exact relation of the earthly and the resurrected bodies. The second life is by reconstitution of the same body after its non-being, says 'Abd al-Ḥamīd Ṭahmāz, and he Who created creation the first time is capable of bringing it back again.[18] Ṭahmāz recognizes that many have raised the question of the dispersion of atoms and molecules of the human body into plants then eaten by other humans, thus becoming part of new bodies. All of these mixtures of atoms, however, are distinct in the eyes of God, he says, and He will reconstitute them in their original forms at the day of resurrection.[19] In much modern commentary, particularly Qur'ānic exegesis, the reassertion of the guarantee of bodily resurrection is intended to counter the threat implied in what modern science now understands about the transformation of matter into new states.

Sometimes contemporary writers suggest elaborate explanations based on modern science and medicine for the reuniting of the bodies. Nawfal, for example, says that on the day of resurrection each cell will know from what body it came, and on the same principle whereby a body rejects an organ foreign to it, no cells will find themselves in strange bodies. This proves that there is such a thing as individuality, he says, despite the interrelationship of cells in different forms. Then referring to the reported comment of the Prophet that an old person will not enter the Garden, he says that we will either gain or decrease in years in the Garden so as to be at the median age; we will also be free from imperfections and physical infirmities.[20]

Others are less willing to specify the exact identity of the present and future bodies. In a private conversation in 1972, Shaykh Faḥḥām, then Shaykh al-Azhar in Cairo, expressed to the authors the common Muslim objection to the cremation of bodies and denied that such a practice could ever be acceptable in Islam. This is not an honorable way of treating the body, he said, for we must remember that there is resurrection of the body "in the form we have now." He refrained, however, from indicating precisely what "in the form" will mean. In the same way, other writers have used terminology open to several possible interpretations or have tried specifically to be flexible in their understanding. Al-Mawdūdī in *al-Ḥadāra al-Islāmīya* cites examples of ways in which death can mean the immediate destruction of the body, such as being devoured by a fish or wild animal, indicating that this cannot be taken as proof against the resurrection. But it is not necessary, he says, to think that on the day of resurrection we will be given the same body, when in fact it may be a different one. Nevertheless anxious to remain open to the other possibility, he quickly affirms that if He so wished, God could completely reconstitute the old body, immediately knowing where all the various parts of it have gone and able to bring them back whole (pp. 247 ff.)

Finally, a sizable body of interpretation denies outright the possibility of the resurrected body being identical with the earthly body. "Life will never return to the actual bodies that have been placed on earth," insists al-Kīk. (*Rasā'il,* p. 159). According to Muṣṭafá Maḥmūd (*Qur'ān,* p. 96) we will be resurrected in bodies not like the ones we now have. They may look like our present forms but will be composed of a different matter, allowing for the multiplication of joys and pleasures in ways that we cannot possibly comprehend. In a very clear and straightforward statement Muhammad Zafrullah Khan scoffs at a literalist interpretation, rejecting wholesale the idea that continuation of life after death means an assembling of bones and flesh after all has been decomposed:

> The body, which is developed for terrestrial existence, is fashioned for the conditions of this life. Life after death cannot and does not mean that the dead will be reassembled and reconstituted upon the earth. Even if that were possible, the earth could not hold a billionth fraction of them. Consequently, the decomposition and disintegration of the human body is completely irrelevant to the possibility of life after death. (*Islam*, p. 185)

With few exceptions, then, contemporary Muslims affirm the resurrection of the body and disagree only on the nature of that body and its relation to the frames we inhabit while on earth. The idea of a purely spiritual resurrection has found few advocates. Addressing the question of whether the resurrection will be physical or spiritual, Maulana Muhammad 'Ali asserts that we cannot conceive of the soul without a body. But it is quite another thing to assume that we will have this same body of clay, he says, in a statement representative of those contemporaries who feel that the *ākhira* can be understood by analogy only: "If the very earth and heaven have changed at the Resurrection, how can the human body remain the same?"[21] The resurrection body, he goes on to insist, has nothing in common with the present body except the name and form by which individuality is preserved.

Some Indo-Muslim writers, however, are less willing to deny that the resurrection will in some way be a bodily revival. Muhammad Iqbal, for instance, raises this issue with great seriousness in *The Reconstruction of Reli-*

gious Thought in Islam (1962). He cites S 50:34,[22] which he says clearly suggests that "the nature of the universe is such that it is open to it to maintain in some other way the kind of individuality necessary for the final working out of human action, even after the disintegration of what appears to specify his individuality in the present environment" (p. 122). We do not know the nature of that other way, he says, but associating the second creation with some kind of body, no matter how subtle, will not afford us any greater insight. Iqbal's thought on the nature of human individuality also has interesting ramifications for his interpretation of the abodes of the afterlife, as we shall see below. Engaging as these ideas are, however, they have not won the approval of Islam as a whole, and the vast majority of Muslims continues to hold to the idea of a bodily resurrection, whatever the nature of that body is to be.

Directly related to the question of revival of the physical body is that of whether the joys and torments of the hereafter are to be understood as physical or spiritual, akin to or totally different from the pains and pleasures we experience in our earthly bodies. While the responses to this question naturally represent a broad range of opinion, they seem to fall naturally into three distinguishable groups: affirmation of the physical nature of ultimate recompense, denial of the physical in favor of its spiritual aspects, and the search for a median or compromise position between these two alternatives.[23] In the context of this discussion often comes some form of reflection on the nature (and location) of the abodes of recompense themselves.

This statement by Ahmad Galwash suggests what has been and continues to be the orthodox position on the realities of the afterlife:[24]

> The felicity of the righteous in paradise, and the pains of the wicked in hell, will vary in degree, according to their merits or demerits, respectively. The happiness and felicity of the dwellers of paradise, on the other hand, and the anguish and pains of the inhabitants of hell, on the other, are according to the orthodox doctrine, *sensuous and material, both body and soul being entitled or subject to them, respectively*. (*The Religion of Islam,* I, 246)

It is the position taken by a number of commentators who feel that efforts to "spiritualize" the rewards both negative and positive fail to do justice to the Qur'ānic intention, bordering on what they see as compromises of the mystics and philosophers. Commenting on S 69:24, which describes eating and drinking in the hereafter, for example, Abū'l 'Azā'im asserts that all of us know that spirits do not eat and drink or get married. Such verses are proof against those who deny the resurrection of the body, he says. Writers who do not wish to consider the hereafter as having physical/sensual pleasures advance the argument (cited above) that because of the disintegration of the physical body at death, a completely physical resurrection is impossible. Abū'l-'Azā'im feels that such disputation is pointless in the light of God's power: the body will be returned on the day of resurrection as it was in this world, with the spirit, and the idea that only the spirit is returned and recompense is spiritual, is false *(Tafṣīl*, pp. 11–13).

The majority of traditionalist doctors of Islam have held to this orthodox view, and it is probably the general response of most Muslim believers today.[25] Some contemporary writers have used the emphasis on the physical nature of the rewards as a means of helping prod the members of the community into living lives of greater moral rectitude. Ṣadīq Ḥasan Khān, for example, commenting in his *Yaqẓat ulī al-i'tibār* (n.d.) on the material nature of the Fire, suggests that while others have written about the Garden and forgiveness, he chose to describe the Fire and its horrors. The Muslim needs the latter more than the former, he feels, because fear does something to the fearful that hope cannot do to the hopeful; recognition of the specific nature of the physical torment will be most effective as a deterrent to moral backsliding. He is particularly graphic in the description of the traditional seven levels of the Fire as places in which flesh is eaten, hands and feet broiled, bones broken, people weep pus and blood, serpents and scorpions torment, and other such grisly details (esp. pp. 79–99).

Many of the modern Qur'ān commentaries, while much less pointed than writers like Khān in their descriptions particularly of the fires of torment, make it quite clear that they hold to the physical nature of recompense.[26] They imply, however, some distinction between the pains and pleasures of this world and the next. It is clearly not that the former are physical and the latter are spiritual, but rather that the former are subject to change and the latter are constant, that the former are temporary and the latter are eternal, particularly in reference to the pleasures of the Garden. (We will consider below the ways in which contemporary thinkers treat the question of the eternality of the Fire and punishment.) These *mufassirūn* share some of the characteristics of what we will describe as our third category of interpretation, although they differ from the writers of that group in that they generally do not deal with the question of the difference between literal and symbolic understanding of particular passages and references. Their interpretations are remarkably literal, with a clear emphasis on the relationship of afterlife realities to earthly realities. Here again we see examples of the didactic and hortatory approach; not only do they warn against waywardness by injecting an element of fear, but they discourage over-indulgence in earthly pleasures by assuring that pleasures will be ample in the hereafter.

At the other end of the continuum of interpretation of the nature of ultimate recompense are writers who posit that the pleasures and pains promised by the Qur'ān are to be understood exclusively as spiritual. In general two subgroups are represented in this school of thought: those whom we have already considered in the group of self-affirmed spiritualists, and a number of Muslims primarily from the Indo-Pakistani sub-continent, who on the whole reflect a less traditional and less literalist interpretation of Islam.

It is not surprising to find that spiritualists of the first subgroup tend to interpret the resurrection and recompense in a spiritual vein. Death in this understanding, as we have seen, is defined precisely as the separation of the physical and the spiritual; while the spiritual being is described as a body, it is clearly not akin to the body of flesh we inhabit while on earth. Thus 'Abd al-Jalīl Rāḍī, in answering the question, Are the Garden and the Fire mental or spiritual states?, responds that man lives through his spiritual body after the disintegration of the physical, and his punishment and well-being are in the form of this new nature.[27] We actually find in most of these writers a blending of what Islamic tradition has seen as two distinct categories or periods of events: the *barzakh* or period between physical death and resurrection, and the event(s) comprising the *ba'th* and determining the ultimate abodes of recompense. For the spiritualists reward and punishment take place immediately after death (a notion shared to a certain extent, as we have seen, by tradition), and the states of the spiritual bodies are in an immediate sense parallel to what tradition has understood eschatologically to be the final abodes of the Garden and the Fire. Thus Ra'ūf 'Ubayd says that the scientific spiritualists have shown that the resurrection occurs at the instant of death and even during the death process itself; it is a second birth completed in the process of separation of the ethereal body from the material body, taking with it the intellect. Spiritualist ideas are not inconsistent with the understanding expressed in all religions about punishments and rewards after death, he says, but these must be seen to be of a purely spiritual nature.[28]

One of the tenets of modern spiritualism is that there are seven spiritual worlds, with varying vibrations. Nawfal, quoting extensively from Arthur Findlay on the existence of seven earths and seven heavens, relates these to the parallel references in the Qur'ān,[29] and Muḥammad Shahīn Ḥamza locates the Prophet Muḥammad and his family, the spirits of the first four caliphs, and the martyrs in the highest of the seven spiritual realms.[30] Reflecting in *Ma'l-fīkr* on the inevitability of the judgment of the human soul, Ḥamza says that the Fire exists inside the spirit as well as around it, and so with the Garden, for recompense is a mental condition. The spiritual or ethereal world is beautiful to the good and contrary to the evil one; conscience, he says, will provide greater punishment for the evildoer than could possibly be felt in the torment of any physical fire (p. 228).

Keeping company with the spiritualists in one sense, though not necessarily sharing their understanding that the abodes of recompense are in effect immediately operative with the death of the physical body, are the other Muslim thinkers who deny the physical nature of ultimate rewards. This view is most commonly held by those influenced by the religious atmosphere of the Indian sub-continent. Sometimes one senses a note of cultural smugness in these analyses, such as the protest of Syed Ameer Ali that "the idea that the Arabian Prophet promised his followers a sensual paradise . . . is a sign alike of ignorance and ancient bigotry" and that "To the wild famished Arab, what more grateful, or what more consonant to his ideas of paradise than rivers of unsullied incorruptible water, or of milk and honey; or anything more acceptable than unlimited fruit, luxuriant vegetation, inexhaustible fertility? He could conceive of no bliss unaccompanied with these sensuous pleasures."[31] Such Qur'ānic descriptions are realistic and almost sensuous, he admits, but to say that they are physical is nothing short of calumny. Ali's own understanding is that Muḥammad in his spiritual development moved from a material to an increasingly spiritualized perspective,[32] and the latter view is the most appropriate to these descriptions.

Some of those who stress the spiritual understanding seem to accept the traditional view of the Garden and the Fire as eschatological abodes. Thus Maulana Muhammad 'Ali testifies that Paradise is for those in whom the good preponderates over the evil, and Hell for those of the opposite condition (*The Religion of Islam*, pp. 219–23). But when pressed as to the location and nature of these abodes, he asserts that "Paradise and Hell are more like two conditions than two places" (p. 294) and assures us that the blessings of the Garden cannot be perceived by the physical senses. Syed Abdul Latif discusses the Qur'ānic picture of Heaven and Hell as "two different states of the human soul," put into an environment completely different from this world. Stressing the commonly-held understanding of the importance of human evolution and progress, he says that in the Qur'ānic sense Heaven and Hell begin for human beings in this life on earth, insofar as the good and evil they do become part of them.[33]

Muhammad Zafrullah Khan in *Islam* concurs in this understanding of evolution when he says, much as did 'Ubayd, that the birth of the soul into a new life, after it has gone through the process of developing its various faculties, is actually what is to be understood by the resurrection (p. 187). He goes on to describe his view of the Garden and the Fire in a way similar to Latif:

> Heaven and hell are not separate, defined and divided regions, but exist, as it were, coextensively. . . . Hell means a state of the soul whose faculties are defective or diseased and whose reactions, consequently, are painful in contrast with the pleasant and agreeable reactions of a healthy soul. It is true that the phraseology employed constantly creates in the mind physical images, but in the conditions of human existence in this life that is inescapable. . . . It is only by means of paraphrase and explanation that an effort can be made to bring the human mind closer to some understanding of these conditions, the reality of which is indeed beyond the ken of man. (pp. 192–93)

One of the clearest denials of the physical (or geographical) nature of the abodes of recompense is seen in this statement by Muhammad Iqbal (*Reconstruction*):

> Heaven and Hell are states, not localities. The descriptions in the Qur'ān are visual representations of an inner fact, *i.e.*, character. Hell, in the words of the Qur'ān, is 'God's kindled fire which mounts above the hearts'—the painful realization of one's failure as a man. Heaven is the joy of triumph over the forces of disintegration. (p. 123)

A sizable number of contemporary interpreters of Islamic doctrine choose to maintain a middle position between the extremes of the physical and the spiritual interpretations of the afterlife. In certain cases they view the nature of recompense as being different in different circumstances. Sayyid Quṭb, for example, in his analysis and chronological classification of all the Meccan and Medinan Suras relative to the resurrection, *Mashāhid al-qiyāma fi'l-Qur'ān*, states that the scenes describing the bliss and punishment after the resurrection and judgment at times are materialistic and sensual and at other times to be understood as ideational [*ma'nawī*] or in some way pointing to a reality more abstract or more spiritual in its true nature. The sensible modes of recompense are often accompanied by other modes intelligible on a different and higher level (pp. 36–46). Quṭb even concedes that suffering might be a psychological condition, although its exact nature must remain unknown to us: "One does not die so he can have rest, nor does he live so he can have enjoyment. But he continues suspended to an eternity, the end of which is unknown (p. 57).'' As always, of course, one must look for the motivating factor in any author's work; it is clear that Quṭb is less concerned with a precise interpretation of the joys and pains of the hereafter than with the analysis of the Qur'ān as a work of literary art as well as a guide for the ethical life of the Muslim community.

Muṣṭafá Maḥmūd, the Egyptian journalist whose numerous volumes on Islamic theology are to be found in every Cairo bookstall, represents well this middle position in the understanding of the afterlife. It is possible for joy and suffering to be spiritual and sensual at one time, he says in *al-Qur'ān* (pp. 85–96). Unwilling to discount completely the physical nature of recompense, he articulates a common understanding of the interpretation, that the nature of the afterlife bodies will be different from that we now know. Thus, he says, suffering and pleasures might be multiplied in sensual and *ma'nawi* ways that we cannot understand. Maḥmūd holds that as we are all in different ranks or levels here on earth, so shall we be in the life to come, and the rank [*daraja*] or state of being that is the highest point of the Garden will probably be elevated above the senses. God will choose the deserving for this level, in which there is no pleasure like the pleasure of eating, drinking, or the *ḥūr,* but only the pleasure of meditating on truth, beauty, and absolute good. ''Thus the Garden will contain all the different ranks from the sensual to the purely spiritual, each one of us getting whatever he deserves.''[34]

Finally, says Maḥmūd in another work, *Riḥlat min al-shak*, there can be no ''how'' to the recompense of the next world because in the hereafter all is ultimately *ghayb*, part of that known only to God. It is possible, he confesses, that the holy books must be understood purely symbolically. In an example that occurs several times in his writings he likens these descriptions to the answer one might give a child inquiring about sexual enjoyment—that it is like sugar or honey—because the child has no experience with which to make comparison (p. 71). Muḥammad Nuwaihī of the American University of Cairo represents himself as in agreement with this kind of understanding and commented in a private interview that ''Personally I believe all references to the Fire or to the delights of paradise to be symbolic.''

In contrast, even the suggestion of symbol or allegory is more than some Muslim writers wish to espouse. Affirming again that the purpose of faith in the last day is to drive man to progress and perfection in this lower life, Maḥmūd Shaltūt says in *al-Islām* that we must be content with accepting the existence of abodes of blessedness and suffering without trying to approximate or understand them. These abodes, he says, are not like this world with its characteristics and descriptions (p. 42). In a powerful denouncement of the ability of the human mind even to imagine what it has never before experienced, Muḥammad al-Mubārak affirms that there is nothing in the Qur'ān or the *ḥadīths* that allows us to think that the description of the hereafter is allegorical. Far from testifying to the literalness of these descriptions, however, al-Mubārak is saying that such allegorical interpretation would relate the descriptions to the realities of this life, when in fact the truths of this world have nothing in common with the truths of the next world.[35] In this understanding al-Mubārak seems to echo the interpretation given by Muḥammad 'Abdu, primus of the Qur'ān commentators of the early part of this century, of some of the verses describing the Fire and the Garden. "We believe in [these abodes] in terms of *al-ghayb*," he says in exegesis of S 2:25, "and we do not speak about the reality of these two matters. We do not wish to add anything categorical concerning these, because the world of the unseen is not understood by analogy."[36]

While 'Abdu admits the possibility of sensuous joys and pains, however, and says that the bliss of the faithful and the torment of the damned will be both physical and spiritual, al-Mubārak insists that they are not literal, spiritual, or allegorical, but simply beyond our comprehension. To discuss these hidden matters, he says, is only to invite dissension and argument; one must recall that only the *mushrikūn* raised these kinds of interpretive questions in the early history of Islam. What is important, he concludes in a manner characteristic of contemporary Islamic thought, is to understand that the significance of remembering the hereafter is in underlining the responsibility of man for his works, the preparation of man for judgment in the hereafter. Stressing psychological and emotional reasons for encouraging faith in the life to come, he emphasizes in a way not unlike Ṣadīq Ḥasan Khān the necessity of instilling a fear of the Fire as well as a desire for the Garden. No matter how elevated his thinking or advanced his knowledge, says al-Mubārak, by instinct man seeks that which gives him pleasure and fears that which gives him pain, either physical or *ma'nawī*. If these emotions are kept alive through the graphic descriptions of the Qur'ān, man will do that which is ultimately pleasing in the eyes of God. He concludes his commentary with the provocative question, Would man's conduct be the same if he believed that there is no afterlife as it would be if he believed in the reality of ultimate punishment?[37]

More important for these writers than the nature of the joys and torments of the hereafter as described in the Qur'ān and traditions, then, is the purpose of these detailed and seemingly sensuous characterizations. Whether inciting fear of what is to be avoided or extending hope for what is to be attained, in the minds of many contemporary Muslims they are intended for the primary purpose of encouraging man to live in this world with the concrete and immediate awareness that he will be called to accountability for his actions in the next. "Thus the hereafter is a reality [the Muslim] lives," says Aḥmad Fā'iz, "and not a distant promise. He is in certitude and has no doubt that each soul will be recompensed for what it has earned. . . . And this is the secret of his piety and awe."[38]

Several other issues are of particular concern to most contemporary commentators on matters of the afterlife, as they have been of interest to Islamic theologians from early on. To a certain extent these issues are interrelated; they include the question of whether or not (and for whom) intercession will be a reality, the matter of punishment and justice as these relate to the eternality of the Fire (or of one's stay in it), and the understanding of what is meant by the vision of God. Central to the development of these themes is the understanding and attempted resolution of the tension that has been present throughout the history of Islamic thought in relation to the divine: God's promise of justice and the hope of God's mercy.

Despite the Qur'ānic insistence that there will be no intercession [*shafā'a*] on the day of resurrection except in certain very qualified instances, Islam quickly expanded this to a more general belief in the possibility of intercession, particularly through the Prophet Muḥammad. Modern Muslim thinkers usually support the affirmation that some form of intercession will be possible, particularly for those in whose hearts is at least a modicum of faith. (There are, of course, some exceptions among those who feel that the firm nature of God's justice at the judgment precludes the possibility of escape from punishment. There is no *shafā'a* and no ransom [*fidya*], insists Sayyid Quṭb, and not a single hair's weight of the judgment balance is affected.[39] While the affirmation of *shafā'a* sometimes takes the form of a repetition of many of the numerous *ḥadīths* on the subject,[40] it is often accompanied by commentary revealing the particular point the author wishes to underscore relative to the divine promise.

Sometimes the reason for stressing the reality of intercession at the last day is to relate it to more popular expectations of intercession on the part of saints [*walīs*] in the course of everyday events. Appendix III describes the belief in this kind of intercession held by many of the Muslim faithful past and present, as well as orthodox response to that belief. Here we should note that for some modern theologians such a possibility of daily intercession by the *walīs* is nothing but superstition, and it is in contrast to the *shafā'a* of the day of resurrection which Islamic tradition has attested to be true.[41] At other times the affirmation of *shafā'a* seems to provide another opportunity to affirm the importance of the Prophet Muḥammad. This stress on the significance of Muḥammad not only as the vehicle of the revelation but also as the supreme leader and ideal educator of the community is a powerful theme in much modern interpretation of Islam. Here he is thrust into the eschatological role, supported by many traditions, of the purveyor of God's mercy.[42]

For many contemporaries the most important issue is the nature of the divine as the guarantor of justice in response to human responsibility and as the final and sole authority in matters of punishment and remission. Thus the issue is not whether intercession will be a possibility, but that authority for this as for all other matters is in the hands of God. "It is impossible for a prophet to change the law of God despite his closeness to God," insists Muṣṭafá Maḥmūd. "To God alone is intercession—none can intercede except by His permission."[43] It is, of course, wholly consistent with the direction of Islamic tradition to deny the authority for *shafā'a* to any save God. These writers emphasize in the spirit of the Qur'ān that no allowance for *shafā'a* will alter the fact that there will be means for holding every individual accountable for his or her actions. This inevitability applies to intercession as well as to punishment and reward: "*Shafā'a* is like the sun; it shines on the good and the bad. But the amount one gets is in relation to the good one has done."[44] One of the clearest statements of this point of view is made by Muḥammad 'Abdu (*Tafsīr*) in exegesis of the eschatological verses which, he says, illustrate the inevitability of accountability and judgment. Recognizing that many verses in the Qur'ān totally deny *shafā'a* on the day of resurrection, he admits the possibility of intercession as acknowledged by many of the ancestors. However, he says,

> This does not mean that God will retract His will for the sake of the intercessor. Rather it [signifies] respect for the intercessor by fulfilling the Eternal Will subsequent to his request. There is also nothing in it to strengthen the self-righteousness of those who disregard matters of *dīn* because of their dependence on intercession. Rather it is that the matter is entirely in God's hands. (I, 308)

The issue of *shafā'a* or intercession with the end of release from torment is closely related to the question of temporary vs. eternal punishment, as well as to whether or not the Fire itself will endure endlessly. Thus many writers treat these issues as a totality, whose central theme is the affirmation of God's mercy as limitless as His authority is absolute. Some feel that because of the nature of certain sins there can be no alternative to eternal punishment. Khalaf al-Sayyid 'Alī, Head of the Islamic Research Center at al-Azhar, for example, said in a private interview with the authors that while in general Islam supports the idea of *shafā'a,* there are three unforgiveable sins for which no intercession could ever be possible: murder, *shirk*, and *kufr*. For such sinners the Fire will continue forever.[45] Galwash affirms that while those who have embraced the true religion of God will be delivered from the Fire after expiation, even if they are guilty of atrocious crimes, the infidels will be doomed to eternal damnation.[46]

For others the very point of traditional affirmations of intercession is to prove God's mercy.[47] Just as the dominant contemporary understanding is that some form of intercession will obtain on the last day, so the great majority come down firmly on the side of ultimate extinction of the fires of torment. Many thinkers, particularly those representative of the "middle position" in relation to the nature of recompense, find the answer to this question in the way one interprets the frequently repeated assertion of the Qur'ān that the people of the Fire will be there eternally [*hum fīhā khālidūn*]. Similar to the early Jahmīya, these interpreters say simply that as long as the Fire lasts, so will at least some of those consigned to it remain there; but because of the mercy of God, we can be sure that the Fire itself will not last eternally. The majority of Qur'ān exegetes[48] generally hold this view. Some insist that not one categorical statement in the Qur'ān supports the eternity of the Fire, the suggestion that the *kuffār* will be in it eternally meaning only that they will remain as long as it exists.[49]

Sometimes the question is dealt with from the perspective of the eternity of bliss as opposed to the non-eternity of punishment. The Qur'ān itself, say such advocates, teaches that while the torment of punishment will come to an end, the joys of the life to come will indeed last forever and even increase. Verses cited in support of this argument are not those dealing specifically with the *kuffār,* but rather those such as S 7:156 and S 11:119, which speak of God's mercy for all humankind.[50] According to this understanding, the purgation of the Fire is not so much a punishment or chastisement as it is a curative, putting man into a proper state to be able to enjoy the bliss of the happier abode. Thus, says Maulana Muhammad 'Ali,

> . . . there can be but little doubt left that Hell is a temporary place for the sinner, whether Muslim or non-Muslim, and this also supports the view that the

> chastisement of Hell is not for torture, but as a remedy, to heal the spiritual diseases which a man has incurred of himself and by his own negligence, and to enable him to start again on the road to the higher life.[51]

This interpretation also supports the view common to many moderns that the afterlife is a state, or rather a series of states, in which continual progress is implicit, and that even those whose actions on earth consign them to a period of purgation will not be exempted from the joy of spiritual progression.

What, then, is the goal of this progression? Or in other terms, how do we categorize or describe the ultimate bliss of the abode of felicity which Islamic tradition has understood as the promise of the divine vision? The first point to be noted in relation to the ideal of seeing God, the *ru'yā Allāh*, is that many contemporary writers do not mention it at all. This is perhaps not surprising, for as al-Kīk observes in *Rasā'il*, it has been a very sensitive issue for Muslims and cannot be handled simply. It involves not only man himself or in relation to other creatures, he says, but is the divine question itself—the question of man and his Lord. Ignoring much of the literalist understanding of Islamic tradition, al-Kīk insists that none in the history of Islam has ever said that we shall see God plainly on the day of resurrection or any other day. Like many of his contemporaries he refrains from trying to speculate on either the reality or the nature of this vision (p. 106).

Those who treat the issue with any specificity do so generally in the context of a particular affirmation about the nature of the life everlasting. Some indicate that the first appearance of God in terms of human understanding will be on the day of resurrection, an idea consonant with many of the *ḥadīths*.[52] The literalist interpretation depicts God as both in sight of and in conversation with the resurrected assembly on that day, directing the progression of events. Others are somewhat more esoteric in their understanding. "Man will look to God and the veil will be removed from the light of God," says Nawfal, "and the light will shine over man covering him and man will gain from it and take from it and the light will emanate from him."[53] This light Muṣṭafá Maḥmūd describes in *al-Qur'ān* as the force so powerful that in effect it defies all efforts at vision. The Lord will make Himself apparent at the resurrection in such a way that everything will melt away in awe, he says. All life disappears—the *fanā'*—because God has removed the veil from His face and all the earth is illumined by His light (pp. 192–94).

More commonly moderns see the idea of viewing the divine or of being in the presence of the divine as the supreme pleasure or reward of the abode of eternal felicity. Beyond the joys of the Garden, however these may be interpreted, is the bliss of gazing upon God's perfection and basking in the radiance of His divine oneness. This is the ultimate joy, the greatest happiness to which a person can aspire, and therefore the supreme goal of the life to come. "The highest purpose of the hereafter is for all the beautiful radiant faces to sit and behold the glory of God," says Aḥmad Fā'iz.[54] This vision is both related to and yet beyond the knowledge or understanding of the divine. In a section devoted to "The Vision of God" in *The Religion of Islam* (II, 240–41) Ahmad Galwash reasons that since God is the highest possible object of knowledge, the greatest pleasure must be in the knowledge of Him. Yet, he says, even this joy falls short of the delight of vision. As a seed grows into a tree, so the knowledge of God one gains in this world will in the next be transformed into the vision of God. As human knowledge differs, so will God be seen in different ways by those of different levels of intuition. This view, appropriate to the contemporary understanding of progress in the hereafter, is articulated by Abū'l-'Azā'im when he says in *Tafṣīl* that the vision is the uncovering of knowledge beyond the material, given to man by God. Each believer is given light whereby he can see God according to his own ability or understanding (pp. 57–58).

Others have related the notion of progress even more specifically to the possibility of apprehending the divine. Maulana Muhammad 'Ali speaks not of the vision but of the meeting with God, the *liqā' Allāh,* as "the great goal to attain which all good deeds are done." Just as Hell means being kept from the divine presence, so Paradise is the place where one meets with God. 'Ali sees this as both an end and a beginning, however. Within the realms of Paradise, present in some measure with the divine, the righteous rise to ever higher stages of progress.[55] This idea of the image of the divine as attainable on the one hand and yet never attainable on the other is a means of expressing the understanding of God as infinitely complex while at the same time utterly simply in His divine oneness. "There is no end to God's beauty and perfection and awesomeness," says M. K. I. Ja'far, "so the believer is continually discovering new horizons of divine perfection without ever coming on all of them."[56] According to Ja'far this is a rational understanding of the Islamic view of the divine, so that each person will be able to see of God's holiness only as much as his own potential allows, as well as what God out of His goodness and mercy chooses to bestow on him.

In the contemporary treatment of eschatological concerns, then—from the events signaling the Hour to the highest joys of the abode of bliss—one can see repeated themes generally characteristic of modern Islamic thought.

Basic to the understanding of the meaning of the resurrection and day of judgment, of course, is the thesis that human accountability is inextricably tied to divine justice, that this world and human actions in it are meaningful only in the light of the next world, and indeed that the main reason for concerning ourselves with any analysis of the affairs of the eschaton is to provide the impetus for moral rectitude in the immediate present.

In commentary on the signs of the Hour we find a ready proving-ground for efforts to reconcile the Qur'ān and even some of Islamic tradition with the findings of modern science. If the physical calamities of that day lend themselves to scientific analysis, so the indications of moral disorder provide an appropriate vehicle for general condemnation of what is seen as moral turpitude in the Islamic world and the world in general, as well as an occasional thrust at the West as the progenitor of many of these forms of degradation. Not unrelated to the concern for scientific analysis is the treatment of the possibility of bodily resurrection. Here one finds the assertion that the physical realities of human decomposition notwithstanding, God could if He so chose reassemble the scattered parts; should this happen, it would not be in opposition to rational, natural laws.

Concerned with maintaining the essence of the Qur'ānic message about the abodes of the hereafter and the nature of recompense, the majority of modern writers take some kind of middle line which either allows for the reality of both sensual and spiritual interpretations or else says that any analogy with experiences of this world is false because the next world is simply beyond our ability to comprehend. The affairs of the life to come, say many of these interpreters, are matters of the *'alam al-ghayb*, part of the knowledge of God, which surpasses any attempts at human understanding.

Such concerns as the possibility of intercession, the duration of punishment, and the vision of God are dealt with first in the context of a constant emphasis on God's mercy, and second with a recurring insistence on the possibility of human progress. If judgment is necessitated by the demands of divine justice, some eventual remission is also assured, say the great majority, through the reality of divine mercy. As progress toward a fuller understanding of God is possible in this world through the living of a morally upright life, so the abodes of the next are viewed by many as the arena of constant movement upward toward higher states of bliss, knowledge, and ultimate contemplation of the divine itself.

Appendix A
Evidence of Afterlife Concerns in Pre-Islamic Arabia

The extreme skepticism and even ridicule with which Meccans received the message of the Prophet Muḥammad that all bodies will be resurrected and revivified seems a clear indication that eschatology as it has come to be understood in Islam was not part of the general belief system of the *jāhilī* Arabs.[1] The Qur'ānic emphasis on a personal God as the ultimate authority over life, on the *āyāt* of God as assurances of His beneficent control and of the positive construction of the universe, and on an eschatological resurrection and subsequent judgment ran directly counter to much of the generally accepted world view of the contemporaries of the Prophet. (Even this assertion, however, has been partly brought into question by some scholars who feel that the variety of terms indicating such events as resurrection and the abodes of recompense in Arabic suggest that these ideas were not foreign to the people of the Prophet's day.[2])

In addition to the evidence of the Qur'ān, of course, passages from pre-Islamic poetry and inscriptions indicate an intense pessimism and even gloom in regard to death and the possibility of continuing existence. The following inscription found on two Ḥimyarite tombs seems characteristic of the atmosphere that to a great extent prevailed up to the coming of Islam:

> The two Lords of Ḥimyar in yonder tombs are laid,
> Their bodies in the earth have rott'd, their bones decayed;
> By the hand of death they fell, by it were destroyed,
> Death, that which on earth none can its sting avoid.
> Lo, at the time of birth their bodies of dust were made.
> And to dust return, when in the earth they're laid.[3]

Such testimony, along with the clear emphasis on success and fortune in the context of this life, has led some Western observers to remark that these peoples had little concern for religion[4] and that any conceptions of life after death were either absent or ill-formed.[5] From what has been brought to light concerning the beliefs and practices of the pre-Islamic Arabs, however, such conclusions seem overgeneralized and not fully justified, although it is quite apparent that the message of the Qur'ān represented a radically new formulation of the possibility of eschatological events.

It is particularly important to recognize, of course, that for a variety of reasons our conclusions about the beliefs of the pre-Islamic Arabs must remain mainly speculative. Despite continuing attempts of archeologists and historians, the actual data are scanty. Even when we seem to have fairly clear evidence about practices, it is a difficult and often presumptuous next step to infer from these data the prevailing conceptions that may have inspired them. In addition to archeological evidence from earlier periods of Arabian history, we have a wealth and variety of information conveyed through the *jāhilī* poetry. Again, however, to construct a consistent world view on the basis of this is to press for more than the material reasonably will bear. While archeological evidence is at least indicative of practices somewhere around the turn of the millenium or earlier, and poetry conveys some understanding of the Weltanschauung of the *jāhilī* period, it is not clear to what extent these sources of information meet or even overlap in time.

As is of course true with the study of many ancient peoples—the inhabitants of the Nile valley in pharaonic times, the Mesopotamians at Ur, the Incas of Northern Peru—a consideration of grave artifacts tells us somewhat more about the living culture of a society than about their hopes or fears of a future life. Nonetheless, certain objects found in what are obviously graves and burial places at least suggest some kind of prevailing conception of life beyond the limits of earthly existence. Scholars are on much surer ground with such speculations in the case of certain cultures than in others, of course, as in the understanding of the beliefs of the ancient Egyptians, where archeological findings include such materials as the Pyramid Texts and the Book of the Dead. For pre-Islamic Arabia the evidence is far less conclusive. Several isolated archeological excavations have given us certain valuable clues, but we are far from being in a position to determine beyond mere speculation how these peoples viewed the life of the grave. That such a life was at least considered a strong possibility does seem a justifiable assumption. From the tombs and funerary stelae we know that they paid a good deal of attention to burial of the dead, and that the deceased were provided with particular objects that had been of use to them during their lifetimes.

From Southern Arabia we have evidence that the dead were put into the ground, sometimes in stone sarcophagi, with their graves marked by piles of stones or individual stelae. Where the area was particularly rocky, the tombs were actually cut into the sides of wadis, as in the Ḥadramaut[6] or constructed like a suite of rooms designed to receive the dead. In a temple mausoleum at 'Awwām, near Mārib, tombs were arranged on shelves around the walls, and at nearby Beiḥān the bodies were placed in small compartments leading off a central aisle.[7] Inside these tombs have been discovered a wide variety of objects such as seals, gems, amulets, utensils, perfume jars and the like. From some of the inscriptions on Southern Arabian tombs referring to rain or to the flowing of water, the hypothesis has been made that a supply of water was considered advantageous, possibly for quenching the thirst of the dead.[8] These suggestions are supported by wishes expressed in poetry that the graves of loved ones be supplied with rain ("May the clouds of dawn keep green thy grave with unfailing showers!"[9]), but it seems likely that this desire is more for the general growth of verdure around the grave than for the refreshment of the deceased themselves.[10] Some stelae bear the image of the deceased; others have epitaphs such as *nṣb, nfs,* or *ṣwr* (respectively, stela, soul, and image) and bear the family name of the deceased along with a warning to would-be predators.[11]

It is common knowledge that from early in the first millenium B.C.E. there was a flourishing culture in Southern Arabia, the land of the people of Sabā' (Sheba). From the last independent kingdom of that culture, the Ḥimyarites, we are fortunate to have a rare collection of grave artifacts dating from around 150 B.C.E. to 200 C.E.[12] The objects found in this Ḥimyarite gravesite are of stone and metal, usually alabaster or limestone and copper, typical of the artistic work of that period. The inscriptions are in the Ḥimyarite language and are often placed at the base of funerary images believed to be those of royalty and important personages. On the basis of what we know to have been attempts to represent the dead in a permanent image, it seems reasonable to conclude that in some sense the figures were intended to be images of the deceased, perhaps in an effort to counter the obviously imminent disintegration of the physical body.[13] Although in the case of full-body representations certain details such as joints, fingernails, and hair are carefully portrayed, there is no attempt to make the statues fully life-like. In many instances the figure is nothing more than a large stone block with bas-relief almond- or diamond-shaped eyes, brows, a nose, and a suggested mouth. It seems clear that the head was considered the most important part of the body, and great care seems to have been given in particular to the construction of the eyes and depiction of the hair. In some instances the funerary monument is nothing more than a piece of stone with a name engraved on the bottom and an animal head represented above. When the full body is portrayed, the feet are placed in such a manner that the figure is seen to be standing rather than walking, hands stretched out in front of him.[14] Along with statues and statuettes the findings include incense burners, small altar-like constructions, items of personal toiletry, and some jewelry with semiprecious stones.

Aside from evidence derived from modern archeological expeditions, we have little to guide us in determining the beliefs and practices of Arabia before the time of the Prophet. Of the few Muslim writers to devote themselves to an interest in this subject, one of the most widely-recognized is the tenth-century geographer and historian al-Ḥamdānī, whose *Iklīl*, Book Eight, gives testimony to many of these Ḥimyarite findings. Describing the excavation of one of these tombs, a millenium before the work of western archeologists, he says: "After a long and tedious effort, we succeeded in opening it, to find in it (the corpse of) a woman decked with so many jewels that one could hardly believe that they could possibly have belonged to one woman. We also could discern the woman's beauty despite the distracting glare of the jewels."[15]

Also recovered from Southwest Arabian burial sites is a series of interesting relief carvings giving us clearer insights into the daily life of the time.[16] These include animal and domestic scenes such as a farmer plowing, a man at table with a woman behind him playing a stringed instrument, and a man on horseback driving a camel. The inscriptions, invoking the protection of the god 'Athtar, indicate that these carvings were used specifically as grave markers. It is tempting, of course, to project the idea that such representations of everyday scenes from this life were intended to describe and/or guarantee the continuation of felicity in the next. Short of finding much more detailed and lengthy inscriptions or some sort of textual explanations, however, such speculations must remain unsubstantiated. That the objects preserved in the graves were precious to them seems indisputable; that they hoped in some way to make use of these objects after death is clearly less certain yet still a reasonable possibility.

In Central Arabia, the region of the Ḥijāz north of Yemen, the tombs like the sanctuaries were often considered part of the sacred domain. Here, too, stelae were erected on the graves,[17] which were usually also marked with a pile of stones, and the tombs were supplied with various objects in current usage. It was apparently the custom to place cut hair on the tomb, connected most likely with specific practices of lamentation.[18] Certain sacrifices were made on the tombs;[19] a commonly-cited practice is that of tying a she-camel or a mare near the grave and allowing it to die of starvation. Various hypotheses have been suggested to explain this practice, among them the idea that the soul of the camel would be ridden by the dead person in his immediate existence beyond the grave. There are numerous references in Islamic literature to the image of individuals riding at the time of the resurrection on camels or other beasts,[20] but it is surely unlikely that any such intention was in the minds of the pre-Islamic Arabs.[21]

The sacrifices and offerings made in connection with the dead seem clearly to have been in the context of social responsibility. There is no evidence to suggest that the dead were regarded as having attained special powers that they could exercise over or on behalf of the living. The practice of caring for graves and providing offerings appears not to have been for purposes of propitiation but rather, as has been true in many cultures ancient and not so ancient, to perform a service in the name of the departed. In a highly structured tribal society, clearly defined familial and social responsibilities are the way of life. Services performed at the grave may well be seen as a way of continuing these responsibilities even after death.[22]

Speaking of the care paid to proper interment so that graves would not be violated, T. Nöldeke comments, "That all this may be done without any notion of benefiting the departed is sufficiently obvious from the usages of modern Europe. The belief which exists among many primitive races, that the dead are malevolent and seek to injure the living, is one of which no traces are to be found among the Arabs" ("Arabs", p. 672). One finds, of course, occasional suggestions to the contrary. W. Robertson Smith feels that the various Arab funeral customs over the ages have been designed primarily to insure that the corpse is not a threat or danger to the living but in some way a source of blessing.[23] Many cultures have held the idea that the spirit of the deceased is a restless ghost, wandering either with malevolent intent or in unhappy confusion around the places it used to inhabit.[24] The concept of restlessness, however, may actually be out of keeping with the general world view of Arab society. Particularly for Bedouins, the wandering aspect integral to nomadic existence is in sharp opposition to the state of the individual at the time of death, when he becomes a sedentary [*muqīm*], a term used both for the grave and its occupant. This idea, developed in early Arab poetry, is supported by the observation that the nomad quickly abandons his departed comrades, who are stilled by the fact of death, to resume his own activities until the end of his appointed time.[25]

The question of whether practices such as offerings and sacrifices actually constituted a cult of the dead or a form of ancestor worship has been the subject of some discussion. One view is that at least the dead heroes of the tribe were worshiped, along with images and certain natural phenomena.[26] In *Kitāb al-aṣnām,* considered to be one of the most important sources of information about the practices of ancient Arabia, a tradition says that the sons of Cain taught the Arabs how to make images of the dead so that they could be remembered. This use became perverted, however, says *Kitāb al-aṣnām*, and as time passed these statues came to be worshipped as idols.[27]

That respect led to veneration, which in turn led to a kind of worship—i.e. that an ancestor remembered for his heroism came to be regarded as a local god—seems not unlikely in light of numberless such occurrences in a variety of other societies and also in consideration of the extreme importance put on the family relationship within Arab society. A Durkheimian analysis may be appropriate: the object of worship, the tribal ancestor, may have been identified with the collective of society itself. Such practices of ancestor worship, if indeed such a term is applicable, could be seen to have their natural continuation in popular Islam in the attribution to certain personages, i.e. the saints or *walīs*, of powers of intercession after death in the lives of those still on earth.[28]

What little we can surmise about specific beliefs concerning the soul of the departed depends mainly on scattered references to its continuing existence. It seems certain, in any case, that no real communication between the living and the dead was considered possible:

> Before the door of each and all a slumber-place is ready set:
> Men wane and dwindle, and the graves in number grow from day to day;
> And ever more and more out-worn the traces fade of hearth and home,
> And ever yonder for some dead is newly built a house of clay.
> Yea, neighbours are they of the living: near and close their fellowship;
> But if thy soul would seek their converse, thou must seek it far away.[29]

That aspect of the individual seen as continuing in or near the grave was referred to or described by the words *ṣadā* and *hāma*. The latter, a verb form, means "to be thirsty," or in the form *hāma 'alá*, "to hover around or about." *Ṣadā*, a noun, has several interpretations interesting in this context.[30] It can signify an echo and is used in such phrases as "his echo became dumb," meaning "he died." It can also refer to the part of the head or brain considered to be the location of one's mental faculties, to an owl-like bird that comes forth from the head of a slain victim (or a revivified bird-form of the bones of the dead), or to thirst itself. Sometime it has also been used to refer to the remains of the dead person in the grave.

These various meanings help to explain the belief, widely held by the Arabs before and at the time of the Prophet, that the "soul" of the departed, associated with the head, became an owlish apparition said to fly from the head of the deceased and hover near the grave. Particularly in cases of murder or violent death it is not difficult to see how the screeching of a bird in a lonely grave site could have been taken to be the voice of the deceased seeking vengeance: ". . . ill bird that shrieks in the gloom of the graves," says the poet.[31] This vengeance was often expressed by the phrase "give me drink, give me drink," apparently referring to the desire of the deceased to drink the blood of his slayer (although it may well be related to the aforementioned idea that the dead were construed as being thirsty): "Oh God, if I die, and Thou give not to mine owl to drink / Oh Lailà, I die, no grave lies thirstier than my grave."[32]

The Arabs have always maintained a clear line between the human species and the inhabitants of the spirit world, or *jinn*. In many aspects the latter have been thought to resemble humanity, but in fact they constitute one half of creation on the earth and human beings the other.[33] Neither made of flesh and blood nor in any way transcendent as are the gods, they appear in many forms, eat and drink, and in a general way participate in the activities of this world. The Qur'ān, of course, makes it quite clear that the *jinn* were created of fire and humankind of clay, although both will be called to judgment at the day of resurrection. It is nonetheless true that certain legends from early Arabian history suggest that beliefs were sometimes held attesting to the relationship of spirits and humans. A. S. Tritton, for example, reports that the *Kitāb al-aghānī* suggests that some of the Jews were considered to be related to the *jinn*, and that the *Ḥayawān* indicates that some tribes were descended from ancestors who were among the *jinn*.[34]

The word *jinn* itself is a collective noun (singular *jinni*), and the entire class of creatures has been subdivided and categorized into a variety of beings, of varying interests and abilities, including *ghūl, ʿifrīt, siʿlāt, rūḥ, shiqq, ʿāmir,* and *shayṭān*.[35] Possession by the *jinn* was considered to be a common phenomenon in the days of the Prophet, evidenced not least by repeated assertions in the Qur'ān that the utterances of Muḥammad were prophetic and not the ravings of one possessed. On the theoretical level, then, the *jinn* are not to be confused with the spirits of the deceased. That the line occasionally gets somewhat blurred, however, is apparent from the many reports of folk beliefs, and it is reasonable to suppose that such may have been the case also in earlier days. In situations of violent death in Egypt, for example, the spirit is often felt to become an *'ifrīt* and to hover around its former habitation for a number of days. Both Sayyid 'Uways, the Egyptian sociologist who has done detailed studies of afterlife beliefs, and the American University of Cairo anthropologist Sausan al-Missīrī assured us that the superstition is widely held that the *'ifrīt* goes out at night begging people for a drink, an interesting parallel to the ancient Arab belief in the thirsty owl-soul.[36]

Whether or not one wishes to argue linguistically for a belief among pre-Islamic Arabs in the idea of resurrection, and the weight of opinion clearly discourages such an attempt, the evidence suggests that there was and had been for some time an understanding of the possibility of life continuing beyond the death of the physical body. Nonetheless, even if these suggestions should find conclusive support, it is still apparent that there was no full-blown concept of life beyond the grave and that the advent of death was deeply dreaded. The evidence of poetry indicates that the early Arabs felt life is to be lived and to whatever extent possible enjoyed in this world, that the tomb is a place of general gloom and sadness. ''O thou dear lost one!'' cries the poet. ''Not meet for thee is the place of shadow and loneliness.''[37] (It is not unreasonable to suppose that this rather dismal conception of the life in the grave, while certainly not unique to this society, may well have influenced the later Islamic doctrine of the punishment of the grave.) Youth and virility were exalted and the passing into old age considered an unavoidable misfortune. In the following poem, actually written in the very early days of Islam, the author, in addressing his own soul at the moment of going into battle, expresses this vision of life:

> I said to her [my soul] when she fled in amazement and breathless
> Before the array of battle—Why dost thou tremble?
> Yea, if but a day of Life thou shouldst beg with weeping
> Beyond what thy Doom appoints, thou wouldst not gain it. . . .
> The pathway of Death is set for all men to travel:
> The Crier of Death proclaims through the Earth his empire,
> Who does not die when young and sound dies old and weary,
> Cut off in his length of days from all love and kindness;
> And what for a man is left of delight in living,
> Past use, flung away, a worthless and worn-out chattel?[38]

If it is possible to surmise any hopeful view of life after death in the South Arabian or Ḥimyarite times, there is little doubt that such had given way to the deep pessimism, informed by the notion of inexorable fate, that seems to have characterized the outlook of the *jāhilī* Arabs. To become a thirsty bird shrieking among the tombs is hardly a happy expectation, and all evidence suggests that the focus one's attention and hopes was to be on life in this world. As in many of the world's cultures, the expectation of immortality was not eschatological; the hope of living beyond death was seen to be achieved by remaining present in the memory of those of one's family and community. As the famous poet Ibn Qutayba recorded,

> A man after death is a tale.
> He vanishes, yet his traces [*āthār*] remain.
> What he concealed during his sleep is canceled out,
> And his secrets will be spread abroad.
> The best condition for a man is when the reports of him after death are good.
> His memory will endure after him,
> Even though his house is empty of his being.[39]

Little wonder is it that the Prophet's message of the relation of *dunyā* and *ākhira*, of the universal judgment, and of the possibility of physical pleasures for all eternity in the presence of a merciful and compassionate deity fell on incredulous ears.

Appendix B
The Special Case of Women and Children in the Afterlife

One of the strongest objections raised to the methodology of the discipline generally known as orientalism is that it has tended to ask questions about Asian traditions and faiths more relevant to the structure of Western thought than to the orientation of the persons about whom it attempts to report. Historians of religion have learned the sometimes painful lesson that to presume the wrong questions, or more specifically to fail to ask the right questions, is to run the grave risk of seriously misapprehending and even distorting the data.

The intent of this work has been, insofar as possible, to view the Islamic understanding of life after death from the inside, studying w what Muslims have seen in the Qur'ān and traditions, and the ways in which the various streams of thought with which the Muslim community has come into contact have affected their understanding. To the extent to which this approach necessitates asking Islamic questions rather than Western ones, it might be argued that the very orientation of the material in this appendix is inappropriate. Muslims traditionally have not, in fact, addressed themselves specifically to the question of what happens to women and children after they die, although their responses to this question are set forth in the course of dealing with other issues. We would suggest that with all due recognition of the tentativeness of this particular study, it may not be indefensible at this time to attempt to construct Islamic responses to questions which until recently might have been seen to be of more concern to Westerners.

It is certainly the case with the growing emphasis on women in Western society today that there is a concomitant rise in interest on the part of students of Islam in women in Muslim society. This interest is now being reflected, perhaps in response, by Muslims themselves. We offer the following study on one particular aspect of the role of women in the hope that it might bring to light some traditional as well as some contemporary thinking concerning the part that considerations of women have played in the total fabric of Muslim understanding. We do this, however, with the full recognition and insistence that the very ordering of this material, and perhaps particularly of the following material on children, brings home the obvious point that in most instances it has been articulated for some direct purpose other than to offer a description of what future life will be like for women and their offspring. By suggesting this kind of focus we hope to help illuminate from another perspective the theological categories in which Islamic questions have been raised, as well as to contribute to the general store of Western knowledge about ways in which the Islamic community has understood the circumstances of the hereafter.

Women in the Afterlife

The occasional conclusion of observers of Islam, particularly in the early stages of Christian missionary outreach to the Muslim community, has been that women according to the Islamic understanding do not have souls.[1] If this were true, of course, it would have grave and obvious implications for the issue of judgment and responsibility in regard to women. Such a misunderstanding, however, is far from the Qur'ānic conception, as contemporary Western scholarship is now fully aware, and is certainly unsupported by the Islamic community as a whole.[2] While certain of the *ḥadīths* have greatly elaborated the suggested fate of women after death from the Qur'ānic intention, it is unequivocably clear in the Qur'ān itself that men and women are on an equal footing when it comes to chances of final felicity or perdition.[3] {And whoever does works of righteousness, male or female, and is a believer, will enter the Garden and will not be wronged in the least}, says S 4:124, and in S 33:73 we are assured that {God punishes the male and female hypocrites [*al-munāfiqīn wa'l-munāfiqāt*] and the male and female idolaters [*al-mushrikīn wa'l-mushrikāt*], and He turns mercifully toward the male and female believers [*al-mu'minīn wa'l-mu'mināt*]. . . . } There has been some suggestion that the expansion of certain Qur'ānic references to include both masculine and feminine forms came in the later revelations, but there is no indication that this was more than an elaboration of the original intention that the masculine forms be understood as generic.[4]

In only a few places does the Qur'ān specifically mention women in the Garden or the Fire, but these make it clear that women are certainly responsible for their own actions. The wives of Lot and Noah mentioned in S 66:10 are said to have been ordered to the Fire because of their faithlessness. This is an interesting example because it describes the wives as "under" two righteous servants, meaning the two prophets who are their husbands, but faithless to them [*khānatāhumā*]. The *ḥadīths*, as we shall see, frequently refer to the direct connection of a wife's fate to her relationship with her husband. Here, while the Arabic might carry that implication, the condemnation of these wives seems to be because they rejected God's message sent through His Messengers rather than because they personally rejected or belied their husbands. This Sura also mentions in the following verse that the wife of Pharaoh can hope for a place in the Garden near to God, which is probably a result of her having saved Moses (S 28:9) and thus preserved a Messenger of God. The only mention the Qur'ān specifically makes of the punishment of a woman is in S 111, where the wife of Abū Lahab is described as wearing a collar of palm fiber around her neck in the Fire.[5] There she will be in the company of her husband, the uncle and avowed enemy of the Prophet and his message. Her punishment, however, is not a result of his misdeeds but probably because she herself is said to have participated in the iniquity by scattering thorns in front of the Prophet to cut his feet and make him stumble.

Only one passage in the Qur'ān could be interpreted to suggest that women in general might be judged according to the deeds (or misdeeds) of their husbands rather than on their own merits. This is S 37:22–23; {Gather together those who have wronged, and their wives [*azwājahum*], and whatever they have worshipped apart from God, and lead them to the way of the Fire.} The word *azwāj* clearly signifies earthly wives in this context and not the companions of paradise or *ḥūr,* since the latter are pure, sinless, and never inhabit any region but the Garden. Commentators have traditionally felt that the consignment of the women to the Fire is because they themselves have sinned rather than because of association with their sinful husbands (although as the Qur'ānic promises in such verses as S 13:23 that the virtuous believer will be in the Garden with his wives and children have been subject to several interpretations,[6] so there might well be some suggestion here that part of the punishment of the male sinner is to see his family with him in his misery).

Modern writers and commentators generally concur that wives are not punished for the misdeeds of their husbands, although one does find an occasional reference to the contrary.[7] Some Qur'ān commentators avoid the question entirely or leave their interpretations as ambiguous as the Qur'ān itself. "Gather them, their partners, those related to them and those like them in the worship of idols," says Ḥijāzī.[8] Others, however, make it clear that consonant with the Qur'ānic assurance that all are personally responsible for their deeds and will be judged equitably, the women here discussed are consigned to the Fire by virtue of their own conduct. "God commanded the angels to drive those *mushrikūn* to the place of the ingathering [*al-maḥshar*]," says al-Khaṭīb, "and to gather with them their partners who are like unto them. . . ."[9] 'Ammār leaves no doubt of personal responsibility when he says, "*Azwājuhum* [meaning] those similar to them in disobedience," but suggests also the possibility that creatures other than wives might be intended: "Some say they are their devilish counterparts [*qurnā'uhum min al-shayāṭīn*] and others that it refers to their women [*nisā'uhum*] who are followers of their *dīn*."[10]

Beyond these limited references, then, the Qur'ān has little to say about earthly women in relation to eschatological concerns. (It does, of course, treat in some detail the engaging subject of the celestial maidens or *ḥūr,* as we shall consider shortly.) In the narrative reports of the first several centuries of Islam, however, one can find much more specific mention of the women of Islam and their fate in the hereafter. It is quite apparent that much of the material found in the *ḥadīths* is indicative of current social attitudes toward women and reflects the legacy of the indigenous culture. Because the reports were oriented to and for males in this context, to look too closely for intended implications for the actual fate of women is probably to misuse the material and not to do justice to the consistent Islamic theological understanding of the equal responsibility of all persons in the sight of God. One must acknowledge, however, that the *ḥadīths* were certainly influential in molding the opinions and understanding of many centuries of Muslims. While they do not necessarily reflect either the revelation of God or the teaching of the Prophet, they are nonetheless significant insofar as they reveal a cultural understanding important to the historical development of Islam.

It is interesting to note first what tradition has said about women in relation to the signs signaling the coming of the eschaton. While these signs do not speak specifically about the future consignment of women to the Garden or the Fire, they do indicate how clearly the general understanding of women has been tied in with cultural expectations. Many references have been made to the cataclysmic events which will signal the coming of the *ba'th* or resurrection. The reversal of the natural order so graphically portrayed in the Qur'ān[11] is preceded in the traditional expansion of the series of eschatological events by other signs signaling the disruption of the ethical, moral, and social order. Some of these signs, clearly seen as disgraceful to the societies out of which the traditions originated, are that a man will have to obey his wife and disobey his parents, men will have to work for women, a woman will go on the pilgrimage with other women but unaccompanied by a man, there will be complete sexual license, and the like.[12] The number of males will decrease so that women will outnumber men fifty to one; ignorance will prevail.[13]

Some contemporary writers considering questions of afterlife and eschatology have elaborated such predications, reflecting the current concern in the Islamic community that many kinds of social changes are destroying the fabric of the Muslim socio-ethical system. Thus describing the specifics of the coming eschaton in light of what is coming to pass today, Abū'l-'Azā'im says that we will recognize the coming of the eschaton by fifteen specific evils, one of them obedience of a man to his wife rather than to his mother. Without saying that the eschaton is necessarily imminent, he discusses how society has moved toward this feared development. "As for obedience to the wives," he says, "it has become a religion that men follow. The woman has become the superior over the man."[14] He goes on to describe how women now handle the financial affairs of the household, shop for clothing from male merchants, and so forth, with no objection raised by their husbands. In complete contrast to this kind of alarm we also find from another element of Islamic society, modern Turkey, a very different understanding of the progression of culture. Far from seeing the newly-defined role of women as negative, for example, M. Sadeddin Evrin of the Institute of Advanced Islamic Studies in Istanbul states that "Equality of women, intelligence in conversation, genial conduct and manner, etc. is increasing in accordance with the advance in culture."[15] It is noteworthy that this commentary is part of a section in his work on eschatology dealing with the *ḥūr*! Observing that the women of today are developing in beauty because of improvements in health care and hygiene, he views the women of today's world as the *ḥūr* in a form of realized eschatology.

If contemporary Muslims disagree as to the relative value of the present role of women, finding ingenious ways of expressing these views in the context of eschatological commentary, we have seen clearly that they do accept and propound the Qur'ānic insistence on individual accountability and reward according to merit. Most modern Muslim writers not only refute the above-mentioned misinterpretation that accuses Islam of denying souls to women,[16] but in expressing their views in terms of the evidence of the Qur'ān, they also ignore the significant number of traditions in which the fate of a woman seems clearly to be in direct relationship to her obedience to her husband. For the most part these reports have very weak chains of transmission [*isnāds*] and are considered not only unreliable to most contemporary Islamic thinkers but clearly misrepresentative of the predominant Islamic view of women and their potential. It is worth noting that a few of these narratives, however, seem to suggest a genre of literature that provides another clear instance of the way in which theology can be interpreted to reflect current social concerns, here serving a function of social and personal control in keeping wives subservient and obedient to their husbands.

Perhaps the most commonly cited report in the manuals of *ḥadīth* concerning the future fate of women is that suggesting, in one form or another, that the majority of them will be consigned to the Fire. This is said to have come from a vision of the Prophet about which he related, "I passed by the Fire and when I noted the intensity of its heat, I tarried; the most of those I saw therein were women who, if you put trust in them, tell that with which they have been entrusted, and if you ask them [about something] they hide it, and if they are given [many things] they are ungrateful."[17] According to another version the Prophet related:

> I saw the Fire and I have not seen to this day a more terrible sight. Most of the inhabitants are women. They [those to whom the Prophet was talking] said, O Messenger of God, why? He said, Because of their ingratitude [*kufr*]. They said, Are they ungrateful to God? He said, No, but they are ungrateful to the companion [*al-'ashīr*, meaning husband] and ungrateful for the charity [*al-iḥsān*] [shown by their husbands to them]. Even if you men continue to do good things for them, and a woman sees one thing [bad] from you, she will say, I never saw anything at all good from you.[18]

One can surmise from this material that the sins of idle prattle and breaking of confidences must have been considered serious in the early centuries of Islam. Other reports omit the direct reference to the fate of women in the Fire but indicate that women are deficient in their religious practice [*dīn*] because of menstruation, which prevents them from fasting at certain times[19] (suggesting punishment for a biological function), and that in many instances the husbands should be permitted the right to determine when and how their wives perform their religious duties ("The Messenger of God said, From now on let a woman not fast except by permission of her husband. . .''[20]). All of this clearly reflects, no doubt, not the considered conclusion of Muslim theologians that women are really more likely to be consigned to the Fire than men, but rather the attempt to legitimate forms of social control over women by suggesting that a wife's relationship to God is in some way determined by her relationship to her husband.

Literalists through the ages have attempted to take from some of the reports describing the Prophet's view of the Fire and the Garden proof that those abodes of punishment and bliss are in fact already in existence. This seems a tenuous argument at best, and it would be quite fruitless to suggest from the above-mentioned narratives that there has been in Islam any developed idea that women are actually residing in the Fire for the period of the *barzakh* or intermediate stage before the resurrection. Parallel to such descriptions one can also find occasional stories about women in paradise (although far less frequently than those noting their position in the Fire), usually designed to meet the same purpose of social and personal control in keeping the Muslim wife obedient to her husband.[21] For the most part, however, the traditional materials refrain from commenting on any particularities of the period between death and resurrection having special reference to women.

Such is also the case with contemporary Islamic writers, who on the whole have little to say about the *barzakh* period with the exception of a group of modern spiritualist writers. The primary concern of these thinkers, of course, is with the life of the spirit immediately after death. While comments with specific regard to women are rare, there does seem to be clear indication that men and women will be alive, functioning, and in general living full and productive lives. Muḥammad Shahīn Ḥamza, for example, cites the following narrative related to him by one who has already died: ''When I opened my eyes from death I saw my mother and father who had preceded me in the land of the spirits. And they were in the form they had when they were youthful.''[22] He later states that the family will be reconstituted in the *barzakh* and all will live in love. Some people who do not marry while on earth will marry in the *barzakh*, although they will have no children. Joy, he says, is beyond mere physical pleasure (p. 193).

'Abd al-Razzāq Nawfal, one of the best-known of the contemporary Egyptian spiritualists, describes his understanding of the way things will be after death. He paints a quite idyllic scene of people walking in fields and meadows, meeting and greeting old friends, then outlines a common spiritualist understanding that there are many different levels in the *barzakh*, with people at each level sharing similar experiences and sensations: ''A great activity is characteristic of this world, for every person, whether male or female, does some work. And the two moral principles governing that world are serving others and loving others.''[23] These narratives emphasize the importance of maintaining (and even creating for the first time) a conjugal structure, but with a characteristically modern stress on sharing and mutual cooperation rather than on simple subservience of a wife to her husband.

Perhaps no aspect of Islamic eschatology has so captured the imagination of Muslims and non-Muslims alike (and often engendered crude and insensitive critique by the latter) as the descriptions of the *ḥūr*, the chaste maidens of the Garden promised in the Qur'ān as an eternal reward to the faithful Muslims. Who are these creatures so graphically portrayed in scripture, and what is their relationship to the female believers of the Islamic community, the *mu'mināt*? The term *ḥūr*, mentioned four times in the Qur'ān (S 52:20, 56:22, 55:72, and 44:54),[24] literally means having eyes with marked contrast of black and white [*al-ḥur al-'ayn*]. All the references are early Meccan, the longest coming in S 55:

> {In them are those who are chaste, with glances restrained, whom neither man nor *jinn* has before touched . . . like rubies and coral . . . is there any reward for goodness but goodness? . . . In them are those who are good, beautiful, . . . *hūr* well-guarded in pavilions . . . whom neither man nor *jinn* has before touched . . . reclining on green cushions and beautiful carpets . . .} (selected from vss. 56–76)

The Qur'ānic descriptions of the *ḥūr*, though restrained, have been sufficient to pique the imaginations of the faithful and have served as the basis for a great deal of later elaboration. In the *ḥadīths* details of their description differ, but they are generally said to be composed of saffron from the feet to the knees, musk from the knees to the breast, amber from the breast to the neck, and camphor from the neck to the head.[25] Working often with multiples of seven, the traditionalists have described them as wearing seventy to 70,000 gowns, through which even the marrow of their bones can be seen because of the fineness of their flesh, reclining on seventy couches of red hyacinth encrusted with rubies and jewels, and the like. The *ḥūr* do not sleep, do not get pregnant, do not menstruate, spit, or blow their noses, and are never sick.[26] References to the increased sexual process of those male believers for whose pleasure the *ḥūr* are intended are numerous;[27] the reports make it clear that the *ḥūr* are created specifically as a reward for males of the Muslim community who have been faithful to God.[28]

There is no question from the way the *ḥadīths* present the descriptions of the *ḥūr* that they are to be understood as entirely different from the female believers. Some narratives relate that each *ḥūr* intended for a *mu'min* and waiting eagerly for him actually looks on the earthly wife as a rival, becoming annoyed when the wife is inconsiderate to the man who will come to her in the hereafter.[29] While details of the conjugal relationships of men in the Garden are elaborate and detailed, it is much less clear in the *ḥadīths* what role the *mu'mināt* in the Garden will play. These women, often referred to as the daughters of Eve to distinguish them from the *ḥūr*, are usually said to have one husband each (the *mu'minūn* are often portrayed as having all of their earthly wives plus seventy or more of the *ḥūr*) If the woman had more than one husband on earth, the situation is unclear; sometimes it is said that she will get the last one as husband in the Garden, sometimes the best one, and sometimes it is reported that she will have her choice.[30]

If the *ḥadīths* are clear that the *ḥūr* and the *mu'mināt* are distinct classes of being, the Qur'ān is perhaps less so, or at least less dramatically so. When one examines the Qur'ānic references to women in the Garden carefully, however, there seems to be a definite distinction, although in some instances (particularly in the use of the term *azwāj* or companions) it is difficult to know to whom the references are made.

The *ḥūr* are described in the Qur'ān as chaste, with glancing eyes like pearls or guarded eggs, of equal age or contemporary with the male believers for whom they are intended as a reward, good and lovely, buxom and virginal. The female community is described as purified, acceptable to God, and is said to abide in the Garden forever. The four specific references to *ḥūr* were probably revealed at the end of the first Meccan period, this kind of affirmation of the Garden as a place where rivers, trees, cool breezes, and chaste maidens are available to reward the virtuous standing in stark contrast to the denouncements of such a possibility voiced by many of the contemporaries of the Prophet.

The *ḥūr* are not mentioned after the Meccan revelations, and the other Qur'ānic references to females in verses dealing with the hereafter are apparently to those who have been part of the earthly Islamic *umma*. Such verses as S 2:25, 3:15, and 4:57 should be seen as references to earthly wives, since they describe purified companions [*azwāj muṭahhara*], and the *ḥūr*, of course, by their very nature are pure rather than purified. Again, this shift in emphasis is coordinate with the growing concern for Islam as a community of believers evidenced by the end of the third Meccan period, with the stress on individual responsibility and accountability to God and the promise of the Garden to the righteous.

Despite the apparent distinction evidenced by the Qur'ān between the earthly women and the paradisiacal *ḥūr*, there are certain verses in which alternative interpretations have been offered, particularly when the term *azwāj* is used. In reference to S 44:54, for example, which discusses the pairing of the righteous with *ḥūr,* al-Bayḍāwī says that people have differed on the question of whether this refers to the pairing with women of this world in the hereafter or to other women.[31] When one looks at some of the modern commentary on the *ḥūr*, one finds that the question of the relationship of the *ḥūr* to the *mu'mināt* is often not fully resolved. Considering S 2:25, {and in them [the Gardens] are pure maidens}, for example, Muḥammad 'Abdu says that these maidens have no bodily defects, as one would have in the natural world, such as menstruation or bleeding after childbirth, and they have no artifice or cunning because they are pure with every kind of purity. He then goes on to say that the women of the Garden are the good believers [*al-mu'mināt al-ṣāliḥāt*] known in the Qur'ān as *al-ḥur al-'ayn*. He obviously chooses not to make a distinction between these categories of female beings, justifying this equation in a manner common to him by saying that the companionship of the *azwāj* in the hereafter is like other unseen matters. We believe in what God has said concerning them, not increasing nor decreasing anything, and not discussing the essence of their natures.[32] Rashīd Riḍá, continuing the *Tafsīr al-Manār* of 'Abdu, says later that he accepts the authenticity of only one tradition about the *ḥūr*, that cited by Bukhārī and Muslim declaring that the happy ones in the Garden will have two women, one *ḥūr* and one earthly wife.[33] It is obvious that for him a distinction is supportable.

Most contemporary commentators specifically avoid discussing the issue of the relationship of the *ḥūr* to the *mu'mināt*, usually repeating with only slight modification the words of the Qur'ān in each particular verse. Commenting on the last Qur'ānic mention of the *ḥūr*, found in S 56:22, for example, they indicate generally that the reference is to women [*nisā'*] but do not specify the nature of these women.[34] Al-Jammāl gives a somewhat fuller description but still avoids suggesting the precise identity of the *ḥūr*:

> They [the believers] will enjoy in the garden beautiful women, white of face and wide of eyes, whom God has masterfully created and poured into casts of beauty and stunning looks. These *ḥūr* are noted for their purity, joy, and whiteness as though they are pearls untouched by human hand. God has given them this bliss because of what they have done in the world and for the improvement of their souls through good works.[35]

With characteristic exactitude, on the other hand, Mawlana Muhammad

'Ali in his popular exposition *The Religion of Islam* makes every effort to clarify the question for his readers:

> Are *ḥūr* the women that go to Paradise, the wives of the righteous? A hint to this effect is given in a ḥadith. The last of the occasions on which the *ḥūr* are spoken of is 56:10–24, and in continuation of the subject there occur the words: "Surely We have made them to grow into a new growth, then We have made them virgins, loving, equals in age, for the sake of the companions of the right hand" (56:35–38). In connection with this, the making them "to grow into a new growth," the Holy Prophet is reported to have said, that by this are meant women who have grown old here (Tr. 44: sūra 56). The meaning, therefore, is that all good women shall grow into a new growth in the new life of the Resurrection, so that they shall all be virgins, equals in age. The Holy Prophet's explanation shows that the word *ḥūr* is used to describe the new growth into which women of this world will grow.[36]

Even he, however, apparently feels the need to cover himself in this equation, for he goes on to say: "But even if the *ḥūr* are taken to be a blessing of Paradise, and not the women of this world, it is a blessing as well for men as for women. Just as the gardens, rivers, milk, honey, fruits, and numerous other things of Paradise are both for men and women, even so are *ḥūr*" (p. 298).

In contrast to the heavy emphasis in the traditions on the specifically physical pleasures encountered with the females of the Garden and the clear indication that if desired the believer can in fact have children,[37] one finds little such discussion in contemporary literature. Occasionally spiritualist writings refer to the possibility of procreation in the hereafter: "God has returned the spirits and life to bodies from which they were separated and they talk, walk, eat, drink, marry and procreate".[38] Most contemporaries agree with Muhammad 'Ali, however, in denying that procreation will have any role in the life to come, and particularly in stressing the understanding that the descriptions of the Garden are not to be taken as sensual in the usual meaning of the term: "What these blessings actually are, no one knows, but the whole picture of Paradise drawn in the Holy Qur'ān strongly condemns the association of any sensual idea therewith."[39] In this interpretation writers like 'Ali follow very much in the tradition of Muḥammad 'Abdu, who urged that the pleasures of the next world are but vaguely prefigured in our experiences in this world.

If anything can be said to be characteristic of contemporary attitudes toward the particulars of the next world, it is this feeling that they are really beyond human comprehension, alluded to analogously in the descriptions of the Qur'ān but finally to be realized only in that renewed state in which we will move beyond time to the ultimately distinct condition of the hereafter. For a particularly clear statement of this understanding see the summary of Ṣoubḥi El-Ṣaleḥ from 'Abd al-Qādir al-Maghribī's *al-Ḥujaj al-ẓāhira fī māhīyat maladhdhāt al-ākhira*:

> Les Bieheureux jouiront au Paradis de la Compagnie des Houris. Les esprits critiques se moquèrent de tous temps de la sensualité promise aux Élus. C'est qu'ils supposent qu'il y aura réellement commerce avec les Houris comme il y a ici-bas rapports sexuels entre hommes et femmes. Mais si on leur répond que la jouissance procurée par les Houris au Paradis est une figuration ou une représentation d'un délice supreme dont la réalité est inaccessible à la compréhension humaine, nul ne pourra se moquer de la mention continuelle des Houris faite par le Coran. Les Croyantes participent alors avec les Croyants à cette jouissance du noble plaisir que dispensent les Houris, ces créatures célestes.[40]

Children in the Afterlife

When we turn to the Islamic material concerning the fate of children in the afterlife, we see immediately that to the extent to which this question has been raised at all it has generally been in the context of theological considerations of divine justice, mercy, and knowledge. The issue does not seem to have been, or to be, so much the specific fate of children as the extent to which conclusions about that fate are determined by two general concerns: how one's understanding of God affects one's estimation of the future of children who have done wrong, or have been virtuous, or are too young to be held responsible; and assurances to the living that they can take consolation in the death of a child because the suffering and forbearance attached thereto may insure a more felicitious state in the hereafter for the parent, and that the parents' happiness in the Garden will be enhanced because they will have the joy of dwelling with their children for all eternity.

The Qur'ān itself offers little that can be taken as clear information about the fate of children. Several verses deal specifically with the theme of whether or not a father and son can intercede for each other on the day of resurrection or otherwise help secure one another a felicitious end, such as S 3:10, 3:116, 31:33, 60:3, and 80:34–36. Since the answer given in each instance is a categorical no, the question seems to be immediately resolved. Two other verses, however, raise the issue of one's progeny in paradise, and a review of exegesis of these reveals some insights into the theological considerations of God's mercy and justice, on which most of the discussion of children in the afterlife seems to focus. The first of these is S 13:23: {. . . Gardens of Eden, which they shall enter, and those who were righteous of their fathers, and their wives and their progeny [*dhurrīya*]. And the angels will enter unto them from every gate.} The second verse, and the one most frequently cited by those dealing with children in this context, is S 52:21: {. . . and those who have faith and whose progeny follow them in faith, We shall join to them their progeny and shall not deprive them of any [fruit of] their works. Every individual is a pledge for what he has earned.}

Working from these verses the exegetes both ancient and modern have generally focused their thoughts on a central issue: affirming God's justice in according the rewards of the Garden only to those who have earned it, while at the same time being faithful to the Qur'ān, which indicates that the faithful will have the blessing of living in paradise accompanied by their children. Instructive here is the attempt to see how some of the best-respected *mufassirūn*, past and present, have attempted to resolve this issue.

It is useful to consider at the outset the *Jāmi' al-bayān* of al-Ṭabarī, not only because he is the giant of the classical Qur'ān commentators and an early codifier of vast numbers of traditions, but because in this case he suggests a variety of alternative explantions among which the interpretations of later writers and commentators seem to range. In the exegesis of S 52:21 he lists the following possibilities: (1) the progeny will attain to the ranks of their fathers in the Garden, even though they have not by their own works achieved those ranks, through God's beneficence to the believing fathers; (2) only the young children who have not yet matured to the point where they can be held accountable will be joined to their fathers; (3) the progeny who themselves have been faithful to God and obedient to Him will be joined to their parents in the Garden along with the younger children; (4) the progeny are joined to their fathers by the merit of the latter, although nothing is, in effect, taken away from the fathers to give to the children.[41] Al-Ṭabarī's own conclusions, offered in consideration of this verse and of S 13:23, seem to indicate his preference that the progeny are themselves righteous persons of faith, although like many of his successors he stresses that while their deeds may fall short, God will raise the progeny to the rank of the fathers through His beneficence.[42] In this al-Ṭabarī seems to lay the groundwork for the predominant understanding of these verses through the centuries.

One might expect that the Mu'tazilī commentator al-Zamakhsharī would put strong emphasis on the importance of faith and works as requisite of the progeny for entrance into the Garden, as a reflection of God's just dispensation of reward. In commenting on S 52:21, however, he provides one of the most explicit statements of God's mercy in raising the progeny of the faithful to the father's rank, even though they may be of a lower station by their own merit.[43] He is far from alone in suggesting this interpretation, although it is unusual in not indicating that such an elevation of rank comes only after one has by his own virtue gained initial entrance to the Garden. Al-Zamakhsharī makes it quite clear that children are raised to the faithful fathers for their pleasure, enjoyment, and fulfillment.[44]

In some contrast to this al-Ṭabarsī says specifically in commenting on S 13:23 that children means believing children, and more explicitly on S 52:21 that "*dhurrīya* means their children both old and young, for the older ones follow the fathers by faith, the younger ones the faith of their fathers."[45] He indicates that if the works of the older children fall short of those of the fathers, their rank will be elevated out of respect for the fathers. This is not, he says, in itself a recompense but a joining for the sake of togetherness. He concludes his reflections with the words of the Prophet, which clearly temper his original stress on the merit of the progeny: "The children of the believers are given as a present to their parents on the day of resurrection."

The tension between earning a place in paradise and the merciful elevation in rank by God as explicated by these commentators is expressed by the later *mufassirūn* with varying degrees of emphasis but with no new insights. Al-Bayḍāwī says on S 13:23 that the fathers are joined by those of their progeny who are good and worthy, though they may not have reached the father's rank. On the one hand, he says, there is clearly an implication of intercession here, yet the insistence on virtue shows that mere relatedness is not sufficient.[46] Ibn Kathīr[47] in reflecting on both of these verses briefly repeats these themes, perhaps with greater emphasis on elevation of rank than on the merit of the children.[48]

Ibn Qayyim, who offers in *Ḥādī al-arwāḥ* a summary of theological positions on questions of children in the afterlife, suggests that the exegetes have differed on the meanig of *dhurrīya* in S 52:21. Is the intention of it, he asks, very little children, somewhat older children, or both? Some say that the verse must refer to older children, for as faith implies speech, action, and intention, only the older ones could have faith sufficiently like that of the father (even though it be less than his) to allow them to be raised to that level. Others say that progeny clearly refers to little ones, who though by necessity are undeveloped in faith attain to a high station by virtue of the faith of their fathers. Some claim that progeny must mean those who have not yet attained adulthood, because all adults are judged according to their own deeds and not those of their fathers. Finally, some say that the verse refers to both young and older children "because the older one draws near to the father by the faith of the father."[49]

For the most part the interpretation of these verses suggested by some contemporary Qur'ān exegetes follows very closely that of their predecessors, although one can perhaps detect a somewhat greater stress on the necessity of personal virtue as a prerequisite for the progeny to enter the Garden. Muḥammad al-Khafājī, commenting on S 13:23, states the case succinctly when he says,

> The gardens of 'Aden are the place of eternal abode in which there is no separation. . . . In them there will be the righteous of their parents and wives and children (i.e. those who have themselves fulfilled the specific duties set forth in the previous verse). And they will enjoy personal happiness and fellowship and will enjoy the happiness of those whom they love—parents, mates, children. The fulfillment of the grave for man is the fulfillment of happiness in seeing his family and loved ones happy.[50]

Al-Khafājī thus suggests that the relatives of the one in the Garden are there because they are themselves virtuous, and because it makes the one in paradise happy (fulfills his grace) to see his loved ones happy and to have them with him, an idea highly compatible with the value placed on the family unit in Muslim society.

Contemporary exegetes generally put particular stress on the first of these reasons. Some of the earlier *mufassirūn*, says M. 'Izza Darwaza on S 52:21, indicate that progeny refers to those who have not attained maturity.[51] This interpretation holds, he says, as long as these progeny have had an upbringing in the faith [*nash'atan īmānīya*]. Suggesting that there is also merit in the idea that God will raise the rank of the lower as a good-will gesture toward the parent, Darwaza nonetheless reminds his readers of the saying that each person is accountable for whatever he has earned. He concludes that this verse really means that progeny who do not follow their parents in faith are recompensed by what they have earned without any benefit to be gained from the faith or the good deeds of the parents.[52]

The contemporary *tafsīr* of 'Abd al-Karīm al-Khaṭīb, *al-Tafsīr al-Qur'ānī li'l-Qur'ān*, is particularly interesting in this connection for his elaboration of S 52:21 concerning what is meant by rank in the Garden. Having established in his earlier commentary on S 13:23 (VII, 105) that he agrees with the others about the necessary merit of the progeny, he here expands on the idea we have seen developed that for the sake of those already in the Garden their progeny will be raised in rank until their circumstances are equal. Very much in agreement with early interpretation, he says that the progeny follow their fathers to the Garden because they believe in God as their parents did, although their ranks differ; their being joined together is part of God's beneficence (XIV, 564). He then raises this question: Given the general understanding that both the Garden and the Fire are actually made up of a series of ascending (and descending) ranks or levels, how is it possible that those of different ranks are joined together? Indicating that levels do not imply a rigid, cold separation setting each group in isolation from the other, he says that the difference between the ranks of the people of the Garden is a difference in the capacity to partake of bliss: "There are great souls who are able to partake of the totality of the bliss of the Garden, and to find pleasure in it, whereas there are small souls that partake of this bliss only as a bird eats" (XIV, 565). What he implies here is not so much that God elevates one soul to a rank higher than it would normally deserve, but that the ranking itself does not suggest the kind of separation between the inhabitants of the Garden that has sometimes been supposed. In this way he offers an interesting resolution of the long-standing issue of the potential tensions between God's justice and His merciful grace.

Clearly considering this question in light of the nature of God, the commentators seem particularly concerned about whether or not, and when, a child can be held responsible. This problem has, of course, caught the imagination of many theologians of Islam, as well as being the subject of a number of *ḥadīths*. One of the well-known sayings of the Prophet is that every child is formed in a "natural condition" [*fiṭra*] in his mother's womb, with the implication that until or unless his parents indoctrinate him into a particular tradition, that *fiṭra* will determine his religious orientation. Modern Muslims have made much of the assertion that the *fiṭra* is indeed the true and natural response to God, the innate religion of Islam. The consequence of this theory suggests that if one should die before attaining an age where he can affirm the choice of religion made by his parents, he is considered to be still in the natural condition that he enjoyed in the womb. The time at which one would affirm or reject the religion of his parents and be held accountable for his own faith and his own actions is generally understood to be coincident with the age of puberty.[53]

It has long been recognized, because of its Qur'ānic assurance, that martyrs will be awarded a place in paradise immediately after death. Reports like the following, which clearly refer to children who have died before the age of responsibility, may suggest that martyrs will not be alone in avoiding what has been called the intermediate or waiting state before the resurrection:[54] "The Messenger of God said, The Prophet is in the Garden and the martyr is in the Garden and the newborn child [*al-mawlūd*] is in the Garden and the new-born girl buried alive [*al-wa'īd*] is in the Garden."[55] Some have carried the references to new-born children farther, suggesting that even the aborted fetus will gain paradise. Al-Suyūṭī says that the aborted fetus is in one of the rivers of the Garden, turning around in it until the coming of the day of resurrection, at which time he will be brought forth as a person forty years old.[56] (This, of course, has implications for the question of whether or not one remains eternally the age he was at death.) The *Kitāb aḥwāl al-qiyāma* is rather more specific about the location of the spirits of children in relation to martyrs, saying that the latter are in Firdaws, while the children (specifically of Muslims) are in the Garden in the form of birds perched on mountains of musk (p. 47). One finds occasional references indicating that Muslim children too young to have reached the age of reason remain on the *a'rāf*, the "heights" referred to in the Qur'ān, whose precise meaning has long been disputed.

Most references to the fate of children, particularly in the *ḥadīths*, indicate that they will be in the Garden. Some of these omit any suggestion of why this is so, while others specify that the children are offspring of believers, of Muslims, or were themselves righteous. Much of this speculation is undoubtedly related to the way in which the Qur'ān treats this question in the verses cited above and to the fact that the Qur'ān does not mention the fate of children of those who are not of the community of the faithful.

One of the more tender suggestions concerning children in paradise is that describing the nurture provided by the Ṭubba tree: "In the Garden there is a tree named blessed [*ṭubba*] which is full of nurture. Every boy [*subyān*] who dies while still at the breastfeeding stage will be able to feed from that tree."[57] This implies that regardless of parental affiliation or degree of personal piety, the young offspring will be provided for. From the several contexts in which the Prophet is reported to have uttered such assurances, it is clear that the intent was not so much to inform about a particular event or condition as to console those who were feeling keenly the loss of their beloved little ones.[58]

The modern traditionist Hajjī Khalīfa cites a variety of *hadīths* suggesting that children of Muslims are on the mountain in the Garden and are taken care of by Abraham and Sara until they are returned to their parents on the day of resurrection.[59] Abraham, who as the father of all Muslims acts as a parent substitute for Muslim children, sees to their needs and raises them during the *barzakh* period.[60] According to al-Suyūṭī, "Every child born in

Islam is in the Garden full and happy, and says, 'O God, bring to me my parents!' "[61]

As we have seen, some references to children in the afterlife are simply to children in general, suggesting an existence in the Garden. Others seem to indicate that particularly the children of Muslims and of the faithful, or youth who in some sense can be said themselves to be faithful, can hope for this pleasant fate.[62] There is also, however, a series of references to the possibility of a less hopeful destiny for some children. In general this fate, too, is linked directly to the sins of their fathers.

One of the questions addressed in this connection is whether or not children are questioned in the grave. Here again Ibn Qayyim is a useful source for a variety of interpretations, this time in his *Kitāb al-rūḥ*. He suggests that the Ḥanbalīs, for example, have had two opinions on the subject. According to one school of thought, God will complete the rational faculties of children, and they will receive some intimation of the appropriate answers to the questions they will be asked.[63] Others of the Ḥanbalīs, he says, held strongly that questioning in the grave will be only for those who while alive on earth heard and understood the message of the Prophet. How, they ask, could a child before puberty be expected to be able to discern whether or not one is a true messenger of God? Even if his rationality were completed for him in the grave, as their opponents suggested, how could one be questioned concerning that about which he had no knowledge of experience? Such an expectation would be contrary to the idea of examination in the hereafter. God, they say, sends His prophets to mankind and orders them to obey His command when they are fully rational (p. 108).

For some the matter of interrogation in the grave is to be seen in contrast to the situation of a general discomfort or mild punishment. These, including al-Suyūṭī and al-Nasafī, feel that while the children of believers in general are exempt from examination or severe punishment, they along with all others must pass through a period of the pressure [*ḍaghṭ*] of the tomb. This view has generally been held by the Shāfi'īs. Ibn Qayyim concurs in saying that there seems little question but that the grave holds certain pains and worries, which in all likelihood will come to the child as well as to the adult.[64]

When we come to the issue of the fate of children of those clearly considered *kāfirs* or *mushriks*, there seems again to be some range of opinion. Many are loath to speculate and prefer to quote the words of the Prophet: "The Prophet, when asked about the children of the *mushrikūn*, replied, God knows best what they have done [*Allāhu a'lam bi-mā kānū 'āmilīn*]."[65]

It appears that on other occasions, however, the Prophet was rather more specific in discussing the fate of such children. Sometimes he seems to have been somewhat pessimistic:

> Khadīja asked the Messenger of God about two children who had died while still in the period of the *jāhilīya*.[66] The Messenger of God said, They are in the Fire. And when he saw the aversion on her face he said, If you saw their place, it would be loathesome to you. She said, O Messenger of God, what about my child by you? He replied, In the Garden. Then the Messenger of God said, Truly the faithful and their children are in the Garden and the polytheists and their children are in the Fire. Then the Messenger of God recited [S 52:21].[67]

At other times he held out more hope: "They [the children of the *mushrikūn*] have no evil deeds for which they must be punished among the people of the Fire, and they likewise have no good deeds for which they are to be recompensed among the angels of the people of the Garden. Therefore they are servants for the inhabitants of the Garden."[68]

It is obvious, of course, that there has been nothing resembling consensus in the Islamic community on this very problematic question of the fate of children of non-believers. It is also true that the real issue in these discussions, while clearly related directly to the understanding of God's mercy and justice, is the firm condemnation of *kufr* and *shirk* and thus the punishment incumbent on offspring because of the sins of the fathers. Abū Ya'la relates that according to certain Ḥanbalī theologians, on the day of resurrection a huge fire will be set, and all children will be ordered to enter it. Whosoever does so willingly will be allowed to enter the Garden, but he who refuses it will be sent to the Fire. Himself a Ḥanbalī, Abū Ya'la indicates that S 52:21 is actually a proof that the children of the *mushrikūn* are with their fathers in the Fire. This, he says, is supported by the above-cited question of 'Ā'isha concerning her children by a husband before her marriage to the Prophet.[69]

The Ash'arīs were in agreement that the children of the faithful are in the Garden with their fathers. They were of several opinions concerning the children of the *mushriks* and *kāfirs*, however, as seems generally to be the case. Some felt they will be in the Fire for the express purpose of causing more pain to their parents, again indicating that the main concern of this discussion often does not lie with the fate of the children themselves. Others support the idea of the fire built to test the obedience of the children, as described above, while still others assign them to a place in the Garden but as servants of the faithful there.[70]

Much of what the Ash'arīs said, of course, was in response to statements of the Mu'tazila on the question of children. In general the Mu'tazila denied that children of non-believers would go to the Fire.[71] Their position, however, was not unambiguous, and as al-Ash'arī himself indicates, encompassed several somewhat alternative points of view.[72] Concerning the fate of children in general, some said that God *could* recompense children with pain for no purpose if He chose (though He probably would not so choose), some that such recompense would not be purposeless but would serve as a lesson to those of age, and some that while recompense without pain is preferable, it is not incumbent upon God to do what seems preferable to us. On the eternality of punishment for children, some said it would be eternal because God decreed it (for the deserving, rather than automatically). Some apparently felt that the children of polytheists will be judged by the same judgment as their fathers, and others that the children of polytheists and faithful together are in the Garden. All Mu'tazila, however, said that it is likely that God will in fact not hurt or even punish children in the hereafter.

'Abd al-Jabbār Ibn Aḥmad, one of the best-known of the fourth-century Mu'tazilī theologians of Baṣra, presents his understanding of the question of the children of the *mushrikūn* in a somewhat less qualified way in *Sharḥ al-uṣūl al-khamsa* (pp. 477–81). It is not permissible, he says, that the children of the polytheists will be punished for the sins of their fathers.[73] This is the case, says al-Jabbār, because to do so would be *ẓulm*, oppression, and God is not an oppressor. He also feels that because God promised in S 17:15 that He will not cause anyone to suffer to whom He has not sent a Prophet, punishment of children is precluded, as prophets were not sent to children. He then quotes the Prophet Muḥammad as having said in a *ḥadīth qudsī*, "We shall suspend the pen from the child until he reaches puberty." Citing what he calls the stupidity of those who believe the fabrication that God will order children to enter a fire on the day of resurrection and the progeny of the *mushrikūn* will disobey, he says that such would make the hereafter a place where people make choices, and we all know that the choices are made in this world and the consequences of them reaped in the next.[74]

Contemporary Islamic writers, despite their extreme concern for individual human responsibility and divine justice, have apparently been little occupied with questions concerning the fate of the children of non-Muslims. In *al-Dār al-barzakhīya* Khalīfa summarizes the issue by saying that while traditionally all have agreed that the children of Muslims go to the Garden, there are three general opinions about the children of the *mushrikūn*: that they go to the Fire as do their parents, that some of them enter the Garden by the will of God, and that they are automatically among the people of the Garden, which last understanding Khalīfa himself supports. These opinions all refer to children who die before puberty; if they are not responsible, they are not held accountable, but if they are of responsible age, then they must face their own judgment. Countering suggestions that some children are predestined for the Fire while they are still in the loins of their fathers, he insists that the child of the unbeliever who dies before maturity goes to the Garden because he is still in the *fiṭra* of God in which he was born (pp. 269–70).

Commentary on the fate of children considered thus far has been intended not just as purely descriptive, but as part of overall theological considerations of the justice and mercy of God and of human responsibility. There remains, however, a relatively substantial amount of material, the orientation of which is not to deal with theological concerns as much as to provide assurance and support for adults. Traditions and elaborations from this perspective fall into three general categories: the desires of an adult for a child in paradise, the ways in which children serve adults in the Garden, and the means by which children assist adults in reaching the place of felicity.

We have seen above that one of the most common interpretations of S 52:21 suggests that God raises the progeny of the believer to his rank because it fulfills the joy of the one in the Garden to be reunited with his family. A number of reports presented in the same vein also assure that the faithful will have all desires granted in that time of happy reward. Some of these do not suggest reunion between parent and child, but rather that one can in fact start the process from the beginning: "The messenger of God said, If a *mu'min* desires a child in the Garden, pregnancy and birth will take place in one hour as he desires."[75] This *ḥadīth*, appearing in a variety of places and with some variations, is often balanced by another indicating that in fact one will probably not so desire.[76] In some instances it is said categorically that the people of the Garden will have no children at all. This again, however, is best understood as an attempt to assure a condition of the greatest ease and comfort in the hereafter rather than as a specifically descriptive statement.

A few narratives mention the actual role of children in the Garden as servants of adult believers. Again, one can discern two perspectives in these reports. Some, as we have seen, suggest that this particular function solves the problem concerning the fate of the children of the *mushrikūn* who of themselves have no good or evil deeds. Quite another purpose seems to be served in the material that indicates that getting married and having children is an advantageous enterprise, among other reasons for the comfort one will thereby gain in the hereafter. In the *Durra*, for example, al-Ghazālī describes the following scene in paradise:

> Some people are drinking water which is cold, sweet and clear; this is because children move around their parents with cups of water from the rivers of the Garden for them to drink. One of the ancestors has related that while he was sleeping he dreamed of the coming of the resurrection. It was as if he were actually there, parched of thirst, and he saw small boys giving drink to people. ''I called to them'', he related, ''saying 'Give me a drink of water.' And one of them said to me, 'Do you have a son among us?' 'No,' I answered. 'Then No!' came the reply.'' Therein is the advantage of marriage.[77]

There is also another instance in which children may be seen as servants of the faithful in the Garden. The Qur'ān makes three references to the fact that in the Garden, youths will be present to serve its inhabitants.[78] These youths are generally described, like the *ḥūr*, as being of perpetual freshness and similar to well-guarded pearls. For the most part Muslim commentators do not elaborate on their nature and generally understand that they are not related to the youths or children of this world. Maulana Muhammad 'Ali in *The Religion of Islam,* however, has this to say:

> In the first case, there is a double indication showing that these boys, called the ghilman, are the offspring of the faithful (see 56:17, 76:19); they are called ghilman-un la-hum or their boys, and it is clearly stated that God ''will unite with them (i.e., the righteous) their offspring'' (52:21). To the same effect it is elsewhere said that the ''offspring'' of the faithful will be made to enter Paradise with them (40:8). Hence the ghilman and the wildan are the young children who have died in childhood. (p. 299)

A third group of materials deals with the ways in which children actually aid adults to attain to the Garden. It is quite clear from the Qur'ān, as observed earlier, that relatives can be of no assistance to each other on the day of resurrection;[79] yet we have also see that in the exegesis of verses such as S 13:23 and 52:21 it is difficult to avoid the implication that progeny will in some sense be helped by their fathers insofar as they are to be elevated to the ranks of the latter. This process also seems to work in reverse in some instances: ''God will raise the rank of the good person in the Garden. This person will say, 'From where is this given to me?' and [God] will reply, 'By the forgiveness sought by your child for you.' ''[80]

Many of the *ḥadīths* carry this implication a good deal farther.[81] In general the rule seems to be that the one in the highest level pulls up the other; i.e. if the position of the father in the Garden is higher than that deserved by the acts of the son, the latter will be raised to the place of the former (which is in accord with the Qur'ān), but also that the opposite is true. The actual import of these narratives, however, seems to put emphasis on the felicity of the parent, an increased reward precisely because he is one of the *mu'minūn*. The purpose in raising the son is to put him within the father's view, so that he can rejoice in seeing his child, while in the second instance the child who is in a higher station seems to be causally instrumental in bringing the father to a more elevated circumstance. One also can find frequent descriptions in Islamic folklore of the ways in which entrance to the Garden is actually seen to be assured by the ministrations of one's own children. Constance Padwick relates that she was told by a Nubian peasant of a belief that children who have died while still in the state of innocence will be given permission to intercede for their parents at the time of final judgment, saying, "This is my father, This is my mother, *shaffa'nī fīhim*."[82]

Many reports indicate that the process of living through the death of one's child can in itself be a means of insurance of salvation:

> The *fātiḥa* [opening chapter of the Qur'ān] should be recited over the [dead] child and one should say, O God! Make him for us a cause of recompense in the world to come and as one going before and a reward.
>
> The Prophet said, No Muslim will have three children die before they reach majority but that it will bring him out of the Fire into the Garden.[83]

The latter of these is repeated in a number of forms, some versions indicating that the death of two or even one child can serve the same function. Al-Adhamī, a contemporary writer citing traditional materials, comments that the death of children should be easy because of the recompense God has prepared for the parents who lose very young children. He too then lists reports about the loss of children.[84] According to the contemporary *Kaffārat al-khaṭāya*, the following *ḥadīth qudsī* comes from the Prophet: "My servant the believer has no punishment with Me if I have taken one of his children from the world and I shall give him no recompense or judgment except the Garden." He then cites some of the above-mentioned variants:

> If a man loses two children in Islam God will cause him to enter the Garden because of His mercy for them. If a Muslim couple have three children who die God will get them into heaven. The Prophet said, He who buries three children,

> he and I will be together in the Garden. If one loses three children who have not reached the age of puberty God will cause them to enter the Garden as a mercy for them. It will be said to the children, Enter the Garden, and they will say three times, No, not until our parents come. It will be said to them, Enter you and your parents.[85]

One possible interpretation of the Prophet's intention here, if these narratives are not apocryphal, is that bereavement is tantamount to suffering in the Fire, while overcoming that and realizing the mercy of God brings one bliss like that of paradise. Other narratives such as the following, however, seem to suggest somewhat more directly that the child can serve to bring the believer directly to the Garden:

> The Messenger of God said, The child will drag the woman who has just given birth by his navel-cord into the Garden on the day of resurrection.[86]

With the exception of such issues as whether or not children will be questioned in the grave, the circumstances of aborted fetuses, and Abraham caring for babies near the Ṭubba tree, commentary dealing with the fate of children has focused primarily on the question of ultimate consignment to the Garden or the Fire. A quite different orientation is suggested by the writings of contemporary Islamic spiritualists (whose general ideas on the life of the spirit are outlined in Chapter Four above).

Islam on the whole has offered little specificity concerning the chronological age of persons in the hereafter, although the Prophet is reported to have told an old woman that all will be brought to a new growth in Paradise (i.e. that none will remain old.[87] There are also occasional references to the expectation that we will be resurrected at the prime of life, with some indication that this will be an age in the mid-thirties. These speculations are somewhat problematic in terms of Qur'ānic assertions about progeny, but not completely irreconcilable. In any case they deal with the time of the resurrection itself rather than with what we have come to call the *barzakh* period between the death of the body and resurrection.

Spiritualism, which deals primarily with this *barzakh* time, has on occasion offered some suggestions in relation to life and growth after death that have clear implications for our understanding of children. One of the basic tenets of the spiritualist approach to the afterlife is that the spirit or soul is given the opportunity to progress upward to increasingly higher levels. This idea of progression, not surprisingly, is carried over into the understanding of one's age in the hereafter. Working on the assumption that full maturity is the time at which one is most fully functioning, however that might be specified in terms of years, the spiritualists suggest that part of what is implied by progressing in the *barzakh* is moving forward (or in some cases backward) chronologically so as to arrive at that time of maturity. Sometimes this is understood as a recuperative period after the death of the body during which time the soul is helped to recover from all that affected the material body to which it was attached: "If the soul is that of a young man, it is treated until it feels that it has left the stage of childhood. The opposite is true in the case of a senile soul, where it is returned to the stage of full growth."[88]

If the child goes into the other world before having been polluted by worldly things, his spirit rises quickly and continues to grow until it becomes a man or a woman. Occasionally one even finds references to the kinds of education that children will receive during that period, even including instruction in Qur'ān and the Islamic sciences.[89]

Despite these indications of growth to maturity in the *barzakh* period, one also finds in spiritualist writing attempts to reiterate the assurances to bereaved parents so characteristic of the commentary viewed above. Ḥamza, for example, after detailing the growth process, which he indicates will lead the child to maturity, then assures his readers that each person will meet with his dead children as soon as he dies (p. 198). Clearly one cannot see in that a chronological confusion, any more than one can take as contradictory Nawfal's double suggestion that children will grow at the time of resurrection and that husbands, wives and children will be together in the Garden.[90] On the one hand at least some writers distinguish between actual maturation and a development in one's perception of his surroundings in the afterlife. An understanding in the spiritualist conception indicates clear development during the time between death and resurrection, without the implication that by the time of the coming of the Hour all children will have reached full maturity.

On the other hand, to the extent to which the spiritualists remain true to the assurances of the Qur'ān as well as to the understanding of the traditions, there are points where consistency and logical resolution sometimes must be set aside in favor of a recognition that the precise modes of God's dispensation cannot yet be known. This, in fact, is in the long run perhaps the most that can finally be said about the Islamic understanding of the fate of children. Despite the many attempts to extrapolate from the understanding of God the ways in which He will deal with his little ones, it remains true that the specifics of the Qur'ānic assurances are meager and that the dominant theme of the traditions is that God alone knows the particulars.

In the following prayer recited in contemporary Egypt on the occasion of a child's death one finds a summary of the best of Islamic thought concerning hope for the little one as well as comfort for those who must face the ordeal of loss:

> O God, he is Thy servant and the son of Thy servant. Thou didst create him and sustain him and bring him to death and Thou wilt give him life. O God make him for his parents an anticipation, riches sent on before, a reward which precedes, and through him make heavy the balance (of their good works) and increase their rewards. Let neither us nor them be seduced by temptation after his departure. O God cause him to overtake the believers who preceded him, in the guardianship of Abraham, and give him in exchange (for his earthly home) a better dwelling place and a family better than his family, and keep him sound from the temptation of the tomb and the Fire of Gehenna.[91]

Appendix C
The Cult of Saints

Islam occasions many manifestations of belief in communication between the living and the dead, as demonstrated repeatedly in the foregoing materials. The dead are reported in a variety of ways to be cognizant of the living and through the media of dreams and other appearances are often felt to be able to communicate their desires and directives to those still alive on this earth. In this section we would like to describe briefly one particular phenomenon evidenced in contemporary popular Islamic piety, reflecting a long-standing custom, which is based on the conviction that at least certain of the dead have both the ability and the inclination to affect the lives of the "living." This is the practice of Muslim worshippers seeking intercession from local saints [*awliyā'*] in both mundane and theological matters, with particular reference to the cult of saints as observed in modern Egypt.

A great number of pious Muslims, both rural and urban, believe that the dead saints figure actively in the affairs of the living in terms of this world and the next. The line between *al-dunyá* and *al-ākhira* is not always an easy one to draw. Petitions to saints are sometimes made that would appear to be related specifically to everyday affairs of this world, but to which are appended the phrase, "Not now, but in the hereafter." One of the reasons for this lack of a sharp dividing line is the well-developed idea of *barzakh*, that intermediate state between physical death and final resurrection, in which the saints are considered to be fully alive, praying and going on the *ḥajj*, and the like. In this state we encounter them, according to both popular and orthodox understanding, participating in the lives of those still in the earthly realm.

The idea of intercession, *shafāʿa*, has played an important role in a variety of ways in the development of Islam. In the most general sense it can perhaps best be described as that activity whereby one individual is able in some manner to act as an intermediary for another. In an obvious sense *shafāʿa* implies intercession between human persons and God, particularly as that relates to questions of the eternal fate of individuals involved. This role has been assigned by the conclusions of orthodoxy to the prophets, in particular to Muḥammad (based primarily on S 43:86). In actuality, however, intercession in many cases is believed to extend to an active participation of certain deceased individuals in the day-to-day lives of others.

Constance Padwick has suggested the following definition of *shafāʿa*: ". . . the intercession of a mediator with the right to intercede, of the greater or more worthy on behalf of the lesser or less worthy."[1] This definition is interesting for two ideas relating to the function of *walīs* as intercessors. The first has to do with worth. Saints are recognized as having a hierarchical worth or value exceeding that of ordinary believers, based very simply on the understanding that they have achieved a special closeness to God. In traditional essays on eschatology they are generally described as being, along with prophets, in the fourth and highest of the realms of spirits awaiting the day of resurrection. From this position they may choose to remain in the seventh heaven, to circle around the earth until the Hour comes, or to devote themselves to a continuing concern for this world.[2] More interesting, or at least more controversial, is the suggestion of the "right to intercede." The orthodox conclusion has been that at least the Prophet Muḥammad has the right, God-invested of course, to intercede at the final hour. But what of the saints? Here one is on much shakier theological ground, although the idea of right is clearly related to that of rank.

The question of whether or not saints are empowered to intercede for the rest of humankind has elicited a variety of responses in the Muslim community. In the opinion of many, intercession of saints is invalid, and the petition for such is an improper activity for Muslims. There has been an action-reaction process throughout Islamic history in which periodic attacks have been made on popular practice in attempts to purify Islam from supposed aberrations. One of the most articulate of those to denounce the custom of visitation—to say nothing of veneration—of saints' tombs was the famous Ḥanbalī legist Taqī al-Dīn Ibn Taymīya[3] (although even he, it must be noted, did affirm the function, miracles, and nearest to God of the *walīs*.[4]) Muḥammad ʿAbdu, who continues to be considered by contemporary Egyptian thinkers a primary spokesman of modern Islamic theology, made it quite clear that in his opinion the Egyptian customs of building tombs for saints and venerating them through celebrations and visitations is nothing less than *shirk* or polytheism.[5] This continues to be the general position of the orthodox establishment, which on the whole condemns the idea of the intercession of *walīs* as false and not to be considered a part of Islam.[6]

Such official condemnation is not without its rather ambiguous exceptions, however. A large proportion of the population continues to observe these beliefs and practices; perhaps out of deference to this some more moderate statements are made by the orthodox establishment. As recently as 1971, the Council of Islamic Affairs in Egypt gave its official approval to a theoretical work entitled *Karāmāt al-awliyā'*, in which the special abilities and functions of saints are clearly recognized. The author, Farīd Māhir, discusses the question of authority in a way that clearly links the ideas of right and rank suggested above. He says that while some feel strongly that believers should communicate directly with God, others recognize that God in fact delegates authority, with the *walīs* commissioned to act as mediators. The *walī* is closer to God than the servant, and it is reasonable to assume that a request from (or through) the one closer is of higher value or at least of more efficacy than that from one lower in station.[7] Muḥammad Ḥasanayn Makhlūf, former Shaykh al-Azhar, says that

> Man petitions through the prophet or the *walī* seeking a prayer . . . as though the petition is saying, "Lord, I implore you through the Prophet or the *ahl al-bayt* or such and such a *walī* . . . that you fulfill my concern or heal the sick (related to me) or return to me that which I have lost or give me abundance or forgive me or cause me to enter your Garden. . . .[8]

An even more problematic question to be considered here, however, is the extent to which the *awliyā'* are not simply prayed *through,* but actually prayed *to*. There is little question that in many rural areas this practice of praying to the saints is observed. An anthropologist who has done extensive study of *shaykh* cults in Upper Egypt has expressed the strong opinion that despite the insistence of the *'ulamā'* that requests are made to God with the reward given through the *shaykh* or *walī* as an intermediary, the great majority of the population considers that the *shaykh* himself grants the wishes and desires of the believers.[9] That a request made directly to any but God is *shirk* would surely be supported in theory by most Muslims. And yet even here the subject is often dealt with rather circuitously. Māhir in *Karāmāt* (pp. 87–90) says that the *awliyā'* can do things beyond the natural. He suggests that while it is perhaps a bit extreme to say, as did the founder of the Tījānīya Order, that prayer *to* them is possible, still God in His divine wisdom has made people in different ranks. The lower takes refuge in the higher, but gifts come from God through the *awliyā'*.

The question of visitation of graves of the deceased has been subject to some varying interpretations in the history of Islam but on the whole has been sanctioned and is recommended in the four major schools of jurisprudence.[10] Certainly it is an ancient and time-honored custom to visit the tombs of loved ones to pray for them, distribute alms in their name, and in general to affirm the memory of the deceased in the mind and heart of the living.[11] Special visits are made to the tombs of the *walīs* to seek some form of intercession, favor, or blessing. This may involve telling the saint about one's problems, asking a particular favor, or simply obtaining blessing [*baraka*] from being in the presence of one of God's blessed ones. In return for the saint's favor the believer may make some kind of vow, distribute money at or on the sarcophagus itself, or even bring agricultural products, the income from whose sale is used for the upkeep of the tomb.[12]

A word should be said here about the condition of the saint's body in the tomb. Despite the still running controversies about the nature of the resurrected body at the day of judgment, most Muslims clearly recognize that the bodies of all ordinary people disintegrate at death and return to their original components in the earth. The case is often said to be somewhat differerent with the bodies of prophets and martyrs, however, which God will preserve from disintegration, being eaten by animals, or any other form of destruction.[13] In the opinion of many this exemption also holds for the bodies of the *awliyā'*, so that the believer who comes to pray and make petition at the tomb of a saint usually understands that the *walī* is there, present and intact in body as well as in spirit. Numerous stories are related about finding portions of deceased saints whole and uncorrupted long after their burial, such as the leg of 'Umar ibn al-Khaṭṭāb, the bodies of persons who died in the battle of 'Uḥud, and many others.[14] Louis Massignon, in describing a variety of occurrences in relation to his study of the necropolis at Cairo, relates that "Les cimetières sont ainsi le théâtre d'événement étranges, de phénomènes matériels troublants...: dormition de corps incorrompus, mouvements par psychokinèse de certains corps saints, suintements de sang, d'huile et de manne, apparitions de fantômes."[15]

Regardless of what one makes of such phenomena, and, as Massignon says, they can really neither be wholly accepted nor wholly rejected, their implications for popular belief are extensive. For many Muslims today as in the past, in most parts of the Islamic world, the saints are indeed alive and aware, ready to receive the petitions of earth-bound creatures who need help in the carrying out of affairs in this world as well as in preparation for the next. Let us look in particular at some of the beliefs and practices of contemporary Egypt to see how the saints, sometimes in bodily forms, are understood to act as beyond-the-grave intermediaries.

The *walī* in general understanding is said to be able to act in one of two ways when given a request from an individual worshipper: he (or she) can take the request directly to God, as in matters related to the eternal salvation of the supplicant, or else he can personally intervene, as is commonly acknowledged in matters related to the affairs of this world. One of the most popular saints in Cairo to be addressed for direct intervention is Imam Shāfi'ī, the founder of the Shāfi'ī school of law and one of Cairo's most illustrious citizens (d. 819). This particular saint is the recipient of a continuous stream of leters, addressed either to the tomb or to the Imam himself.[16] Many written and verbal requests are offered to him in person by the faithful who come to circumambulate the *maqṣūra* (the railing or screen surrounding the coffin [*tābūt*]). The large headpiece with its bright green turban gives the believer the impression that he is in a rather graphic way speaking directly to Shāfi'ī. The area immediately surrounding the *tābūt* generally is spread with personal notes and money given as votive offerings. The constantly enacted scenes around the shrine are widely varied: a mother dressed in black prays, "O Imam, please find a decent man for my daughter!"; a woman gently rubs her handkerchief around the railing, cleaning it and at once receiving blessing from it; two old men sit by the back wall softly murmuring, "Let us be among the children of the Garden of Paradise."

Imam Shāfi'ī's specialty is considered to be complaints about money, family problems, and concerns of personal injury.[17] Doubtless as a carry-over from his judicial functions when alive on earth, he is believed to mete out justice between supplicants and their oppressors. This he does by means of an underworld high court (in which some see the suggestion of continuity from the pharaonic theology of Osiris) called *al-maḥkama al-bāṭinīya*. Clearly not a generally accepted part of orthodox Islamic understanding of the afterlife, this court is believed to carry the implication of an intermediate judgment before the final one on the day of resurrection. Imam Shāfi'ī is assisted in the dispensing of justice by the four *imāns*, the four *aqṭāb* or founders of Sufi orders, 'Alī's daughter Sayyida Zaynab and her brothers Ḥasan and Ḥusayn, grandsons of the Prophet.[18]

It is not surprising that Sayyida (Sitt) Zaynab and Sayyidnā Ḥusayn are the two most popular, even venerated, of the saints of Cairo. They are part of the group of historic saints whose appeal and prestige goes far beyond that of the numerous local saints whose tombs are ubiquitous up and down the Nile. Egypt is, of course, a Sunnī state, but it continues to follow the practices of the Shī'a in their high regard for the members of the family of the Prophet, the *ahl al-bayt*. Many of these are believed to be buried in Cairo—such as Ja'far al-Ṣādiq (Muḥammad al-Ga'farī), Sayyida Nafīsa and Sayyida Ruqqaya, as well as Ẓaynab and Ḥusayn—and are highly cherished.

Only the head of the martyred Ḥusayn is believed to be enshrined at the mosque in Cairo, supposedly brought there at the end of the fifth Islamic century from Ascalon in Syria. (He is also considered by others, of course, to be buried in Karbala, Medina, Damascus, Palestine, Raqqa, Aleppo, and Merv.)[19] Legend has it that the Prophet himself appeared to a certain Shaykh al-Bahā'ī to assure him that the real head is buried at the Cairo shrine;[20] in any case the mosque and area surrounding the *tābūt* are the major centers of popular Islamic piety in that city.[21] Ḥusayn as the martyr is considered to be the master of the people of the Garden. Martyrs, of course, are taken immediately to the Garden at death and do not have to wait for the day of judgment.[22] Thus he is in a position of particular advantage to intercede for mankind now as well as on the final day. The strength of the devotion to Ḥusayn is displayed in this poem written in 1975:

> I came here today to proclaim by mouth—
> O master of the martyrs, your love is in my blood.
> I came to entrust my loved ones to you,
> To love in your presence and to seek refuge.
> I smelled the incense proceeding from you;
> I cried in desire for the greatest intercessor. . . .[23]

Sayyida Zaynab's mosque tomb is generally felt to be one of the most sacrosanct areas of Cairo, although the authenticity of the tomb as well as her identity as the daughter of 'Alī is seriously questioned. The depth of emotion expressed by those who pray and call forth her name is perhaps more intense than at any shrine in Cairo, with the exception of that displayed by those circumambulating the *tābūt* of Ḥusayn. In Zaynab's shrine the area surrounding the *tābūt* is divided into a men's section and a women's section; the *tābūt* is visible from each side, although the men look from the head and the women from the foot. Egypt has many female saints whose powers of intercession are considered equal to that of male *awliyā'*. There are also shrines for Zaynab in Lebanon, the Sudan, and Damascus, each claimed by devotees to be the actual grave of the saint.[24]

Prayer at Zaynab's grave is especially efficacious because she is the head of the assembly [*diwān*] of *walīs*. Countless legends are related about her interaction with devotees, some, such as the following, suggesting the importance put on her bodily presence, despite the fact that she has been dead in ordinary terms for fourteen centuries: Repenting for having stolen some money, a man prayed for Zaynab's help in repaying it, then lay down to sleep by her grave. Suddenly she came up from the tomb and told him to follow her, during which journey they passed through walls and otherconcrete objects until they came to the mosque [*masjid*] of Ḥusayn. She then disappeared, leaving behind a scarf with a ten pound note in it for his use.[25]

Zaynab is considered to be especially sensitive to human suffering, as she in her own life agonized over the successive deaths of her loved ones.[26] The following poem addressed to her suggests the importance of the role she plays in the lives of many Cairene Muslims:

> O vision of the holy light, my guide, my Ka'ba
> O daughter of him who wore the robe of salvation on the awesome night
> You who with the light of God destroyed all darkness
> And stood upright in the face of all evil . . . Zaynab al-Raḥmāt . . .
> I hurry, O my mother, to your quarter preceded by my tears.
> I get close and am silent, the tears explain my complaints
> I who have hidden from all people my pain.
> You, the comfort of my soul, the smile of my feelings in my loneliness
> But for you there would be no comfort in my life, in the depth of my yearning.
> I, in the crowd of those on the way, I march after my love.
> It is my weapon on the day of crowdedness [*yawm al-zaḥām*], and if I am asked my reason,
> (It is that) in your shadow I see the light of great beauty. . . .[27]

Also considered as patron saints of Cairo, and next in importance to Sayyida Zaynab as female *awliyā'* in Egypt, are Sitt Nafīsa and Sitt Ruqqaya. Like her, they are members of the family of the Prophet, the *ahl al-bayt*. The great-granddaughter of Imam Ḥasan, Nafīsa is said to have had a spiritual romance with Imam Shāfi'ī, who prayed constantly at her mosque.[28] Ruqqaya was the daughter of 'Alī by a wife other than Fāṭima. Both shrines are objects of constant visitation by men and women making vows and praying for intercession. Young men coming to Cairo from rural areas of Egypt for the first time are often instructed by their families to visit the tombs of Zaynab, Ruqqaya, Ḥusayn and the others so that they can be watched over and cared for by the deceased but still living *awliyā'*.

Visitation of tombs and requests for intercession continue to be popularly practiced in Cairo, although new city construction has caused the demolition of some of the less famous of these shrines. As might be expected, visitations are even more widespread in the rural areas. *Walī*ship there is generally hereditary. Almost every village in Egypt houses the tomb of a favorite saint, to whom is given the same kind of votive offerings as are the city saints. Interaction of believers and *walīs* is a complex process involving expectation of reward, fear of reprisal for neglect, and a highly structured set of particular responsibilities for specified members of the community.[29]

The tomb itself is generally located in a small white building [*maqām, ḍarīḥ*], covered by a dome [*qubba*]. Inside the building is located the *tābūt*, with a covering [*kiswa*] on which designs and inscriptions are painted or woven. Strings are often stretched over this with small articles, money, or letters hung as votive offerings.[30] Details about the building of the shrines are sometimes communicated through dream appearances, in which the dead *shaykh* or *shaykha* comes to a member of the community to convey his or her wishes. We have observed that throughout the history of Islam there have been recurring instances of the conviction that dreams are a clear medium for the transmission of messages of one kind or another from the deceased to the living.

The usual practice is for one entering the shrine to remove his shoes, circumambulate the *tābūt* (perhaps kissing the *kiswa*), and repeat portions of the Qur'ān. Requests for intercession cover a wide range of topics; as is the case with the city saints most local *walīs* are considered to have particular specialities in terms of which requests are made.[31] One of the most important problems for which the assistance of a saint may be sought is that of marital difficulty. Most often women patronize the tombs of *shaykhs* considered to be specialists in this area, particularly in such cases as the husband deserting his wife or taking a second mate of whom the first disapproves. Practices here suggest not only petition but often some forms of coercion. Sayyid 'Uways reports such examples as that of a frustrated wife lighting a candle near a *walī's* grave from the bottom rather than the top, supposedly annoying him until he fulfills her wish, or of rubbing the grave of another with garlic to make sure he is fully awake and aware in his tomb to receive her petition.[32]

Typical of the cult of saints in many religious traditions, the request for curing of physical ailments is one of the most common to be brought to the *walīs*. To this end the physical surroundings of the saint's shrine are very important and themselves often seen as having a role in the curative process.

If water, symbolic of life-giving properties, is not already present in the form of a well or stream, special water pots are placed nearby. Trees associated with the *shaykhs* are also felt to possess *baraka* for curing, the leaves of which can be used for sore eyes and other ailments. This practice too, along with other special properties of the tombs, has been identified by some as having antecedents in the beliefs and practices of pharaonic times.[33]

Whatever the case may be concerning the holdover of ancient ideas in the present practices of saint worship in Egypt, it is nonetheless clear that Islam itself has made a place for them in its own belief structure. While the bodies of most dead persons are known physically to disintegrate in the graves, those of saints are believed by many to remain intact, hearing and responding to the petitions of the living. The traditional understanding of the location of spirits of the deceased in the *barzakh* has ample room for the belief that the saints have the option to remain involved in the affairs of this world if they so choose. The medium of dreams, through which their desires are made known to the living, is a commonly accepted vehicle for communication. Despite the directness of the basic relationship between human and divine in Islam, the general understanding has long prevailed that this relationship can be facilitated and secured through the mediation of one who clearly has found favor and achieved status in the eyes of God.

Glossary of Arabic Terms

The brief definitions given below are those used in the context of this particular study.

'abd servant, slave
'ādhāb al-qabr punishments of the grave
ahl al-sunna wa'l-jamā'a people of custom and the community, used to refer to the Sunnī community
aḥwāl al-qubūr conditions of the graves
ajal fixed term of individual human life
ākhira next world, hereafter
'ālam al-dunyá earthly realm, world of the senses
'ālam al-ghayb the world unknown to all except God
'ālam al-jabarūt intermediate or celestial world
anbiyā' prophets
a'rāf heights, the place of those whose good and bad deeds are equal
aṣḥāb al-a'rāf companions of the heights
aṣḥāb al-kahf people of the cave
awliyā' (sing. *walī*) saints
āyāt God's signs
badan physical body
baraka blessing, efficacy
barzakh barrier, the time/place beyond the grave
basmallah invocation, "In the name of God, the merciful, the compassionate"

ba'th calling forth for judgment at the resurrection
bid'a innovation
bilā kayf without questioning precisely how something is true
ḍaghṭ pressure (of the tomb)
dahr time
dār al-ākhira abode of the hereafter
dār al-barzakh abode of the *barzakh*
dār al-dunyá abode of this world
dār al-qarār abode of everlastingness
al-dhāt al-insānīya human essence
dīn religion, individual religious response
dunyá closer or lower world, this-worldly existence
fanā' extinction or annihilation of all save God
fisq depravity
fitan trials that will usher in the eschaton
fiṭra natural disposition of humans to be Muslim
ghayb unknown to all except God
ghusl ritual washing
ḥadīth narrative report from or about the Prophet
ḥadīth qudsī holy *ḥadīth*, or saying coming directly from God
ḥajj pilgrimage
ḥaqīqat al-insān human essence
ḥashr gathering of all living beings at the resurrection
ḥawḍ pond of the Prophet at the day of resurrection
hāwiya pit of the fire of punishment
ḥijāb partition
hijra emigration of the Prophet Muḥammad from Mecca in 622
ḥisāb reckoning
ḥūr virginal maidens of paradise
'ibāda religious duty
'ifrīt restless spirit (of the dead)
ihtizāz vibration
ijmā' consensus
ijtihād individual interpretation
'iliyīn uppermost heaven
imām religious leader
īmān faith
ishārāt al-sā'a signs of the Hour signaling the day of resurrection
isnād chain of transmission of a *ḥadīth*

isrā' night journey of the Prophet Muḥammad
jahannam abode of punishment
jāhilīya time of ignorance before the revelation to the Prophet Muḥammad
janna (pl. *jannāt*) garden
jism physical body
jism laṭīf subtle body
kabā'ir grave sins
kāfir (pl. *kāfirūn, kuffār*) one who rejects the message brought by the Prophet from God
kalām speculative theology
khalīfa vicegerent
khulūd, khuld eternity
kufr rejection of the message brought by the Prophet from God, ingratitude
liqā' Allāh meeting with God
ma'ād return of all souls at the time of resurrection, used to refer to the entire series of events at the resurrection
mahdī lit. guided one, the savior to come at the end of time
ma'nawī ideational, pointing to an abstract or spiritual reality
al-ma'ṣiyāt bad deeds
al-milla al-ḥanīfīya the religion of the pious monotheists
mi'rāj heavenly ascension of the Prophet
mīzān (pl. *mawāzīn*) balance
mufassir (pl. *mufassirūn*) exegete of the Qur'ān
mu'min (pl. *mu'minūn*) person of faith
mushrik (pl. *mushrikūn*) one who commits *shirk*
mutakallimūn doctors of theology
nafs (pl. *anfus*) soul
al-nafs al-lawwāma the self-reproaching or blameworthy soul
al-nafs al-mutma'inna soul at peace
al-nār the fire of punishment/purgation
nasama soul
nizā' death struggle
qaḍar destiny, foreordainment, divine will
qibla prayer direction
qiyāma resurrection, rising up
riḍá (God's) satisfaction or will
rijs uncleanness
rūḥ (pl. *arwāḥ*) spirit
rū'ya Allāh vision of God

sā'a hour at which the day of resurrection will arrive
saghā'ir lesser sins
salaf pious ancestors
ṣalāt ritual prayer
al-ṣāliḥāt good deeds
samā' (pl. *samawāt*) heaven
ṣaum fasting
shafā'a intercession
shahāda testimony to the oneness of God and the status of Muḥammad as Messenger of God
sharī'a religious law
sharr sin
shaykh elder, venerable one, important religious personage
shayṭān (pl. *shayāṭīn*) satan
shirk association of any other thing with God
shūra consultation
ṣiddiqūn truthful ones
ṣirāṭ bridge of the reckoning
ṣirāṭ al-jahīm bridge over the top layer of the Fire
sujūd prostration during prayer
sunna way of the Prophet
ṭā'a obedience
tābūt coffin, sarcophagus
tafsīr exegesis (of the Qur'ān)
taqdīr predestination
tashbīh anthropomorphism
tawba repentance
'ulamā' (sing. *'ālim*) learned doctors of Islam
umma community
waṣāṭ middle position
wuḍū' ritual washing
zabānīya angels guarding the gates of the Fire
zakāt almsgiving
zamān time

Notes

PREFACE

1. Ṣoubḥi El-Ṣaleḥ, *La Vie Future selon le Coran* (1971), pp. 26–28.
2. Ṡayyed Abul A'la Maudoodi, *Towards Understanding Islam* (1960), p. 130.

CHAPTER ONE

1. See also such verses as S 17:49, 17:98, 19:66, 37:16–17, 50:3 and 75:3, all of which convey the Meccan conviction that such an idea as bodily resurrection is absurd. For a fuller treatment of some of the beliefs and practices of pre-Islamic Arabia related to questions of death and afterlife see Appendix A.
2. The Islamic understanding(s) of *qadar* will be considered in more detail below; there is some evidence from the traditions that in early Islam God Himself was occasionally identified with *dahr*. See W. M. Watt, "*Dahr*" in *El*, II, 94–95.
3. Cf. the famous lines of the ancient poet Labīd, cited by the Caliph al-Mu'taṣim in memory of his brother al-Ma'mūn: "Yet do not grieve, if Time has parted us for ever; the day must come when Fate falls upon every man. Men are as desert encampments, whose brief inhabitants one day quit with the dawn, and they remain desolate; troop by troop they depart, and it abides after them like the palm of a hand, fingers clutching an emptiness. Man is naught but a shooting flame whose effulgency flashes awhile broadly, but then sinks into ashes," A. J. Arberry, *The Seven Odes* 1957, p. 126.
4. See the study of Toshihiko Izutsu, *Ethico-Religious Conceptions in the*

Qur'ān (1966), pp. 45–54. "The 'eternity' of which there is much talk in pre-Islamic poetry, and which undoubtedly constituted one of the most serious problems among the pagan Arabs just before the rise of Islam, meant primarily an eternal life on this very earth" (p. 48). Izutsu reflects in *God and Man in the Qur'ān* (1964), p. 123, that the very recognition of the unattainability of *khulūd* in the sense of eternal life was the major factor in what he calls their "pessimistic nihilism."

5. See Louis Massignon, "Time in Islamic Thought" in J. Campbell, ed., *Man and Time* (1958), p. 109: "But the only perfect, self-sufficient instant is the Hour *(Sā'a),* the Hour of the Last Judgment, the final summation of the decrees of all responsibilities incurred; this Hour must be awaited with sacred awe. . . ."

6. It is clear that we die by God's decree but less apparent from Qur'ānic stipulation exactly when that decree is made. There is nothing in the Qur'ān, in other words, to suggest that the time of one's death is preordained at any particular point either before or after birth. S 6:2 mentions *ajal* twice; some see both references as pointing to the time between birth and death, while others suggest that the second refers to the period between death and resurrection.(See Daud Rahbar, *God of Justice* 1960, p. 98.)

7. Ragnar Eklund, *Life Between Death and Resurrection According to Islam* (1949), p. 21, says that "not only the expected judgment but also the death of the individual is valid as an introduction of *'āḫira*. The term embraces everything that comes after death." In the sense that *dunyá* and *ākhira* represent the only two alternatives of existence, which is certainly consonant with the Qur'ānic view, such a description is accurate.

8. See Izutsu, *God and Man,* pp. 85–87, who feels that *dunyá* was a common concept in pre-Islamic Arabia, perhaps influenced by the Jews and Christians of the area, for whom the idea of a lower world is in clear contrast to the understood greater significance of the world to come.

9. *Ākira* is also contrasted with *al-ūlá,* the first or former, as in S 53:25 and 92:13, which attest that to God belong the last and the first, or the latter and the former.

10. See M. M. Bravman, *The Spiritual Background of Early Islam* (1972), pp. 32–39, who shows that in pre-Islamic poetry *al-dunyá* expresses a secular concept, from which it developed into the Islamic understanding of *dunyá* in contrast to *ākhira*. The secular concept of *dunyá* as the opposite of the glorious going out to war *(dunyá* is near; to go to war is to go far), he says, led to the religious concept of this world as opposed to the world to come, especially since to fight and die for Islam was immediately to gain the hereafter.

11. S 25:53 and 55:20 also mention *barzakh,* but with the meaning of a barrier separating the sweet and salt waters of the earth.

12. Eklund, *Life Between Death and Resurrection,* p. 22.

13. Thus Ibn Qayyim al-Jawzīya in his popular fourteenth-century manual

of eschatological concerns, *Kitāb·al-rūḥ* (A.H. 1357), discusses three abodes: the *dār al-dunyá,* the *dār al-barzakh,* and what he calls the *dār al-qarār,* abode of everlastingness, that which the Qur'ān calls the *dār al-ākhira.* One narrative from the Qur'ān, often cited as "proof" of the possibility of resurrection, is that of the *aṣḥāb al-kahf*, the people of the cave, said by some interpreters to be a version of the seven sleepers of Ephesus tale. It provides a good illustration of the middle category, if one can call it that, between *dunyá* and *ākhira.* This narrative from S 18:8–26 was elaborated by later tradition; the story apparently refers to seven young men who fled during the Decian persecution of Christians (201–51 C.E.), and finding shelter in a cave went to sleep for some 300 years. Upon awaking, one of them went to the city to bear witness to the faith, only to find the persecution over and Christianity reestablished. The notables of the city all came to wonder at the youths before they again went to sleep, this time to rest until the day of resurrection. Some contemporary writers have preferred to opt for actual death rather than sleep as the condition of the youths, saying that they were perhaps Christian hermits who died while at prayer and were mummified that way, their bodies swaying in the breeze giving the impression of life. J. M. S. Baljon, *Modern Muslim Qur'ān Interpretation* (1961), pp. 31–32, citing Aḥmad Khān and Maulānā Kalām Azād.

14. Margaret Smith, "Transmigration and the Sufis," *Muslim World,* 30 (1940), 351; cf. A. S. Tritton, *Muslim Theology* (1947), pp. 136–39, who discusses in some detail the teachings on transmigration of some of the disciples of al-Naẓẓām and others.

15. Of the Sufi saints who have been accused of teaching a doctrine of transmigration we can point to Manṣūr al-Ḥallāj, Shihāb al-Dīn al-Suhrawardī al-Maqtūl, Farīd al-Dīn 'Aṭṭār, Jalāl al-Dīn Rūmī and many others. While in some cases the charges may have had validity, the issue is extremely complex and its understanding requires an intimate knowledge of the teachings of the various masters. The vast majority of Sufis have rejected outright such a possibility. Some of the philosophers, of course, also held to certain notions of transmigration, such as al-Rāzī, al-Farābī, and the Ikhwān al-Ṣafā'. See A. J. Arberry, *Reason and Revelation in Islam* 1957, pp. 38–39; Majid Fakhry, *A History of Islamic Philosophy* 1970, pp. 119–20, 145–47. For detailed references to *tanāsukh* in Persian Muslim thought see E. G. Browne, *A Literary History of Persia* (1969), pp. 310–28.

16. Pp. 13–15; see also his "The Syrian Isma'ilis and the Doctrine of Metempsychosis," *Milla wa-Milla,* (1964), 48–51.

17. Cf. S 2:29, 23:17, 58:3, 71:15.

18. In the later and more fully developed cosmological scheme, paradise was conceived as a kind of eight-tiered pyramid above the earth. In it are not only the magnificent Gardens of the blessed, but also the books in which human actions are recorded, the pen which inscribes them, the trumpet that will sound the resurrection, the balance, and the Bayt al-Ma'mūr or archetypal Ka'ba. See

Carra de Vaux, *La Doctrine de l'Islam* 1909, Chapter Four, for a detailed description of these elements.

19. The literature on this event is voluminous; see especially M. Asin Palacios, *Islam and the Divine Comedy* (1926); J. Horovitz, "Muhammeds Himmelfahrt" in *Der Islam,* IX (1919), and *"Mi'rādj," SEI,* pp. 381–84; G. Widengren, *The Ascension of the Apostle and the Heavenly Book* (1950). The *ḥadīths* generally elaborate the whole experience in two sections: the trip from Mecca to Jerusalem and the journey from Jerusalem through the heavens. Although the versions differ, they usually begin with a description of Gabriel opening up the body of the sleeping Prophet, washing it out with water from the well of Zamzam, and filling it up with faith and wisdom.

20. See Qassim al-Samarrai, *The Theme of Ascension in Mystical Writings* (1968), I, 206 ff.

21. The usages of *jabarūt* and *malakūt* vary with individual authors; sometimes they both refer to the divine region above the realm of the *dunyá*, sometimes the *malakūt* is placed above the *jabarūt* in ranking, and sometimes both are subordinated to even higher realms called the *lāhūt* or world of the divine being and the ultimate realm of the divine names. Cf. Sayyid Hossein Nasr, *Science and Civilization* 1968, pp. 92–93.

22. "The reference to this great mystic story of the Mi'rāj is a fitting prelude to the journey of the human soul in its spiritual growth in life. The first step in such a growth must be through moral contact—the reciprocal rights of parents and children, kindness to our fellowmen, courage and firmness. . . . " M. Abdel Moneim Younis, "The Religious Significance of Mi'raj," *Majallat al-Azhar* (November, 1967), p. 7.

23. See, e.g. Muṣṭafá Maḥmūd, *al-Qur'ān* (1970), p. 81, who discusses the seven steps in the color wavelengths.

24. Muḥammad Zafrulla Khan, *Islam, its Meaning for Modern Man* (1962), p. 194.

25. Muḥammad Shahīn Ḥamza, *al-Rūḥīya al-ḥadītha* (1968), pp. 172–76; 'Abd al-Razzāq Nawfal, *al-Ḥayāt al-ukhrá* (1965), pp. 98–100.

26. See al-Khaṭīb, *al-Tafsīr al-Qur'ānī li'l-Qur'ān* (1967–70), I, 514–16; Darwaza, *al-Tafsīr al-ḥadīth* (1962–00), II, 181. Some modern writers, however, hold the position that the human soul pre-exists its life in the embryo, just as it will continue to exist after the death of the body. 'Abd al-Razzāq Nawfal, *Yawm al-qiyāma* (1969), pp. 59–60, says that there are numerous proofs that the spirit had a previous life, such as instances of people remembering things they could not have known from this life: "The life that the person feels he has experienced before is the spiritual life in another world." (Cf. Muṣṭafá Maḥmūd, *Riḥlat min al-shak ilā al-īmān* (n.d.), p. 58; *al-Qur'ān,* p. 78. Nawfal insists that this is not an argument for transmigration of the spirit into a succession of different bodies (see his *Ṭarīq ilá Allāh* [1962], p. 109). Nawfal's

ideas on the pre-existence of the spirit are thoroughly disparaged by Muṣṭafá al-Kīk, *Rasā'il ilayhim* (1972), pp. 16–75.

27. Cf. Abdul Qasem, *The Ethics of al-Ghazali* (1975), p. 45.

28. See, e.g. S 6:12, 15:26, 32:7, 36:77–78, 40:67, 76:2, 77:20–21, 80:17–19, 86:5–7, 96:2.

29. S 10:12, 16:53–55, 17:67–70, 29:10, 30:33–34, 31:32, 39:8, 41:49–51, 42:48.

30. See S 11:9–10, 74:23, 75:33, 89:15, 90:5–7.

31. {O children of Adam! Let not *al-shayṭān* seduce you as he made your parents leave the Garden . . . } [S 7:27].

32. A. S. Tritton, "Man, *nafs, rūḥ, 'aql,*" *Bulletin of the School of Oriental and African Studies,* 34, (1971), 33, suggests that the three-fold division of the soul into vegetal, animal, and rational in the philosophical sense may have influenced this religious division into the lusting soul, the censorious soul, and the soul at rest.

33. 'Abd al-Wadūd Shalabī of the Idārat al-Azhar in Cairo, e.g., expressed to the authors this view: "I am one of those who does not like to plunge into this kind of study of the unknown . . . and I am distressed at having to give a decisive opinion in it because it is among the affairs of the *ghayb* which God alone knows; al-Islam, as *dīn*, by its nature is uncomplicated and far from *ta'wīl* and philosophizing . . . and so I prefer silence."

34. In an interview in April, 1967, 'Abd al-Ḥalīm Maḥmūd, then Shaykh of al-Azhar, replied to a question about the difference between *nafs* and *rūḥ* only that *"al-rūḥ min amr rabbī,"* as S 17:85 expresses.

35. For a full treatment of the understanding of *nafs* and *rūḥ* in the Qur'ān and in the subsequent development of Islamic thought see D. B. Macdonald, "The Development of the Idea of Spirit in Islam," *Muslim World,* 22, no. 1 (January-April, 1932), 25–42.

36. Originally used as breath, with the plural meaning winds, says Macdonald, *rūḥ* "in the theological sense 'spirit' came into Arabic with Muḥammad and the Kur'ān."

37. E. E. Calverly, *"Nafs," SEI,* p. 434.

38. The emphasis on the corporeal nature of the spirit was related, of course, to the constant effort to avoid *shirk* by affirming that only God is finally non-corporeal.

39. See J. I. Smith, "The Understanding of *nafs* and *rūḥ* in Contemporary Muslim Considerations of the Nature of Sleep and Death," *Muslim World,* 49, no. 3 (1979), 151–62.

40. See esp. al-Zamakhsharī, *al-Kashshāf* (1966), IX, 131; al-Rāzī, *Tafsīr* (1934–62?), XXVI, 283–84; al-Marāghī, *Tafsīr* (1953), XXIX, 11–12; al-Jammāl, *al-Tafsīr al-farīd* (1973), IV, 2682–83; al-Ṭabāṭabā'ī, *al-Mīzān* (1970–00), XVII, 268–69. For the most part, exegesis of this verse does not

occasion among modern *mufassirūn* lengthy analysis of the terms *nafs* and *rūḥ;* one exception is al-Khaṭīb (*Tafsīr* [1967–70], XII, 1160–67), who concludes that (1) *rūḥ* gives life; man and animals have spirits and the difference between them, as between the spirits of men, is in rank and not in kind; (2) the *nafs* distinguishes man from animal, the human essence [*al-dhāt al-insānīya*] being created by the meeting of the *rūḥ* and the body.

41. Cf. a private communication from Prof. Maḥmūd Ibrāhīm of the University of Jordan, 8 May 1978: "The *rūḥ* is the name of the human essence [*ḥaqīqat al-insān*] before its connection with the body and after its separation from it . . . and when it is connected to the body . . . it is called the *nafs*."

42. "Thus," says Aḥmad Ṣubḥī of Ṣan'ā' University in the Yemen, "I am of the opinion that the two terms *nafs* and *rūḥ* are quite different and one cannot be substituted for the other. The word 'yatawaffá' [in S 39:42] which means 'causes to die' is ascribed to *nafs*, not to *rūḥ*. *Rūḥ,* being a glimpse of God's spirit, never dies; it is immortal" (private communication, 5 April 1978).

43. One of the most detailed expositions of the various interpretations given to the terms *nafs* and *rūḥ* is that of the Damascene Ḥanbalī Ibn Qayyim al-Jawzīya in his *Kitāb al-rūḥ* (cf. also his *Ḥādī al-Arwāḥ* [n.d.]), a work that will be cited frequently in the succeeding chapters as an authoritative exposition of orthodox Islam. But his own understanding, representative of the general concensus of Islamic thought, is that spirit, *rūḥ,* is of a material substance, is created, and insofar as it applies to a constituent element of the human person, is to be equated with *nafs*. Thus he uses the terms interchangeably in his many and lengthy descriptions of the circumstances of the soul after death.

44. For a detailed discussion of the different views on the nature of the resurrected body see Louis Gardet, *Dieu et la Destinée de l'Homme* (1967), pp. 260–72.

45. See esp. W. M. Watt, *Free Will and Predestination in Early Islam* (1948); A. J. Arberry, *Revelation and Reason in Islam* (1959). Watt, in attempting to contrast the Qur'ān and the traditions on this issue, found that the *ḥadīths* with few exceptions were unequivocally predestinarian: "The verses of the Qur'ān, which are anti-fatalistic," he says, "are thus twisted [in the traditions] and made to fit in with semi-fatalistic conceptions" (p. 27).

46. A more general term for sin than the *sayyi'āt,* which are particularly onerous deeds because of the implications for others, is *sharr.* See also other Qur'ānic terms such as *dhanb, ithm, khaṭī'a.*

47. Technically *kufr* means rejection of the message brought by the Prophet from God, while *shirk* refers to the associating of any other thing with God. In some discussions *shirk* is considered a more heinous offense than *kufr*; both terms are used in this sense of the ultimate apostasy.

48. T. Izutsu, *The Concept of Belief in Islamic Theology* (1965), p. 37.

49. Muslim, *Īmān,* traditions 141–44 cited in A. J. Wensinck, *The Muslim Creed* (1965), p. 39. It is interesting to note in this connection that in the early

centuries of Islam suicide came to be accepted with little dispute as *kabīra* or grave sin; various traditions attest to the fact that one of the punishments of the Fire for the person who commits suicide will be the continual repetition of the act by which he took his own life. Al-Ghazālī in the *Durra al-fākhira,* for example, cites the Prophet as having said, "Whoever kills himself with a sharp knife will be found on the day of resurrection with it in his hand, stabbing himself in the belly in the fire of *jahannam*, where he will remain eternally" (MS p. 36). See Franz Rosenthal, "On Suicide in Islam," *Journal of the American Oriental Society,* 66 (1946), 239–59.

50. See Chapter Three below.

51. See also S 2:123, 254; 7:53; 26:100–01; 40:18, 74:48.

52. See S 10:18; 30:13; 36:23.

53. D. B. Macdonald, "Immortality in Mohammedanism," *(Religion and the Future Life* [ed. E. A. Sneath]), p. 313, calls this "the victory of the solidarity of Islam over the ethical faith of its Prophet."

54. Some have argued that the notion of intercession had deep roots in Semitic beliefs and that despite the assertions of the Qur'ān, it could not be fully eradicated from the understanding of the faithful. Intercession as a theme has figured prominently in both the Jewish and Christian traditions, and suggestions have been made that the Qur'ānic emphasis may have been a direct counter to such teachings (John Macdonald, "The Day of Judgment in Near Eastern Religions," *Indo-Iranica,* 14, iv [1961], 46), while others make the point that the very ambiguity of the Qur'ānic interpretation may reflect a corresponding hesitation in these other traditions about the efficacy or legitimacy of intercession. See J. W. Bowker, "Intercession in the Qur'ān and the Jewish Tradition," *Journal of Semitic Studies,* 11 (1966), 69–84.

55. A.b.Ḥ., IV, 404; Taqī al-Dīn Subkī, *Shifā' al-saqām fī ziyāra khayr al-anām* (A.H. 1315), p. 163.

56. Burkārī, as cited by al-Subkī, p. 161.

57. One finds differing references in the creeds; al-Ash'arī's *Maqālāt* (R. J. McCarthy, *The Theology of al-Ash'arī* [1973], art. 27), for example, mentions the intercession of God's messenger (sing.); art. 25 of the *Waṣiyat Abī Ḥanīfa* (Wensinck, *The Muslim Creed*) says only that the intercession of the Prophet Muḥammad is a reality, while the *Fiqh Akbar II* (Wensinck, *Creed,* art. 20) and the *'Aqā'id* of al-Nasafī (E. E. Elder, *A Commentary on the Creed of Islam* [1950], chap. 12) speak of the intercession of the messengers (pl.).

58. *Iḥyā' 'ulūm al-dīn* (n.d.), IV, 509–12. Never ridicule anyone, says al-Ghazālī, for God has hidden His *wilāya* in His servants! Cf. the contemporary 'Abbās Maḥmūd al-'Aqqād, *al-Falsafa al-Qur'ānīya* (n.d.), pp. 216–17, and Ṣadīq Hasan Khān, who cites many relevant traditions in his *Yaqẓāt ulī al-i'tibār* (n.d.), pp. 194–253.

59. See, e.g. Taqī al-Dīn Ibn Taymīya, *Qā'ida jalīla fī al-tawassul wa'l-wasīla* (A.H. 1374), pp. 7–18.

60. Appendix C provides particulars of the cult of saints, especially in the Egyptian context.

61. These five elements are said to have been the response of the Prophet when asked what constitutes *īmān* in distinction from *islām* (Tir., II, 101; Ṭay., p. 5; A.b.Ḥ., I, 27, 51–52; II, 104, 426). See Maḥmūd Shaltūt, *al-Islām: ʻaqīda wa-sharīʻa* (1975), p. 41; Sayyed Abul Ala Maudoodi, *Towards Understanding Islam,* pp. 136–37. This was affirmed in personal interviews with Khalaf al-Sayyid ʻAlī and ʻAbd al-Wadūd Shalabī of al-Azhar.

62. See Ustadh ʻAntar Aḥmad Ḥishād, "Al-īmān bi yawm al-ākhar and its effect on character," *Majallat al-Azhar* (April, 1975), pp. 315–20.

63. "If there is nothing to follow, the coordination of values in this life would have little meaning and, indeed, would become almost impossible. There would be no accountability and consequently no responsibility. . . . [Thus] Islam insists on belief in the life after death. There are several matters of belief which Islam regards as essential, but belief in the life after death is concomitant with belief in the Existence of God" (Khan, *Islam,* p. 184).

64. Khalaf al-Sayyid ʻAlī of the Islamic Research Center at al-Azhar, interview in 1976; Abū'l-Aʻlā al-Mawdūdī, *al-Ḥaḍāra al-Islāmīya,* pp. 225–27.

65. Sayyid Quṭb, *Mashāhid al-qiyāma fī'l-Qur'ān* (1961), pp. 11–12.

66. See Muḥammad al-Mubārak, *Niẓām al-Islām* (1970), pp. 136–50.

67. Aḥmad Fā'iz, *al-Yawm al-ākhir fī ẓilāl al-Qur'ān* (1975), pp. 34–51.

68. See, e.g. Muṣṭafá Maḥmūd, *al-Rūḥ wa'l-jasad* (1974), pp. 29–30, who says that we might do what is not acceptable to God, but we cannot do what God does not will. All events and actions occur within the divine will, even if some are outside the divine *riḍá*.

69. "This," says Maudoodi, "is the ethical ideal which takes shape naturally from the conception of human vicegerency." *The Ethical Viewpoint of Islam* 1953, p. 50.

70. "The belief in Future Life, and in the accountability of his (or her) actions in this world, is the most vital force that incites man to perfection and elevation in his present life, in order to attain the highest grade in the hereafter." A. M. Mohiaddin Alwaye, "The Belief in the Day of Judgment and its Effects on the Life of Man," *Majallat al-Azhar,* June, 1969, p. 1.

71. Shaltūt, *al-Islām,* pp. 41–42.

72. Fā'iz, *al-Yawm,* pp. 18–19.

CHAPTER TWO

1. See Chapter One, p. 5.

2. For a discussion of these interpretations see the authors' "Afterlife Themes in Contemporary Qur'ān Commentary," *Journal of the American Academy of Religion* (Supplement), December 1979.

3. As we shall see, the traditions are replete with references to the belief that the dead actually hear very well. Various attempts have been made to justify these traditions in light of the Qur'ān, including that of the Ibn Qutayba, who said that this verse refers simply to the ignorant among the people of the graves, who are insensitive to the message of the Prophet (Eklund, *Life Between Death and Resurrection,* p. 67).

4. Many commentators suggest that there is a double meaning to these verses; the reference is both to the circumstance of the *kāfirs* after their deaths and to the historical events at the battle of Badr when angels beat the backs of the retreating enemies of Islam.

5. For an excellent exposition of many of the basic works and themes dealing with the *barzakh* period see Ragnar Eklund's *Life Between Death and Resurrection According to Islam.* Eklund himself, while structuring his work generally in terms of the historical sequence of these works, says that "When we contine our historical survey of the material belonging to the Hereafter. . . it may be emphasized that in some ways the traditional material is timeless and firm as an anchorage in the theological development . . . " (p. 130).

6. See al-Ash'arī's *Maqālāt al-Islāmiyīn* and *Ibāna 'an uṣūl al-diyāna* (R. J. McCarthy, *The Theology of al-Ash'arī* [1953], pp. 235–54); al-Ṭahāwī's *'Aqīdat ahl al-sunna wa'l-jamā'a* (E. E. Elder, "al-Ṭahāwī's 'Bayān al-sunna wa'l-jamā'a' " in *The MacDonald Presentation Volume* [1933], pp. 131–44); The *Sharḥ al-'aqā'id al-Nasafīya* (E. E. Elder, *A Commentary on the Creed of Islam* [1950]); the *Waṣīyat Abī Ḥanīfa* and *Fiqh Akbar II* (A. J. Wensinck, *The Muslim Creed* [1965]).

7. While some mention only the negative form of recompense *(Maqalāt* and *Ibāna* [p. 245]; *Wasīyat Abī Ḥanīfa* and *Fiqh Akbar II* [pp. 129, 195–96]), in others there are also references to some kind of reward for the virtuous. "The grave is either one of the meadows of the Garden," says al-Ṭahāwī, "or one of the pits of the Fire" (p. 141). Commenting on al-Nasafī's affirmation of the bliss accorded to the obedient in the grave, al-Taftazānī says that this is far better than only mentioning the punishment of the grave as the majority of writers do (p. 99). Al-Ash'arī says that prayers for the dead are helpful (p. 251) and the *Fiqh Akbar II* that the reunion of the body with the spirit in the tomb is a reality (p. 195).

8. This work was first translated into French by Lucien Gautier (1877) as *Ad-dourra al-fakhira, la perle précieuse*. Citations here are taken from the English translation of J. I. Smith, *The Precious Pearl* (1979). References are to the page numbers of the manuscript printed in Gautier, from which the English translation was made.

9. D. B. Macdonald calls it "A good statement and study of the position of the corporeal school, which is undoubtedly the fundamental position of orthodox Islam. . . . " See "The Development of the Idea of Spirit in Islam," *Muslim World,* 22, no. 1 (Jan.-Apr., 1932), 33.

10. All references are to the translations of the *Kitāb al-ḥaqā'iq wa'l-daqā'iq,* given by John Macdonald in the following articles in *Islamic Studies:* "The Angel of Death in Late Islamic Tradition," 3 (1964), 485–519; "The Creation of Man and Angels in the Eschatological Literature," 3 (1964), 285–308; "The Day of Resurrection," 5 (1966), 129–97; "Paradise," 5 (1966), 331–83; "The Preliminaries to the Resurrection and Judgment," 4 (1965), 137–79; "The Twilight of the Dead," 4 (1965), 55–102.

11. Translated into the German by Monitz Wolff as *Muhammedanische Eschatologie* (1872), this work is identical in almost every detail with Imam 'Abd al-Raḥīm ibn Aḥmad al-Qāḍī's *Daqā'iq al-akhbār fī dhikr al-janna wa'l-nār* (probably eleventh-century), which has been translated into English by 'Ā'isha 'Abd al-Raḥmān and published under the title *The Islamic Book of the Dead* (1977).

12. *Mukhtaṣar tadhkirat al-Qurṭubī* (A.H. 1307), p. 23. Cf. the following description from the *Kitāb aḥwāl al-qiyāma* (pp. 13–14): "It is said in Muqātil ibn Sulaymān's *Kitāb al-sulūk* that the angel of death has a seat in the seventh heaven, or in the fourth heaven, created by God of light. He has 70,000 feet and 40,000 wings. His body is all filled with eyes and tongues. . . . He has four faces. One face is in front of him and the second on his head and the third at his back and the fourth under his feet. He takes the spirits of the prophets and angels from the face on his head and the spirits of the *mu'mins* from in front of him and the spirits of *kāfirs* from behind his back and the spirits of the *jinn* from under his feet. One of his feet is on the bridge of Jahannam and the other is on the seat of the Garden. It is said that he is so enormous that if the water of all the seas and rivers were poured on his head not a drop would fall on the earth. . . ."

13. P. 12, cf. Macdonald, "Angel," p. 487.

14. Macdonald, "Angel," pp. 491–92; *Kitāb aḥwāl al-qiyāma,* pp. 15–16.

15. See Chapter One above for a detailed discussion of this issue.

16. P. 32; cf. Macdonald, "Twilight," pp. 70–71. Macdonald suggests that the first angelic visitors are a late addition to the narrative of the after-life events in Islam.

17. Macdonald, "Angel," p. 498.

18. For a description of the various processes connected with the preparation of bodies for final burial see A. A. Tritton, "Muslim Funeral Customs," *Bulletin of the School of Oriental and African Studies,* 9 (1937–39), 653–61.

19. *Kitāb aḥwāl al-qiyāma,* pp. 26–27. This whole sequence of suffering while observing the preparations for one's own burial is greatly elaborated in the *Kitāb al-ḥaqā'iq wa'l-daqā'iq.* (See Macdonald, "Twilight," pp. 60–63.)

20. P. 21; cf. Macdonald, "Angel," pp. 499–502.

21. Such unhappy descriptions of the resting-place of the departed are a common part of folklore concerning death from very early times. In ancient Mesopotamia such a habitation was called Arallu and pictured as "the house

where he who enters is deprived of light, where dust is their sustenance, their food clay, light they see not, in darkness do they sit'' (from "The Descent of Ishtar'' as cited by R. W. Rogers in "State of the Dead [Babylonian],'' *ERE*, p. 828); cf. similar descriptions of the Hebrew Sheol, as in Job 17:13–16: "If I look for Sheol as my house, if I spread my couch in darkness, if I say to the pit, 'You are my father,' and to the worm, 'My mother,' or 'My sister,' where then is my hope? . . . Shall we descend together into the dust?''

22. MS p. 22; cf. Macdonald, "Angel,'' pp. 502–05.

23. Cf. A.b.Ḥ., II, 364 ff.; IV, 287 ff.; Ṭay., Nos. 753, 2389; Nas., XXI, 9; I.M., XXXVII, 31. Common to Persian, Greek, and even Hindu mythology, and taken into medieval Christian thought, is the journey of a hero or saint in some sort of comatose state through the nether and upper worlds to learn of the structure of the universe and the possibilities of the hereafter and to communicate this knowledge to others upon return.

24. Ṭay., p. 102: "The restful soul will come out as a drop in water.''

25. Sometimes the soul is described as already smelling deliciously of musk as it emerges from the body.

26. *Durra,* MS p. 11.

27. The Sidrat al-Muntahá is the name given to the lote-tree in the seventh heaven, whose shade covers the waters and the abode of the blessed; see S 53:14.

28. *Durra,* MS p. 14. The *Kitāb aḥwāl al-qiyāma* and *Kitāb al-ḥaqā'iq wa'l-daqa'iq* develop the above-mentioned visit of the angels to the dying soul before it has departed from the body an make only brief mention of this ascension. The *Bushrá* and the *Durra* neglect the earlier angelic visitation in favor of a more elaborate description of this *mi'rāj*-type journey, which is also detailed in various other accounts such as al-Bagawī's *Mishkāt al-Masābīḥ,* Ibn Qayyim's *Kitāb al-rūḥ,* and al-Ja'farī's *Kitāb al-'ulūm al-fākhira fī al-naẓar fī umūr al-ākhira* (A.H. 1317).

29. *Kitāb al-rūḥ*, p. 59.

30. Ibid.; *Bushrá,* p. 15.

31. Macdonald, "Twilight,'' p. 73; *Kitāb aḥwāl al-qiyāma,* p. 33 (" . . . that it might see what is left behind of its body . . . ''); Ṭay., p. 102 ("Return him to the earth for I have promised that from it We have created them, to it We shall return them, and from it We shall bring them forth again'').

32. *Durra,* MS p. 15. The text continues for several pages describing accounts given to the living by the dead through dreams, in which God and the ascended soul actually engage in rather argumentative conversation concerning the conduct of the departed when still on earth. Al-Ghazālī concludes the section with this summary: "There are some people who, upon finally reaching the Throne, hear the cry, 'Send him back!' Then there are some who are thrust back from the veils of the Throne. Only those who know God reach Him, and

only the people of the fourth station and beyond actually stand before Him" (MS p. 17).

33. See the *Fiqh Akbar II* (Wensinck, *Muslim Creed),* art. 23. Ibn Qayyim, *Kitāb al-rūḥ,* p. 59, raises the question of whether or not the spirit returns to the grave at the time of the questioning and answers it clearly in the affirmative. Eklund comments that "This conception in which the notion of survival after death is thus linked to the human being as a whole—characteristic of Semitic anthropology—is consequently the predominant feature of these traditions" (*Life Between Death and Resurrection,* p. 11). We will consider below ways in which Islamic thinkers have tried to articulate the nature of this relationship between the physical and the non- (or less-) material.

34. P. 33; cf. Macdonald, "Twilight," pp. 73–74.

35. It is certainly not unique in the history of human reflection about questions of justice, judgment, and human responsibility that what appear to be logically inconsistent interpretations are all part of a larger picture. One might look, for example, at the case of ancient Egypt, perhaps the first culture to develop in detail a doctrine of human ethical responsibility as directly related to eschatological judgment. In such a collection of materials as *The Egyptian Book of the Dead* one can see attestations to the importance of magical formulae, the absolute justice administered under the out-spread wings of *maat,* and the need for the individual to profess his innocence to a court of judges at the same time that he is instructed by various means in the proper responses for making his way through the dread hall of double justice.

36. Among the verses that have been considered in this connection are S 6:93, 8:52, 9:102, 14:32, 25:21, 32:21, 40:11, 40:49, 47:29, 52:47, and 71:25.

37. The meaning of the names is unclear, though as verbal forms of *nakira* (not to know, to deny) they might stand for denial and denied, negation and disclaimed, loathesome and shocking.

38. Stanley Lane-Poole, "Death and Disposal of the Dead (Muhammedan)," *ERE*, IV, 547, says that tombs are often constructed with arched roofs so that the corpses can more easily sit up. The period of sitting is sometimes said to be seven days for the faithful and forty for the unfaithful.

39. Macdonald, "Twilight," p. 75.

40. Suyūṭī, *Bushrá*, p. 15; cf. *Kitāb al-rūḥ,* pp. 76 ff.

41. *Kitāb aḥwāl al-qiyāma,* p. 38.

42. The parallelism with the Zorastrian *daēnā* is immediate. The Avesta indicates that every person will meet his own *daēnā* three days after death; the personification there, however, is specifically a woman, either a beautiful young maiden or a horrible old hag, representing the quality of one's deeds done on earth. For a fuller discussion of the import of the word *daēnā* see W. C. Smith, *The Meaning and End of Religion* (1963), pp. 99–100.

43. Cf. S 17:13: {We have fastened the fate of every man on his neck and We

will bring out for him, on the day of resurrection, a book which he will see spread out.}

44. See Chapter One above.

45. Unusual as this may be in the Islamic narratives, however, it has strong parallels with afterlife beliefs in other traditions in which some sort of double-figure related to but not identical with the soul of the individual acts as a guide or helper through the immediate after-death experiences. See, for example, the function of the *ka* in ancient Egyptian texts and the *daēnā* in Zoroastrian lore.

46. In the *Kitāb al-rūḥ* (p. 78) we read that people on horseback often avoid the graves of Jews and Christians and *munāfiqūn* "because the horses hear the punishment of the graves ... and are afraid." Some sources relate that the Prophet, too, could hear these shrieks: "The Prophet said, 'It is certain enough that such are punished in their graves, and if I were not afraid that you would leave off burying, verily I would call on God to give you the power of hearing what I now hear'" *(Mishkāt*, I, 39).

47. al-Subkī, *Shifā'*, p. 148.

48. Suyūṭī, *Bushrá,* pp. 33–34. See the *Kitāb al-rūḥ,* p. 82, for references to the pressure of the tomb, as well as the lengthy discussion on pp. 83–132 of the general subject of recompense in the grave.

49. Of course one can find traditions which also describe punishments taking place until the eschaton. Eklund discusses the variations on this idea *(Life Between Death and Resurrection,* pp. 46–47), saying that some have felt that grave sinners would be punished continuously until the resurrection and less serious sinners for a much shorter time.

50. For a more detailed historical and textual analysis of these developments see Gardet, *Dieu et la Destinée de l'Homme,* pp. 253–57.

51. Gardet, pp. 248–49, describes the position of 'Abd al-Jabbār, who, while negating the possibility of suffering in the tomb immediately after death, did admit its possibility during the time between the two trumpet blasts at the resurrection.

52. Macdonald, "Twilight," p. 82.

53. "Another [of the dead] was seen [in a dream] and was asked what God had done to him, and he said, 'The washer who washed me [at death] handled me roughly, lacerating me on a nail sticking out of the washingroom, and I have suffered from it'." *(Durra,* MS p. 28).

54. One finds this particularly in the exegesis of S 39:42, which says that God, who takes the souls on both occasions, returns them when the sleeper awakes. See, e.g., the modern *tafsīrs* of Maḥmūd Ḥamza (XXIV, 11–12), M. Maḥmūd Ḥijāzī (XXIV, 7), and Tanṭāwī Jawharī (XVIII, 161). Ibn Qayyim, *Kitāb al-rūḥ,* p. 42, elaborates at length the similarity of the sleep and death conditions, suggesting that the *rūḥ* of the sleeper ascends to God, who speaks to it and gives it permission to do prostration [*sujūd*] if it is pure.

55. Macdonald, "Twilight," p. 75.

56. *'Uqalā' al-majānīn,* p. 128, as cited in Margaret Smith, *Rābi'a the Mystic* (1928), p. 28.

57. Although not suggested in the Qur'ān, this idea finds support in a great many reliable *ḥadīths*.

58. *Kitāb aḥwāl al-qiyāma,* pp. 43–44; Macdonald, "Preliminaries, " pp. 151–52.

59. *Kitāb aḥwāl al-qiyāma,* p. 43.

60. Macdonald, "Preliminaries," p. 152. Note the implied distinction between soul and body not only in the description itself but in the mention of weeping "for me and for you."

61. See J. I. Smith, "Concourse Between the Living and the Dead in Islamic Eschatological Literature," *History of Religions,* 19, no. 3 (1980), 224–36. An obvious exception to this idea is the belief still current in Egypt today that when there is a violent death, such as murder, the spirit becomes an *'ifrīt.* Although people often leave their lights on to deter the restless spirit, there is, according to Egyptian sociologist Sayyid 'Uways, little genuine fear displayed that the dead can actually harm the living. Cf. the report from E. W. Lane's *An Account of the Manners and Customs of the Modern Egyptians* (1833–35), in which he indicates that the fear element is present: "The term efreét' is commonly applied rather to an evil ginnee than any other being; but the ghosts of dead persons are also called by this name; and many absurd stories are related to them; and great are the fears which they inspire. There are some persons, however, who hold them in no degree of dread" (p. 311). See Appendix A for a discussion of such beliefs in pre-Islamic Arabia.

62. *Kitāb aḥwāl al-qiyāma,* p. 44.

63. *Kitāb al-rūḥ,* pp. 6–7.

64. See Eklund, *Life Between Death and Resurrection,* p. 10, for a discussion of these narratives.

65. *Kitāb al-rūh,* p. 28. Ibn Qayyim cites many pages of traditions relating experiences in which the spirit of the sleeper meets the spirits of the dead—his friends, relatives, and others.

66. In the *Kitāb aḥwāl al-qiyāma,* for instance, we read that the dwelling place of the spirit, whether it is said to be among the people of the Garden or the Fire, is in one of the holes of the Trumpet which will announce the coming of the Hour (there being enough holes to accommodate all living creatures), or that the spirits of believers are in the beaks of green birds in 'Iliyīn and of *kāfirs* in the beaks of black birds in the Fire.

67. The Bayt al-Ma'mūr, literally the well-populated house, refers to the Ka'ba (see S 52:4) or the celestial archetype of the earthly Ka'ba. See Appendix B for a discussion of the guardianship of Abraham over the souls of children who have died.

68. Different narratives of the *mi'rāj* journey of Muḥammad suggest varying placements of the prophets in the seven heavens.

69. al-Ghazālī refers to these not by name but respectively as the Friend *(al-khalīl),* the Spokesman *(al-kalīm),* the Spirit *(al-rūḥ),* the Chosen *(al-safīy),* and the Beloved *(al-ḥabīb).*

70. Pp. 46–47. This interesting idea that the souls are returned to the bodies during the night reflects a belief common to many religious traditions that spirits who had been in some sense present near their former surroundings during the night depart when the day breaks.

71. *Kitāb al-rūḥ,* pp. 48 ff.

72. The term often used for soul in this tradition is *nasama,* as in "the *nasama* of the *mu'min* goes on the earth wherever it wishes" (pp. 135, 161).

73. The spirits of the martyrs are said to be in green birds near the Throne, coming and going from the meadows of the Garden, greeting their Lord each morning (p. 137).

74. See note 27 above.

75. Eklund, *Life Between Death and Resurrection,* p. 39, says of such references to Barhūt that they are examples of "local traditions undoubtedly pagan in source."

76. See the *Durra,* MS p. 29: "Another [of the dead] came to his son while he was sleeping and he said, 'O my son, repair the place where your father sleeps, for the rain has damaged it.' So when morning came he sent someone to his father's grave and he found that a little water had come upon it from a river and the tomb was filled with water."

77. Sayyid 'Uways in his study of modern Egyptian beliefs concerning death and afterlife (*al-Khulūd fī ḥayāt al-Miṣriyīn al-mu'āṣirīn* [1972]) says that the practice of the living praying for the dead is an inextricable part of the Islamic cultural heritage, as is the idea that the dead also pray. It is commonly held that one gains a kind of merit by praying over the dead, and that all but unbelievers should have prayers said over them.

78. Numerous traditions support the idea that the dead are punished as a direct result of being mourned; see, e.g. A.b.H., I, 26, 36, 41 ff.; II, 31, 38, 134–35; IV, 39, 57, 78 ff.; Ṭay., Nos. 15, 33, 42, 855; Mu., XI, 16–38; Tir., VIII, 23–25.

79. *Kitāb aḥwāl al-qiyāma*, p. 30.

80. Ibid.; cf. Macdonald, "Twilight," p. 67.

81. *Kitāb aḥwāl al-qiyāma*, p. 30; cf. Macdonald, "Twilight," p. 68.

82. Macdonald, "Twilight," pp. 66–67.

83. *Kitāb aḥwāl al-qiyāma*, p. 30.

84. This idea is not unique to Islam; Zoroastrian lore even posits a river in the world of the hereafter composed of the tears shed by the living over the departed. The passage over this river is made increasingly difficult for the de-

ceased at the time of resurrection in relation to the amount of lamentation done by those on earth.

85. *Durra*, MS p. 30.

86. MS pp. 31–32. He assures us that the Zindiqs deny this, which he no doubt mentions to give strength to his own argument.

87. P. 28; cf. Macdonald, "Twilight," pp. 63–64.

CHAPTER THREE

1. The following creeds make mention of one or more of the particulars assigned to the period beginning with the signs of the Hour and leading through the specific events of judgment: al-Ṭahāwī, *'Aqîdat al-sunna wa'l-jamā'a* (Elder, *The Macdonald Presentation Volume,* pp. 134–44); the *Waṣiyat Abî Ḥanîfa* and *Fiqh Akbar II* (Wensinck, *Muslim Creed*); the *Sharḥ al-'aqā'id al-Nasafîya* (Elder, *Commentary*); al-Ash'arī's *Maqālāt* and *Ibāna* (McCarthy, *Theology*).

2. John Macdonald comments that "The emphasis in Islam's sister religions on the suddenness of the Day is perhaps greater than it is in Islamic teaching, where there is more emphasis on its functions" ("The Day of Resurrection," p. 138).

3. Cf. S 7:180, 31:34, 41:47, 43:85, 53:58.

4. The silence of the Qur'ān on the question of when the eschaton will arrive, of course, has not discouraged some writers from speculation. The Prophet is supposed to have said that the end of the world will come 200 years after the *hijra*, although this can as easily be understood to be 200,000 years (al-Barzinjī, *al-Ishā'a li-ishrāṭ al-sā'a* [A.H. 1374], p. 68). Cf. A.b.Ḥ., II, 88, 369.

5. See Shinya Makino, *Creation and Termination (1970),* pp. 32–35.

6. Pp. 70–75. See below for contemporary expressions of some of these same fearful expectations.

7. II, 1136. For other traditions specifying the degradation of that time see Bu., XCII, 22; A.b.Ḥ, I, 384 ff., IV, 391 ff.; VI, 26 ff.; Tir., XXXI, 17, 73.

8. Richard Bell, *The Origin of Islam in its Christian Environment* (1926), pp. 201–02, in arguing for a Christian influence on Islamic eschatology, says, "That there will be dissensions and civil wars among Moslems before the end comes is probably a deduction from the actual course of events. But the idea of the *harj*, the great slaughter which will come at the end of the world, has suggestive similarity with Christian chiliastic beliefs. . . ."

9. *al-Ishā'a*, p. 89.

10. For fuller descriptions see al-Suyūṭī, *al-Durar al-ḥisān*, p. 14; al-Barzinjī, *al-Ishā'a*, p. 105; *Mishkāt*, II, 1144; A. J. Wensinck and B. Carra deVaux, "al-Dadjdjāl," *SEI*, p. 67; cf. Mu., III, 89–91; Ṭay., No. 865; A.b.Ḥ., VI, 283ff.

11. Genesis 10:2; Ezekiel 38:2, 39:6, I Cor. 1:5; Rev. 20:8.

12. S 18:94, 21:96. Bell, *Origin,* p. 202, says that their specific mention in the Qur'ān suggests that they were an earlier part of the Islamic understanding than the beast of the earth.

13. Macdonald, "The Day of Judgment," p. 40, discusses the Gog and Magog legend in Jewish, Christian, Samaritan, and Islamic sources.

14. Cf. *Mishkāt,* II, 1143.

15. Al-Barzinjī's description of Yājūj and Mājūj, reflecting the general orientation of the traditional material, portrays them as tall like cedar trees, extremely wide and cubeshaped, having tiny eyes and ears so large they use one for a pillow and one for a blanket (pp. 152–53). He reflects a certain ethnic bias in suggesting that they have wide faces and may be of Turkish origin.

16. Because of the peculiarites of the Arabic, this verse can be (and has been) interpreted variously to refer to 'Īsá as a sign (*'ālam*) of the Hour and to the Qur'ān itself as the knowledge (*'ilm*) that the Hour is coming.

17. Cf. A.D., XXXVI, 14; Tir., XXXI, 62; A.b.Ḥ., III, 367 ff., IV, 216 ff.

18. Macdonald, "The Day of Judgment," p. 41.

19. R. A. Nicholson, *A Literary History of Islam* (1962), p. 216; Bell, *Origin*, pp. 205–07; cf. Margoliouth, "Mahdi," *ERE* VIII, 337: ". . . the only Mahdi to be awaited was 'Isa b. Maryam, i.e. the Christian Savior; and, since orthodox Islam looks forward to His returning to judge the world—according to the law of Muhammad—it is not quite easy to find room for another Deliverer."

20. Margoliouth, p. 337.

21. *The Muqaddimah* (1958), II, 142/156 (tr. F. Rosenthal); see pp. 156–200, for a complete discussion of this subject.

22. For an interesting consideration of early Shī'ī *mahd*ism see W. M. Watt, "The Muslim Yearning for a Saviour: Aspects of Early 'Abbasid Shī'ism" in *The Savior God*, ed. S. G. F. Brandon (1963). Also see A. Abel, "Changements politiques et littérature eschatologique dans le monde musulmane," *Studia Islamica,* 2 (1954), esp. 31 ff.

23. Barzinjī, for example, says that he will be between thirty and forty years old and provides an abundance of minutia including that he will have a mole on the end of his nose (*al-Ishā'a*, pp. 87 ff.). Cf. A.b.Ḥ., III, 21 ff., 26 ff.; Tir., XXXI, 52; I.M., XXXVI, 34 for further descriptions.

24. Having cited many pages worth of *ḥadīths*, Ibn Khaldūn concludes: "These are all the traditions published by the religious authorities concerning the Mahdi and his appearance at the end of time. One has seen what they are like. Very few are above criticism" (*Muqaddimah*, II, 163/184).

25. See note 1 above.

26. In Arabic *al-ṣūr, al-ba'th*, and *al-ḥashr*. The term *qiyāma* or resurrection has come to signify the entire series of events to take place on that day,

although technically *al-sā'a* means the actual hour, *al-qiyāma* means the literal rising up at the resurrection, *ba'th* signifies the calling forth for judgment, *ḥashr* means the specific gathering together, and *al-ma'ād* (the return) is the general term used by theologians for the entire process.

27. *Kitāb aḥwāl al-qiyāma*, pp. 49–50.

28. The trumpet is called *al-ṣūr* in S 6:73, 23:101, 39:68, and 69:13 and *al-naqūr* in 74:8.

29. Pp. 54–55. Cf. Abū'l-Layth al-Samarqandī: "Then God commands [the Angel of Death] to seize his own spirit. He comes to a place between the Garden and the Fire, and casts his gaze up to heaven. Then he withdraws his spirit and utters a loud cry, which, were all the creatures still alive, they would die for (hearing) it!" (Macdonald, "The Day of Resurrection," p. 148).

30. While this kind of total extinction makes a neat theological category and in fact was the understanding of the early community, it is also true that with the passing of time various traditions and commentaries did come to suggest that some elements would be exempt from the complete annihilation or the *fanā'*, always according to the will of God. Included in that category were the Throne, the Guarded Tablet, the Pen, sometimes the Garden and the Fire, the prophets (along with the martyrs, who are assured a place in the Garden in the Qur'ān), and the *ḥūr* or maidens of the Garden. Later theology even posited that human spirits will not perish at the *fanā'* but will remain, along with the top of the spine, from which the resurrected body begins its growth. Cf. Gardet, *Dieu*, pp. 264–65.

31. *Durra*, MS pp. 40–41.

32. According to some traditions the tail-bone is the only part of the human anatomy that will not suffer the natural disintegration of the body in the grave (*Mishkāt*, II, 1165; cf. Mu. LVII, 142–43).

33. The rock of the Temple of Jerusalem, over which the Dome of the Rock was built.

34. See al-Ghazālī's *Tahāfut al-falāsifa*, Problem XX, "Refutation of their Denial of the Resurrection of Bodies" (tr. S. A. Kamali, [1963]), in which al-Ghazālī replies point by point to objections raised by Muslim philosophers to the fact of physical resurrection. This position was countered by Ibn Rushd in his *Tahāfut al-tahāfut*, in which he contends that only the soul survives the death of the physical body.

35. Ash'arī theology taught that the resurrection of the body is not an element of faith common to Judaism, Christianity, and Islam, but that it was revealed in its full understanding for the first time in the Qur'ān.

36. *Durra*, MS p. 45.

37. Macdonald "Day of Resurrection," pp. 149, 151.

38. *Kitāb aḥwāl al-qiyāma*, pp. 59–60; cf. Macdonald, "Day of Resurrection," pp. 159–60.

39. *Mishkāt*, II, 1168–69, as cited from Ibn 'Abbās; cf. Mu., LI, 56–58;

A.b.Ḥ., I, 220, 223; III, 495. To this is often appended the *ḥadīth* relating 'Ā'isha's question to the Prophet whether or not this means that men and women will be staring at each other undressed, to which replied that they will have other concerns than nudity on that day.

40. MS p. 48, in reference to S 66:8.

41. The *Mishkāt*, II, 1170, quotes Būkharī and Muslim: "On the day of resurrection mankind will sweat to such an extent that their sweat will penetrate the earth seventy cubits, and it will cover their mouths, reaching to their ears."

42. Cf. A.b.Ḥ., III, 16; Ṭay., pp. 289–90.

43. The Arabic of this verse begins, "*yawma yukshifu 'an sāqin* . . .," which in the Pickthall translation is rendered "On the day when it befalleth in earnest. . . ."

44. Dā., XX, 83; Ṭay., No. 2179; A.b.Ḥ., III, 16 ff.

45. Some authoritative traditions suggest that 70,000 (a mystical number occurring in a variety of contexts in Islamic eschatology) will not have to face the reckoning, but this, of course, is nowhere substantiated by the Qur'ān.

46. Based on S 80:11–15; 82:10–12; 87:7, 18.

47. {We have fastened the fate of every individual on his neck and We will bring out for him, on the day of resurrection, a book which will spread out.}

48. See, e.g. Gardet, *L'Islam, Religion et Communauté* (1970).

49. See especially the modern commentaries of Ḥijāzī (XXV, 15–16), al-Qāsimī (XIV, 5235), al-Khaṭīb (XIII, 37), and 'Īsá (p. 641).

50. The idea of a bridge crossing to the underworld has found expression in a number of different religious traditions: "In the lower world of Shades will there not be a bridge to be crossed, a bridge spanning the dark stream of death, nay, it may be, the very mouth of hell itself? The idea became a fixed belief in nations far sundered geographically" (Knight, "Bridge," *ERE*, II, 852).

51. ". . . pursued by the malevolence of the evildoer Wrath who bears a bloody spear, (the soul) will come to the Bridge of the Requiter, lofty and dreadful, for thither must saved and damned alike proceed." *Dāstan-i Mēnōk-i Krat*, tr. R. C. Zaehner, as cited by S. G. F. Brandon, *The Judgment of the Dead* (1967), p. 158. The Chinvat Bridge is referred to many times in both Avestan and Pahlavi literature.

52. See, e.g. al-Suyūṭī, *al-Durar* (p. 19): "The *ṣirāṭ* is finer than a hair and sharper than a sword; on its edges are metal hooks that grab onto one. If a person falls it involves a 3000 year journey—1000 climbing back up, another 1000 trying to travel along the bridge, and again another falling down."

53. A.b.Ḥ., II, 533 ff.

54. A.b.Ḥ., I, 334 ff.; V, 189 ff.; VI, 409 ff.; Mu., XLIII, 33–38; Ṭay., Nos. 995, 1969, 2135; I.M., XXXVII, 36.

55. *Iḥyā'*, IV, 378.

56. *Shifā'*, p. 163.

57. Makina ("The Structure of the Retribution" in *Creation and Termination*) observes that even in the Qur'ān, while retribution for evil accords exactly with the nature of the wrongs committed, God always adds something in reward to the good works so that in effect the good, by God's mercy, get more than their due (S 19:78–79, 4:22).

58. In the concluding description of the day of resurrection given by al-Ghazālī in the *Durra* one finds that even the Qur'ān and Islam are personified so as to be able to call on God's mercy for as many souls as possible: "On the day of resurrection the messengers will be on their thrones, and the Prophets and the *'ulamā'* will be on smaller thrones somewhat below them. The throne of each messenger will be in proportion to his rank or standing. The *'ulamā'* who have performed well will be on seats of light; the martyrs and the virtuous, such as the Qur'ān readers and those who give the call to prayer, will be on a mound made of musk. . . . It is even said that the Qur'ān itself comes on the day of resurrection in the form of a man with a beautiful face and figure. He seeks permission to intercede, and it is granted. In the same way Islam comes to argue its cause, and is victorious. . . . After it has pleaded its case, God joins whomever He wills to it, and Islam leads them to the Garden" (MS p. 107).

59. II, 1186 from Bukhārī and Muslim.

60. Cf. Macdonald, "Paradise," pp. 36–41.

61. Analysis of the Qur'ān reveals that the more detailed and seemingly natural descriptions of paradise as well as the rather gruesome details of the Fire predominate in the (chronologically) earlier portions, while the Medinan Suras indicate less concern with these kinds of particulars.

62. "The real explanation," suggests A. A. Bevan ("The Beliefs of Early Mohammedans Respecting a Future Existence," *Journal of Theological Studies* [October, 1904], p. 26), "seems to be that at first the idea of a future retribution was absolutely new, both to Mohammed himself and to the public which he addressed. Paradise and Hell had no traditional associations, and the Arabic language furnished no religious terminology for the expression of such ideas; if they were to be made comprehensible at all, it could only be done by means of precise descriptions, of imagery borrowed from earthly affairs."

63. *Jahnnam* is used seventy-seven times, *jaḥīm* twenty-five, *sa'īr* sixteen, *saqar* four, *ḥuṭāma twice, and hāwiya* and *laẓā* each once. See the analysis of these appellations by Thomas O'Shaughnessy, "The Seven Names for Hell in the Qur'ān," *Bulletin of the School of Oriental and African Studies,* 25 (1961), 444–65.

64. A.b.Ḥ., IV, 14, 185 ff.

65. From the Greek version of the original Hebrew Ge-Hinnōm, a valley

near Jerusalem where in early times human sacrifices were made to the god Moloch (Macdonald, "The Day of Judgment," p. 51).

66. For a full collection of *ḥadīths* describing the structure of the Fire and the torments of the damned see Soubhi El-Saleh, *La Vie Future Selon le Coran*, chap. 2.

67. A.b.Ḥ., III, 25 ff.; Ṭay., No. 2643.

68. See S 74:30, which lists them as nineteen in number. The *Kitāb aḥwāl al-qiyāma* (p. 92) describes these angels in the following way: "The angel of the Fire has as many hands and feet as there are people in the Fire. With each foot and hand he makes [those whom he wants] stand and sit and puts them in shackles and chains. When he looks at the Fire, the Fire consumes itself in fear of the angel. . . ."

69. On this subject see the interesting comments of Fritz Meier, "The Ultimate Origin and the Hereafter in Islam," *Islam and its Cultural Divergence,* ed. G. L. Tikku (1971), pp. 101–03.

70. ". . . les auteurs musulman qui ont décrit les peines de l'enfer (il s'agit surtout, rappelons-le, des traditionnistes et commentateurs du Coran), ont décrit avant tout d'atroces peines du sens" (Gardet, *Dieu*, p. 330).

71. As Soubhi El-Saleh comments, the Qur'ān allows one to fantasize, but the traditions, with their insistence on a plethora of detail, do not.

72. Five descriptions are used in conjunction with Janna, singular or plural: the garden of eternity [*al-khuld*] (S 25:15), the gardens of Firdaws (S 18:107), the gardens of refuge [*al-ma'wan*] (S 32:19), the gardens of bliss [*al-na'īm*] (S 5:65), and the gardens of Eden (S 9:72). Two are in conjunction with *dār,* abode: abode of peace [*salām*] (S 6:127) and abode of repose [*qarār*] (S 40:39); the last is *'iliyīn* (S 83:18).

73. See B. Carra de Vaux, "Djanna," *SEI*, p. 88.

74. Scholars differ as to whether or not the intent of the Qur'ān is to equate the Garden of Eden with the Garden of eternal felicity awarded to the righteous.

75. Gardet (*Dieu*, p. 335) cites the view of Bājūrī (*Ḥāshiya*, p. 107) that this was the majority opinion.

76. All of the names are Qur'ānic, although they are not specified there as four rivers. See S 76:5 on the water of Kāfūr, of which the righteous shall drink; 83:27–28 on the waters of Tasnīm drunk by those brought near to God; 76:18 on the water of a spring named Salsabīl; and 108:1, which speaks only of abundance [*kawthar*]. The last is sometimes applied to a river running through the Garden and sometimes to the *ḥawḍ* of the Prophet Muḥammad.

77. See Soubhi El-Saleh (*La Vie Future*, chap. 1, pt. 3), who cites numerous traditions describing these gates. He categorizes them respectively as the gates of (1) prayer, (2) holy war, (3) almsgiving, (4) fasting, (5) repentance, (6) self-control, (7) submission, and (8) the door reserved for those whose entry

to Paradise will be without preliminary judgment. Al-Samarqandī (Macdonald, "Paradise," p. 343) gives a similar classification, although the order and some of the particulars differ; cf. *Kitāb aḥwāl al-qiyāma,* pp. 105–106, which presents the same description.

78. Carra de Vaux ("Djanna," *SEI*, p. 88) comments, apparently somewhat insensitive to the Muslim view of the divine origin of the Qur'ān, that "All these descriptions are quite clearly drawn pictures and seem to be inspired by the art of painting. Muhammad or his unknown teacher must have seen Christian miniatures or mosaics representing the gardens of Paradise and have interpreted the figures of angels as being those of young men or young women."

79. Some texts indicate that Riḍwān is the name of the guardian of paradise who receives the faithful into the Garden.

80. "A crier will call, 'You will have the privilege of being healthy and never ailing, you will have the privilege of living and never dying, you will have the privilege of retaining your youth and never becoming decrepit, you will have the privilege of being in affluent circumstances and never being destitute" *(Mishkāt, II,* 1198).

81. Macdonald, "Paradise," p. 349. Cf. *Mishkāt,* II, 1201: "The inhabitants of paradise will enter paradise hairless, beardless, with their eyes anointed with collyrium, aged thirty or thirty-three years."

82. For Western analyses of this question see Richard Bell, "The Men on the A'raf," *Muslim World,* 22 (1932), 43–48; Louis Gardet, *Dieu*, pp. 330–34; Tor Andrae, *Les Origins*, p. 85; Rudi Paret, "Al-A'rāf," *EI* (New Ed.), I, pt. 1–10, pp. 603–04; Asin Palacios, *Islam and the Divine Comedy,* pp. 81 ff.

83. See al-Ṭabarī, *Jāmi' al-bayān*, VIII, 188–97; al-Rāzī, *Tafsīr*, IV, 86–90.

84. One of the fullest listings of possibilities is that of al-Qurṭubī quoted by al-Sha'rānī in *Mukhtaṣar* (pp. 62–63), most of whose suggestions are included in the categories treated by al-Ṭabarī and al-Rāzī.

85. Cf. *Tafsîr al-Rāzî*, IV, 87.

86. Contemporary commentators, while occasionally citing other views in reference to the companions of the *a'rāf*, are virtually unanimous in saying that they are those whose good and bad deeds are equal and who must remain the last to enter the Garden. (One apparent exception to this is al-Qāsimī, VII, 2691–92, who inclines toward the interpretation that because *A'rāf* means the loftiest part, these folk are to be understood as the best of the *mu'minūn*, such as the martyrs, prophets, etc.) The principle of divine justice is underscored in the insistence that recompense is exact and in the implicit recognition that God will not unfairly punish or unduly reward. See, e.g. Khafājī, VIII, 119–20; 'Ammār, I, 170; Wajdī, p. 199; Marāghī, IX, 159; Ḥamza, VIII, 90–92. Al-Jammāl, II, 988, summarizes all the opinions of the traditional commentators into three groups, saying that the *rijāl* are (1) those

whose good and bad deeds are equal, (2) the children of deficient parents, and (3) prophets, martyrs, and the pious. The whole passage, says Ḥizāzī, points to the fact that every person deserves the recompense of his work with accuracy (VIII, 59). As justice is always seen to be tempered with (or, more exactly, fulfilled through) mercy, however, the verse provides the opportunity to expand on this twin aspect of the divine in relation to ultimate recompense. Thus, says al-Khaṭīb, "These men are similar to observers (or arbiters) witnessing from a place between two opposing groups. They look first at one group, then at the other, and they are in a circumstance of wonder and perplexity, of happiness and affliction, of hope and fear. It is a kind of punishment that is touched by the kindness of God, and the mercy of God surrounds them" (IV, 405).

87. Cf. *Mishkāt,* II, 1185–86.

88. *Waṣīyat Abī Ḥanīfa*, art. 18 and *Fiqh Akbar II*, art. 21 (Wensinck, *Muslim Creed*); al-Ṭahāwī, *'Aqīda* (Elder, "al-Ṭahāwī's 'Bayān . . .,' " p. 141); al-Nasafī, *'Aqīda* (Elder, *Commentary*, p. 105); al-Ash'arī, *Ibāna*, art. 53 and *Maqālāt*, art. 51 (McCarthy, *Theology*).

89. As al-Taftazānī comments on this article in the creed of al-Nasafī: ". . . as for what has been said about the Garden and the Fire being destroyed even though for a moment in order to verify the statement of Allah that 'Everything perishes except His face' (Qur'ān 28:88): this meaning is not inconsistent with their abiding. You well know that there is nothing in the verse to indicate passing away" (Elder, *Commentary*, p. 106).

90. The commonest Qur'ānic expression of this is *"hum fīhā khālidūn."* they are in it eternally, which occurs in descriptions of the inhabitants of both the Garden and the Fire.

91. There were, of course, some exceptions to this, such as the followers of Jahm ibn Ṣafwān, who denied the eternality of both the Garden and the Fire.

92. ". . . a doctrine of purgatory was required in Islam," says D. B. Macdonald, "and . . . it duly appeared. Mohammed himself had not, I think reached any such idea; but the complex of facts which he recognized led to it of necessity" ("Immortality in Mohammedanism," p. 311).

93. Gardet, *Dieu*, p. 329.

94. See Chapter One above.

95. *Waṣīyat Abī Ḥanīfa*, art. 20 (Wensinck, *Muslim Creed*).

96. *Fiqh Akbar II,* art. 21.

97. This view, as we shall see, is held by a number of contemporary Muslim thinkers. James Robson, in "Is the Moslem Hell Eternal?", *Muslim World,* 28 (1938), p. 392, argues against Muhammad 'Ali's insistence that this is the true Islamic understanding. "It is clearly taught in Tradition," he says, "as also in the Koran, that for some Hell will serve the purpose of the Roman

Catholic Purgatory, but it is not taught, as Muhammad Ali would have us believe, that this applies to everyone."

98. The pardon of the people of the Fire is attested to in the creeds of al-Ṭahāwī, al-Ash'arī (*Maqālāt* and *Ibānā*), and al-Nasafī.

99. *Mishkāt*, II, 1206.

100. See Izutsu, *The Concept of Belief in Islamic Theology*, for a discussion of the ways in which both the Mu'tazila and the "orthodox" Muslims used this issue as a means of accusing the other group of *takfīr*.

101. al-Ṭahāwī (Elder, "al-Ṭahāwī's 'Bayān . . .,' " p. 135).

102. *Fiqh Akbar II*, art. 17 (Wensinck, *Muslim Creed*); cf. *Waṣīyat Abī Ḥanīfa*, art. 24, which describes the meeting of God with the inhabitants of paradise, and the *Maqālāt* and *Ibāna* of al-Ash'arī (McCarthy, *Theology*, p. 242).

103. Soubhi El-Saleh, *La Vie Future*, chap. 1, pt. 4.

104. Ibid., chap. 1, pt. 7. Cf. *Mishkāt*, II, 1202–03, recognized as a *gharīb* (obscure) tradition.

CHAPTER FOUR

1. *al-Yawm al-ākhir fī ẓilāl al-Qur'ān* (1975), pp. 81–82.

2. See Muḥammad 'Abd al-Ẓāhir Khalīfa, an inspector at the Azhar, whose book *Kitāb al-dār al-barzakhīya* offers more material on the *barzakh* than is found in most modern writings. He takes this opportunity to repeat the old Ghazālīan story about Iblīs accompanied by certain Shayṭāns in the image of the dying person's mother and father coming to tempt him to convert to Judaism or Christianity (pp. 19–20), as well as other satanic tricks perpetrated on the dying person. He describes 'Izrā'īl as either great and frightening to the *kāfir* or gentle and careful with the souls of the pious (pp. 30–33). Reviving the tradition about the drop of soil in each mother's womb, he tells us that each person will be buried in the earth from which he was originally created (p. 52).

3. Fā'iz, *al-Yawm*, pp. 89–90; Khalīfa, *Kitāb al-dār al-barzakhīya* (1973), p. 191.

4. These questions, says Muḥammad 'Awwād, will be asked of every dead person though he be inside the belly of a fish or a lion (unless he is one of the exempt such as the prophets or the angels) (*Ḥayāt al-Islām* [n.d.], p. 50).

5. Fā'iz, *al-Yawm*, pp. 87–88; Khalīfa, *al-Dār*, p. 191.

6. 1964, pp. 67–71. This work is the commentary on a creed entitled *Tiḥfat al-murīd 'alá jawharat al-tawḥīd*.

7. Muḥammad Kamāl al-Dīn al-Adhamī calls it "the science of those who are good and those who are bad at the time of death," quoting a tradition from Tirmidhī about God's mercy or wrath reflecting itself in the dying process (*Kitāb al-tadhkīr li'l-marji' wa'l-maṣīr* [A.H. 1349], p. 23).

8. " 'Uthmān b. Affān used to stop by the graves and cry until his beard became wet. [Someone] said to him, 'You remember the Garden and the Fire and do not cry and you remember the grave and you cry.' He replied, 'I heard the Prophet say, The grave is the first abode of the abodes of the hereafter. If one is saved from it, then what follows is easier. If one is not saved from it, then what follows is worse' " (Fā'iz, *al-Yawm*, p. 87).

9. See, e.g. Bayjūrī, *Sharḥ*, p. 65; Muṣṭafá Muḥammad al-Ṭayr, *Hādī al-arwāḥ* (1971), pp. 25–30.

11. See below in this chapter for a discussion of spiritualist interpretation of this frequently reiterated notion.

12. "What you do to a dead body is felt by the body the same as if he were alive," says al-Adhamī, *Kitāb al-tadhkīr*, pp. 45–46.

13. *al-Dār*, p. 29.

14. *al-Dār,* pp. 20–21. On pp. 272 ff. he suggests a number of things the living can do to facilitate the circumstances of the dead, such as fasting, reading the Qur'ān, visiting the grave, etc. He reiterates the old theme that too much lamenting and weeping actually disturb the dead.

15. *Hādī al-arwāḥ*, p. 33.

16. The Egyptian sociologist Sayyid 'Uways *(al-Khulūd fī al-turāth al-thaqāfī al-Miṣrī)* has conducted a most interesting survey of contemporary Egyptians from the urban and rural areas representing a wide age range. His findings indicate that the majority of Egyptians apparently continue to hold to most of the traditional ideas about life after death as they have been outlined in the preceding chapter. Of those polled, the same percentage of persons from city and country (c. 92%) believe that there is some kind of life in the hereafter. Of those raised in the city, 46% affirmed life in the grave, compared with 76% from rural areas or villages. Over 90% of all persons polled said they had duties toward deceased relatives such as participation in the funeral proceedings, visitation during proper seasons, prayer for the dead, and distribution of alms in their names.

17. *Al-Ḥadāra al-Islāmīya* (n.d.), pp. 219–20. Al-Mawdūdī actually represents a somewhat different perspective from that of many others whom we are calling modernists. He is, in fact, a kind of traditionalist-modernist, considered by some to be the *mujaddid* of Islam in the sense of restorer rather than innovator. His aim is to uphold the traditional faith as closely tied to the Qur'ānic teachings as possible (with much less concern for the accumulated traditions than those viewed above as traditionalists) in order to present Islam as God's way for humankind from creation to eternity. His primary concern, then, is to affirm the authenticity and validity of the traditional faith for life in the twentieth century.

18. Muṣṭafá Maḥmūd, *Riḥlat*, p. 29.

19. Muḥammad Zafrullah Khan, *Islam,* p. 187.

20. Muṣṭafá Maḥmūd, *al-Qur'ān*, p. 198.
21. N.d., pp. 127 ff.
22. Khan, *Islam,* p. 184.
23. *Riḥlat,* pp. 39–44.
24. *al-Mawt wa'l-ḥayāt* (1973), pp. 41–42.
25. al-Mawdūdī inverts the usual formula that we need to do justly because we will be recompensed in the hereafter, saying that society needs ethical standards and thus needs a belief in the afterlife to support these standards (*al-Ḥadāra,* p. 226). Cf. Muḥammad al-Mubārak (*Niẓām al-Islām*, pp. 153–55) who compares life to a journey in which the travelers behave in different ways depending on the purpose of the trip. Would man's conduct be the same, he asks, if he believed that there is no afterlife as if he believed he would be punished?
26. Khalaf al-Sayyid 'Alī, Head of the Islamic Research Center at the Azhar, in a private communication in April, 1976 says: "Islam is the *wasaṭ*, both *dîn* and *dunyá,* the way of life for this world as well as for the next." Cf. 'Abd al-Razzāq Nawfal (*Islām dîn wa-dunyá* [n.d.], p. 126), who stresses that extremes are weakening, that Islam is the religion that avoids excesses.
27. *Yawm al-qiyāma*, pp. 162–70.
28. A. M. Muhya al-Dīn Alwaye, "The Belief in the Day of Judgment," *Majallat al-Azhar*, June, 1969, pp. 1–6.
29. *The Religion of Islam* (n.d.), pp. 270–71. Ali broke with the main group of the Aḥmadīya in 1913–14 and established a separate group in Lahore, whose intent has been to remain within the confines of Sunnī orthodoxy.
30. "How will the bliss [take place]? God knows. How will the punishment [take place]? God knows." See above, note 26.
31. *Islam*, pp. 185, 187.
32. *Eschatology in Islam* (1960), p. 32.
33. *The Mind al-Qur'ān Builds* (1952), pp. 58–62.
34. *The Religion of Islam*, I, 241–42.
35. *The Religion of Islam*, II, 227–28.
36. *al-Qur'ān*, p. 175.
37. See, e.g. M. Alwaye, "Life After Death," *Majallat al-Azhar*, Oct., 1973, p. 3; Maulana Muhammad 'Ali, *The Religion of Islam*, pp. 268–69. 'Ali (p. 271) makes reference to a *ḥadîth* which speaks of the righteous being elevated to a higher rank after forty days. This, according to him, is another indication that there is progress even in the state of *barzakh*.
38. See, e.g. Khan, *Islam*, p. 187.
39. *al-Ḥadāra*, pp. 255–56. Mawdūdī sees the universe as based on any idea of moral progression. In the next world, which he calls the next evolutionary stage of the universe, moral rather than physical laws will prevail. See also his *Towards Understanding Islam*, pp. 135 ff. Commenting on the under-

standing of death, Maulana Muhammad 'Ali, *The Religion of Islam*, p. 264, says: "Just as from the small life-germ grows the man, and he does not lose his individuality for all the changes which he undergoes, so from this man is made the higher man, his attributes being changed, and he himself being made to grow into what he cannot conceive at present."

40. *The Mind al-Qur'ān Builds*, p. 65.

41. *Islam*, pp. 186–88.

42. *The Religion of Islam*, p. 271.

43. See Chapter One for a typical example of the attempt to reinterpret Islam from the perspective of the classical understanding of the sub-continent concerning issues of reincarnation.

44. These ideas are particularly espoused in many Western writings on the afterlife, sometimes on theoretical or theological bases influenced by exposure to Eastern religions and sometimes in a more scientific way as based on the experiments of such people as Ian Stevenson of the University of Virginia.

45. *al-Ḥadāra,* pp. 228–35. Cf. his *Towards an Understanding of Islam*, pp. 132–33, and Syed Abdul Latif, *The Mind al-Qur'ān Builds,* p. 64.

46. The Egyptian Muṣṭafá al-Kīk also addresses the question of reincarnation and Islam in his *Tanāsukh al-arwāḥ* (1970). Beginning with a historical survey of various individuals and splinter sects in Islam who have held to the doctrine, he proceeds to refute it as a possible interpretation of any verse of the Qur'ān (such as S 40:11, 42:11, and 53:47). He says that there are some 400 fabricated *ḥadīths* on *tanāsukh* (p. 38), and that actually the idea first came into Islam through Judaism (p. 41) and gained credence by the influence of certain Shī'a sects. The entire book, of course, is a categorical rejection of transmigration as appropriate in any way to the Islamic understanding.

47. Both of their Qur'ān commentaries are devoted to affirming the importance of religious inquiry in the light of scientific investigation. While the modern European scientists have been advancing, says Jawharī, the *umma* of Islam has long been asleep. Those things we call miracles are all explainable by modern science (*al-Jawāhir* [1931–35], II, 163–68).

48. Pointing to what he sees as a persistent human question about the idea of life after death, for example, Mohiaddin Alwaye says that the Qur'ān has dealt with it repeatedly and that "The answer given is quite consistent with scientific knowledge" ("Belief", p. 4). Muṣṭafá Maḥmūd asserts that man knows that he is composed of both body and soul—that he owns an eternal being which transcends disintegration and death—through science, reason, and knowledge (*Riḥlat*, p. 55).

49. See, e.g. 'Abd al-Ṣāḥib al-Muẓaffar, *Nihāyat al-kawn bayn al-'ilm wa'l-Qur'ān* (1967), p. 29.

50. This was particularly evident in the nineteenth-century Egyptian periodical entitled *al-Muqtaṭaf*.

51. A professor at Dār al-'Ulūm and one of the original faculty at Cairo University, Jawharī was demoted because of his spiritualist leanings to a teaching position in a high school, where he stayed until his retirement.

52. *al-Jawāhir*, II, 160–61.

53. Abū'l-Khayr was a professor of biology and director of educational media for the Egyptian Department of Education ('Ubayd, *al-Insān*, p. 206). He translated Findlay's *On the Edge of the Ethereal World* into Arabic, along with several other Western writings. On the basis of Findlay's research he began to experiment in spiritualist healing, the validity of which was attested to by persons from many stations in life.

54. 'Ubayd, *al-Insān*, p. 207.

55. Author of such works as *al-Aḍwā' 'alá'l-rūḥīyah, al-'Ālam al-ghayr al-manẓūr, Arwāḥ mursala, Safīr al-arwāḥ al-'ulyā,* and editor of the journal *'Ālam al-arwāḥ*.

56. Some would see that spiritualism is the legitimate continuation of, and in fact can be equated with, classical Sufism in Islam. What traditionally has been called *kashf* [unveiling] is now called visual and auditory *jalā'* [clarification].

57. "[The discovery of] electricity and the inventions resulting from it have brought the mind closer to understanding the possibility of the transformation of matter into energy and the change of energy into matter. Spiritualism has explained to people something of that about which they have previously been in disagreement; it has helped them to understand the separate existence of the spirit and the possibility of its . . . speed in moving over distances" (al-Maraghī in the introduction to Ḥusayn Ḥaykal's *Ḥayāt Muḥammad*, as cited by 'Ubayd, p. 210).

58. See Muḥammad Muḥammad Ḥusayn, professor of modern Arabic literature at Alexandria University, who goes so far as to say that spiritualism is a glorification and defense of materialistic communism and that one of the sources of the corruption is international Judaism and the Zionist movement, which is using spiritualism as a tool for the destruction of Islam and Christianity (*al-Ḥayāt al-rūḥiya* [1960], pp. 35 ff.).

59. Pp. 36–37. He does affirm that whatever the cause, such healing is compatible with the will of God; otherwise it would not be successful.

60. See Ḥamza, *al-Rūḥīya*, pp. 28–36.

61. See, e.g. his *al-Ḥayāt al-ukhrá* (1965), *al-Islām, dīn wa-dunyá* (n.d.), *As'ila ḥarija* (1970), *Ṭarīq 'ilá Allāh* (1962), and *Yawm al-qiyāma* (1969).

62. *Ṭarīq*, p. 92.

63. *Ḥayāt*, pp. 31–33. He equates the aura, apparently scientifically verifiable, with the light said to be between the hands on the day of resurrection in S 66:8 (*Ṭarīq*, pp. 100–05).

64. *Ḥayāt*, p. 48.

65. *Ḥayāt*, pp. 93–95. This idea of vibration is common to forms of West-

ern spiritualism, in which the spirit body is said to be a replica of the physical body but of a much higher vibration.

66. *Yawm,* pp. 76–87.

67. *al-Insān*, p. 617.

68. *Yawm,* p. 59.

69. As one might suspect, these ideas, which are rather loosely supported both by the scientific proofs he elicits as well as by Qur'ānic references, are sharply attacked by others in the Islamic world. Muṣṭafá al-Kīk incorporates a number of letters he wrote to Nawfal criticizing his theories (as well as those of some other writers) into a book entitled *Rasā'il 'ilayhim*. Here he accuses Nawfal of drawing on his imagination, of inadequately prooftexting his materials from the Qur'ān, and of forming premature conclusions on the basis of too little fact and too much individual interpretation.

70. *Ṭarīq*, pp. 109–10.

71. Ḥamza, *al-Rūḥīya*, pp. 80–90. In a subsequent section Ḥamza describes the familiar silver cord binding the spiritual body to the physical body and providing the body with the means of life. If this thin line of light is severed, death takes place. It is possible, he says, for the soul to materialize in more than one place at a time, giving such examples as someone praying at four different mosques at a single moment (pp. 100 ff.). Cf. 'Abd al-Jalī Rāḍī, *al-Aḍwā' 'alá ruḥīya* (1961), pp. 79–80.

72. Ibid., p. 72. Cf. Muḥammad Ḥassanayn Makhlūf, *Ḥukm al-Islām* (1974), pp. 35–36, who says that the ancients wrote about good and evil spirits, and now we have the evidence to prove that this distinction is valid.

73. In a later section (pp. 189–90) he indicates that this guidance may be in other matters too. Every invention that has appeared on earth appeared first in the *barzakh*, and what is considered genius in this world is nothing but inspiration from the spiritual world. He even goes so far as to claim that "The spirit of Edison has said that it is busy creating a special instrument that will transmit the voices of the people of the *barzakh* to the people on earth, that understanding may become direct without mediation."

74. See, e.g. Nawfal, *Yawm al-qiyāma*, pp. 55, 62; Rāḍī, *al-Aḍwā'*, pp. 79–80; Ḥamza, *Rūḥīya*, pp. 65, 115–29; Ḥamza, *Ma'a'l-fikr al-Islāmi* (1970), pp. 141–47; 'Ubayd, *al-Insān*, pp. 617–18. Kīk, *Rasā'il*, pp. 120–21, attacks Nawfal in particular for suggesting that the Qur'ānic *nafs* should be interpreted as the *rūḥ*, failing to observe that this has been the general practice of exegetes and theologians since well before Ibn Qayyim.

75. Ḥamza, *Ma'a'l-fikr*, p. 142.

76. Sayyid 'Uways, *al-Khulūd*, cites the statistics that of the persons he interviewed in his survey of modern Egyptian beliefs about life after death some 50% said that their dead relatives had visited them in dreams and 12% that they had had communication with their relatives by way of seances.

77. *Ḥayāt*, pp. 75–85.

78. *Ḥayāt*, pp. 80−81.

79. For the full text of the statement see Nawfal, *Ṭarîq*, pp. 118−19; Ḥamza, *Ma'a'l-fikr*, p. 227.

80. Nawfal, *Ḥayāt*, p. 103, says that the angels and relatives remain in a long struggle with the new soul, trying to organize its vibrations and stimulate its knowledge to suit the new environment.

81. 'Ubayd even projects that 4/5 of all earthly marriages are ended and new partners are found in the ethereal world. Even these relationships can end in separation if the partners are unhappy (*al-Insān*, pp. 422−23).

82. Sometimes it is said, however, that the spirits do learn languages and dialects in order to be able to communicate with people on earth.

83. 'Ubayd, *al-Insān*, p. 426.

84. Ḥamza, *Ma'a'l-fikr*, p. 229.

85. *al-Rūḥîya*, p. 161. Cf. al-Ghazālī, *Durra*, MS p. 36. Rāḍī, *al-Aḍwā'*, p. 89, reports that in some instances the spirit of one killed in an accident is unaware that he has died and keeps returning as an *'ifrît*, hoping to resume its old life. In such cases the family of the deceased in the spirit world can be of particular help in aiding the *'ifrît* to overcome its fixation on the accident.

86. *al-Insān*, p. 431. In *Ma'a'l-fikr*, p. 153, Ḥamza says that the halo or aura [*ḥāla*] around the head of the *kāfir* in the *barzakh* is blue-black and that around the *mu'min* is light and bright.

87. *Ḥayāt*, p. 114.

88. *al-Insān*, pp. 424−25.

89. "Spirits say that a soul, upon being resurrected, spends a period in a kind of medical recovery treatment because it is affected by whatever had affected the material body during its life on earth" (Nawfal, *Ḥayāt*, p. 106).

90. From Ḥamza, *al-Rūḥîya*, p. 169.

91. 'Ubayd, *al-Insān*, p. 615.

92. *Ḥayāt*, p. 103.

93. *al-Aḍwā'*, p. 83. Rāḍī also tells of a *shaykh* of an important Sufi order in the Suez who insisted on visiting every mosque in the area (in his coffin) before burial. When thirty soldiers tried to keep him from flying into one mosque, they were all lifted into the air too! (p. 84).

94. One is reminded here of the early Muslim discussions of the nature of the spirit/soul in which that distinguished from the body was still considered to be of a material (though *laṭîf*) nature. See Chapter One above.

95. Ḥamza, *al-Ruḥîya*, p. 64, attempts to shed some light on the *ruḥ/nafs* question when he says: "It is possible to call the ethereal body the *nafs*. If you add to this body or *nafs* the intellect, which is an independent body existent by itself, then you have the *rūḥ*. Thus the *rūḥ* is the ethereal body and intellect joined together."

96. Nawfal, *Ḥayāt*, pp. 107−08, quotes Arthur Findlay as saying that even these thought images are invested with certain qualities resembling the physi-

cal for the enjoyment of the spirits. Thus one can feel and smell the trees and flowers, etc.

97. 'Ubayd, *al-Insān*, pp. 415–16, says that each will choose the work that he enjoys or that is suitable to his artistic or intellectual capacity. One may be engaged in such pursuits as philosophy, literature, languages, natural and social sciences, engineering, chemistry, and medicine (which, he says, is practiced without surgery and is mixed with psychology).

98. Makhlūf, *Ḥukm al-Islām*, p. 19.

99. George Lawton, in *The Drama of Life after Death* (N.Y.: Holt, n.d.) has suggested a series of major common themes with which most Western spiritualist writers seem to agree. Not surprisingly, these reflect to a high degree some of the concerns we have just seen articulated by the modern Muslim spiritualists: (1) there is progress as well as motion upward according to the stages of one's development; (2) the other world is empirically observable with an environment recognizably like our own; (3) the universe is friendly and based on the principle of love; (4) guidance is available from the spirits of loved ones; (5) there is no judgment day, no decisive post-mortem separation into saved and damned and predestination; (6) there is every reason to be optimistic about life after the death of the physical body.

CHAPTER FIVE

1. These are (1) the appearance of the Mahdī, (2) the Dajjāl, (3) the descent of Jesus, son of Mary, (4) the appearance of Yājūj and Mājūj, (5) the Beast who will write "*mu'min*" or "*kāfir*" between the eyes of the deserving, (6) the appearance of the smoke [*dukhkhān*] which will last on earth forty days, (7) the destruction of the Ka'ba by the people of Ethiopia, (8) the death of Jesus, (9) the elevation of the Qur'ān from the rest of the texts, and (10) the decline of all the people of the earth to a state of *kufr* (*Sharḥ al-Bayjūrî*, II, 77).

2. There is no consistent understanding of this beast; it is not usually identified with Dajjāl but is interpreted to be some kind of huge creature who will witness to the unfaithful about the power of God.

3. See, e.g. Khalīfa, *al-Dār*, p. 330–36; Ḥāmid Maḥmūd Līmūd, *Jawhar al-tawḥîd* (1974), p. 49.

4. See the lengthy analysis of Muḥsin 'Abd al-Ṣāhib al-Muẓaffar, *Nihāyat al-kawn bayn al-'ilm wa'l-Qur'ān* (1967), p. 29–125, in which he justifies by scientific theories and findings such Qur'ānic assertions as the stars losing their ability to shine, the sky being torn asunder, and the sun losing its heat.

5. *The Eternal Message of Muḥammad* (1964), p. 271.

6. *Tafṣîl al-nash'a al-thānia* (1973), pp. 39–52.

7. The Aḥmadīya movement has been exempted from the realm of Islamic

orthodoxy since it was declared by the state to be a non-Muslim minority in Pakistan following the riots of 1974–75.

8. "Ta'ammulāt fī al-bayān al-Qur'ānī: al-ṣūra al-Qur'ānīya," *Minbar al-Islām,* 33, no. 10 (October, 1975), 17–18.

9. See his *As'ila ḥarija*, for example, where he says that all the commentary about such creatures as the Dajjāl is interpolation, not mentioned in the Qur'ān (pp. 91–92).

10. Muṣṭafá al-Kīk, a harsh critic of Nawfal, attacks him also on this understanding in *Rasā'il ilayhim*, p. 127.

11. *Yawm al-qiyāma*, p. 93. He declines, however, to say whether or not it will come tomorrow, during the present year, or even in this age (p. 96).

12. Maḥmūd, *Qur'ān,* pp. 180–87.

13. Muḥammad 'Awwād, *Ḥayāt al-Islām*, p. 50.

14. Līmūd, *Jawhar al-tawḥīd*, p. 49, agrees that these particulars will be exempted from the *fanā'*, especially the souls/spirits of human beings.

15. Cf. Khalīfa, *Dār,* p. 334: "God will return bodies on the day of resurrection as they were on earth." Bayjūrī, *Sharḥ*, p. 67, agrees: "Bodies will be reconstituted after the day of resurrection identical to the first bodies."

16. See al-Khaṭīb, *al-Tafsîr* (1967–70), XII, 956; Ḥijāzi, *al-Tafsîr* (1962–69), XXIII, 16.

17. See Wajdī, *al-Muṣḥaf* (1968), p. 586.

18. *Ḥayātunā wa'l-maw'id al-majhūl* (1973), pp. 85–97. Cf. 'Ā'isha 'Abd al-Raḥmān, *al-Qur'ān wa-qaḍāya al-insān* (1972), p. 160, who cites S 45:62 as proof of the divine power illustrated in the creation of man. Is He not capable of repeating it?, she asks. Man can kill a fly, as a fly can cause him death, but despite his technological achievements, man cannot create a fly.

19. Taḥmāz affirms the commonly-held notion that the bodies of prophets, martyrs, and saints will be preserved from disintegration in any case. Cf. 'Ammār, *al-Tafsîr* (1970), p. 75: "God . . . will return the specific (original) parts to each person; all things can be integrated and disintegrated, disjoined and joined again."

20. *Yawm*, pp. 117–20. Muṣṭafá al-Kīk, *Rasā'il*, p. 136, takes another opportunity to refute Nawfal by insisting that the resurrected body will be different from the earthly body.

21. *The Religion of Islam,* pp. 281–83.

22. {When we are dead and have turned to dust [shall we be brought back]? That would be a far return}, a saying, as the Qur'ān makes clear in S 50:2, that is from the mouths of the *kāfirūn*.

23. Some who treat eschatological events are content to describe the resurrection in strictly traditional ways with no attempt at interpretation. See, e.g. Līmūd, *Jawhar*, pp. 47–53; Bayjūrī, *Sharḥ*, pp. 82–88; al-Ṣaffār, *al-Ta'ābir al-Qur'ānīya wa'l-bī'a al-'arabīya fī mashāhid al-qiyāma* (1966), chaps. 3–6. One of the most complete catalogues of traditional eschatological events is

the aforementioned work of Aḥmad Fā'iz, *al-Yawm al-ākhir fī ẓilāl al-Qur'ān*.

24. In the second volume of his work Galwash includes a section entitled "Kinds of Spiritual Hell" in which he sees such things as forced separation from worldly things, shame, disappointment, and failure as alternative ways in which punishment may be experienced (pp. 228–30).

25. Prof. Aḥmad Maḥmūd Subḥī of the Faculty of Theology, University of Alexandria, agreed in a private interview in 1976 that theology affirms the resurrection of the body and the sensual description of the Garden and the Fire. Like many contemporaries, however, while insisting that resurrection is a complete re-creation, he was loathe to elaborate on his understanding of the nature of the new body or of what "sensual" means for our present understanding of the eternal abodes.

26. See, e.g. such commentators as al-Jammāl, *al-Tafsīr al-farīd;* al-Khaṭīb, *al-Tafsīr al-Qur'ānī li'l-Qur'ān;* Darwaza, *al-Tafsīr al-ḥadīth;* al-Qāsimī, *Mahāsin al-ta'wil.*

27. *al-Aḍwā' 'alá al-rūḥīya,* p. 49.

28. *al-Insān*, pp. 614–16.

29. *al-Ḥayāt al-ukhrá*, pp. 98–101.

30. *al-Rūḥīya*, pp. 172–76.

31. *The Life and Teachings of Mohammed* (1891), pp. 394, 396.

32. ". . . in the later *suras* we observe a merging of the material in the spiritual, of the body in the soul . . ." (p. 399).

33. *The Mind Al-Qur'an Builds*, pp. 55–58.

34. P. 96. Cf. his *al-Rūḥ wa'l-jasad,* p. 31, in which he says that the Fire exists on many levels—from the actual fire which burns the skin to the other pole in which the pain is psychic.

35. *Niẓām al-Islām*, pp. 152–53.

36. *Tafsīr al-Qur'ān al-karīm,* I, 231–32. Rashīd Riḍā in commenting on 'Abdu's interpretation of the hereafter says the following: "This speech is what *al-ustādh* ['Abdu] said concerning his example of faith in the unseen without earthly analogy. He does not deny that man in the hereafter is a man and not an angel, and that his pleasure is human yet more perfect than what is on the earth. Among these pleasures are eating and drinking and human concourse . . ." (*Tafsīr*, II, 234).

37. *Niẓām al-Islām*, pp. 146–55.

38. *al-Yawm al-ākhir*, p. 187.

39. *Mashāhid al-qiyāma,* p. 36. Cf. 'Antar Aḥmad Ḥishād, "Al-īmān bi-yawm al-ākhar," p. 317.

40. See, e.g. Fā'iz, *al-Yawm,* pp. 241–48; 'Awwād, *Ḥayāt al-Islām*, pp. 51 ff.

41. In a personal interview in April, 1976 Dr. 'Abd al-Wadūd Shalabī, then the Editor of *Majallat al-Azhar*, insisted that the official orthodox understanding is that the intercession of *walīs* is false and not part of Islam, while the

intercession of the Prophet on the day of resurrection is true.

42. "Muḥammad has a special *shafā'a* that other prophets do not have," says al-Bayjūrī, "and only when he is through interceding for his followers will the door of *shafā'a* be opened for the rest of them" *(Sharḥ*, p. 88).

43. *al-Qur'ān*, p. 221. Maḥmūd also affirms in his *Riḥlat* (p. 68) that Gehennah is the ultimate of love [*maḥabba*] since there is no other way to show God's justice. It is a mercy because it reaches those who have refused to learn from all the books and prophets.

44. Ṭanṭāwī Jawharī, *al-Jawāhir,* II, 55.

45. 'Alī did say that if they repent, God will forgive them, as long as it is not a last-minute repentence. If one is on his death bed and the spirit has not yet reached his throat, there is still time; but if it has, it is too late.

46. *Religion,* I, 245.

47. This understanding of God as merciful bears on several issues related to the nature of punishment, of which eternity is only one. In recent interviews with some Egyptian thinkers the authors posed the question of whether or not those who do not know about Islam will be punished (for whatever length of time) for their ignorance. The answer in each instance was a denial of such a possibility according to the mercy of God. Muḥammad Nuwayhī of the American University of Cairo, for example, indicated that in his opinion in 90% of the cases where people have heard the message of Islam it has been in such distorted forms that they could not be blamed for not accepting it. Urging again the significance of divine mercy, he reflected on how much better it is for God to promise wrath and then show mercy than the opposite.

48. al-'Aqqād, *al-Falsafa,* pp. 216–17, says that this view is supported by the many reliable *ḥadīths* illustrating God's mercy in delivering from the Fire those in whose hearts is even an atom of faith.

49. See, e.g. Shaltūt, *al-Islām*, pp. 43–44.

50. See Muḥammad Khān, *Islam*, p. 196.

51. *The Religion of Islam*, p. 314. Cf. Syed Abdul Latif, *The Mind al-Quran Builds,* pp. 58–59, who cites the Qur'ānic suggestion that from "state to state shall ye be carried forward" in support of what he calls the march towards perfection. He makes the interesting point that by the very understanding of *tawḥīd* we cannot but admit the temporary nature of purgation, for otherwise we would have "a multiplicity of undying units possessing or claiming the quality of co-existence in eternity with God. . . ."

52. Fā'iz, *al-Yawm*, p. 239, cites the *ḥadīth* from Abū Hurayra in which the Prophet affirms that God will be seen on the day of resurrection as one can see the sun or moon when there are no clouds.

53. *Yawm al-qiyāma*, p. 44.

54. *al-Yawm*, p. 345.

55. *The Religion of Islam*, pp. 300–03.

56. *Fī al-dīn al-maqāran* (1970), p. 285.

APPENDIX A

1. See Chapter One above for Qur'ānic references to Meccan opposition, as well as brief discussion of the understanding of time and fate in pre-Islamic thought.

2. Jawād 'Alī, *Tārīkh al-'Arab qabl al-Islām* (1956), V, 250–52, discusses, for example, the question of whether or not at least some of the *jāhilī* Arabs believed in resurrection [*ba'th*] and ingathering [*ḥashr*] of bodies after death. Lamenting that we have no solid evidence on this score, he nonetheless states: "If it is true as reported that the people of the *jāhilīya* believed in the *ba'th* and *ḥashr*, it is not farfetched to say that those who believed in it saw judgment similar to the judgment of man for his deeds here on earth. One takes note that *qiyāma*, *ba'th, ḥashr, janna* and *nār* are true Arabic words. It would not be too much to say that the meaning of these in the *jāhilīya* is very close to their Islamic meaning."

3. From N. Faris, *The Antiquities of South Arabia* (1938), p. 16, a translation of the eighth book of *al-Iklīl* by Abū Muḥammad al-Ḥasan ibn Aḥmad al-Ḥamdānī.

4. See P. K. Hitti, *History of the Arabs* (1960), p. 96: "Judged by his poetry the pagan Bedouin of the Jāhilīyah age had little if any religion. To spiritual impulses he was lukewarm, even indifferent."

5. See Nicholson, *A Literary History of the Arabs*, p. 166: "Such notions of a future life as were current in pre-Islamic Arabia never rose beyond vague and barbarous superstition. . . ."

6. One of the principal sources of our information on this area, which is east of Shabwa, is the extensive description provided by archeologist Gertrude Caton-Thompson in *The Tombs and Moon Temple of Hureidha (Hadhramaut)* (1944). She says (p. 93) that the evidence gives an upper dating limit of somewhere around the fifth to fourth centuries B.C.E. but that determining a lower limit is impossible. Near an ancient temple dedicated to the moon god two cave tombs were extensively excavated. One of these had clearly been plundered many centuries earlier, but the remaining artifacts indicate, as did those of the earlier Ḥimyarite tombs, that the best the culture could provide was buried along with the dead.

7. W. E. N. Kensdale, "The Religious Beliefs and Practices of the Ancient South Arabians," Philosophical Society, University College of Ibadan (1953), p. 5.

8. For details of these inscriptions see p. 323 of the excellent article by G. Ryckmans, "Les religions arabes preîslamiques" in *Histoire général des religions*, 4 (1947), 307–32. He indicates that in some instances a small cavity was carved on top of the tomb for receiving and storing rain and that sometimes a camel was sacrificed on the tomb for the purpose of providing food and water for the deceased.

9. C. J. Lyall, *Translations of Ancient Arabian Poetry* (1885), p. 55.

10. T. Nöldeke, "Arabs (Ancient)" in *ERE*, I, 672.

11. Ryckmans, "Les religions arabes," p. 323.

12. These artifacts were found in the area beyond Aden between Ḥodeida and Ṣan'ā'. For a full discussion of their artistic qualities see Léon Legrain, "Archeological Notes: In the Land of the Queen of Sheba," *American Journal of Archeology*, 38 (1934), 329–37.

13. Legrain says positively that the images "represent the deceased person, and were intended for his 'double,' a support for his soul, after the inanimate body had been buried in the grave" (p. 332).

14. "It is the gesture of presentation or welcome," says Legrain (p. 334).

15. Faris, *Antiquities*, p. 85 (VIII, 161 of *al-Iklīl*).

16. For a more complete description and accompanying photographs see Jack Finegan, *The Archeology of World Religions* (1952), pp. 478–79 and plates.

17. Diana Kirkbride describes the remains of Nabatean tombs from the Wadi Rum and what she determines to be funerary stelae in "A Stone circle in the Deserts of Midian: Cryptic Carvings from the Wadi Rum," *The Illustrated London News*, August 13, 1960, pp. 262–63. She discovered small figures carved on rocks placed in a large circle, in which were also some burial cairns. "Since these little figures give every indication of being individual portraits it is easier to envisage them as memorial *stelae* set up in a sanctuary than as a circle of idols such as we know existed in the Jaheliyeh . . ." (p. 263).

18. Ryckmans clearly identifies this as an offering made to the dead, given along with other items such as water and wine, p. 323.

19. Nöldeke, "Arabs," p. 672. Nöldeke mentions that the slaughter of animal sacrifices has been practiced to the present in various parts of Arabia. From Doughty's *Arabia Deserta* (1888), I, 240–41 we read: "I found also among these Bedouins, that with difficulty they imagine any future life; they pray and they fast as main duties in religion, looking (as the Semitic Patriarchs before them) for the present life's blessing. There is a sacrifice for the dead, which I have seen continued to the third generation. I have seen a sheykh come with devout remembrance, to slaughter and to pray at the heap where his father or his father's father lies buried: and I have seen such to kiss his hand, in passing any time by the place where the sire is sleeping, and breathe out, with almost womanly tenderness, words of blessing and prayer;—and this is surely comfort in one's dying, that he will be long-time so kindly had in his children's mind."

20. Cf. al-Ghazālī's *al-Durra*, MS p. 49, in which the dead are described as riding two, three, four, five, and ten on a camel. "The meaning," says al-Ghazālī, "is that God has mercy on those who are in Islam and creates for them out of their works a camel on which they ride." Jawād 'Alī, *Tārīkh al-*

'arab, V, 250–51, comments on the belief of some Muslims that if they sacrifice an animal at the time of death, it will allow them to ride instead of walk on the day of resurrection, suggesting that this is a residue of pre-Islamic belief even though Islam does not condone it. He says somewhat improbably that the *jāhilī* custom of tying a camel or cow or sheep to the grave was related to the belief of some in a resurrection and judgment.

21. Cf. Lyall, *Translations*, p. xxx.

22. See J. Henniger, "La religion bédouine préislamique," *L'antica società beduina*, ed. F. Gabrieli (1959), p. 130.

23. *The Religion of the Semites* (1972), p. 370.

24. J. G. Frazier, "On Certain Burial Customs as Illustrative of the Primitive Theory of the Soul," *J. Anthrop. Inst.* 15 (1886), 65, indicates that the practice of adding a stone to the pile on top of a grave is an attempt to keep the restless soul of the occupant of the grave confined to his place, particularly if that soul be of a murderer or his victim.

25. See M. M. Bravmann, *The Spiritual Background of Early Islam* (1972), pp. 288, 292.

26. Abdul Hamid Siddiqi, "Religion of the pre-Islamic Arabs," *Iqbal,* 16i (1967), 79.

27. Kirkbride, "A Stone Circle," p. 263.

28. Henniger, "La religion bédouine," pp. 130–31. See Appendix C for a discussion of the intercessory functions of *walīs*.

29. Lyall, *Translations,* p. 53.

30. For a full analysis of these meanings with references see E. W. Lane, *An Arabic-English Lexicon* (1863–93), Bk. I, pt. iv, p. 1670.

31. Lyall, *Translations*, p. 76. Ragnar Eklund, *Life Between Death and Resurrection*, pp. 18–20, discusses the possible carry-over into Islam of this bird idea, indicating that classical scholars have generally understood the *hāma* of Bedouin poetry to have been the predecessor of the bird form into which the martyrs of Islam are said to go immediately at death. Eklund points out, however, that the differences between these two images is considerable and notes that the Prophet himself denied the existence of the *hāma,* while the birds as the souls of martyrs are mentioned frequently in the traditions.

32. Lyall, p. 67: "The poet conceives himself as slain by love for Laila, and his ghost as thirsting for her as his slayer, and requiring to be appeased by her blood." 'Alī in *Tarīkh al-'arab* expresses the opinion that while revenge is an obvious element in the screech-owl phenomenon, it was generally held that all deceased took the form of a bird: "Death according to the *jāhilīya* is the spirit leaving the body for some reason, leading to its disintegration. The spirit leaves through the nose or the mouth, and that is natural death. However if death is caused by a wound, the spirit becomes a bird and flutters over the grave and continues thus until the dead man is revenged. And it keeps saying 'give me to drink.' It could be that this is the reason why they put

some animal next to the grave. If one studies the reports [*akhbār*] a bit more it appears that it is not only the spirit of the murdered one that turns into a bird, but that of everyone. As to how long they stay, what they do and where they go, there is very little information'' (V, 279–80).

33. J. Wellhausen, *Reste Arabischen Heidentums* (1897), p. 148.

34. ''Spirits and Demons in Arabia,'' *Journal of the Royal Asiatic Society* (1934), pp. 720–21. Cf. W. Robertson Smith, *Religion of the Semites*, p. 88.

35. Tritton, ''Spirits and Demons,'' pp. 715–27, talks about the various classes and activities of *jinn* from pre-Islamic times as discussed in a variety of Muslim sources. The question of the relation of the *jinn* to the angels is complex; concerning it the Qur'ān commentators and others have given a variety of opinions. For an analysis of these opinions see the Ph.D. dissertation of Peter J. Awn, ''Iblīs in Sufi Psychology'' (Harvard University, 1978).

36. From a series of private interviews, April–May, 1976, Cairo. Cf. W. S. Blackman, ''Some Beliefs among the Egyptian Peasants with Regard to *'afarit*,'' *Folklore*, 35 1924, 176–84, in which she discusses the relationship of these spirits to the *jinn*.

37. Lyall, *Translations*, p. 54.

38. Lyall, p. 17.

39. Thurayyā Malḥas, *al-Qiyam al-ruḥīya fī al-shi'r al-'arabī* (1964), p. 159.

APPENDIX B

1. D. B. Macdonald, ''Immortality in Mohammedanism,'' p. 316, remarks that ''There is much evidence that amongst Turks, at least, and these not only of the uneducated masses, women are regarded as not having souls, at any rate on the same footing as men. . . . This will, probably, be more than confirmed by every missionary at the present day to the Turks.'' See also the authors' ''Women in the Afterlife: The Islamic View as Seen from Qur'ān and Tradition,'' *Journal of the American Academy of Religion,* 18 1975, 39–50, from which some of the material in this section is taken.

2. In fact, far from denying that women have souls, in some instances contemporary Islamic thinkers have suggested that the spirit [*rūḥ*] is stronger in men than in women and that the woman has a preponderance of soul [*nafs*], the seat of emotion and desire. See, e.g. Muḥammad Khalīfah, *al-Dār al-barzakhīya*, pp. 227–28. Macdonald (p. 317) continues his appraisal of the Islamic view by affirming that ''. . . no Moslem theologian would dream of denying that women have souls, of exactly the same kind as men, and in exactly the same degree as men. The attitude of the Turks is probably a lingering relic of their pre-Moslem beliefs; there are many such contradictory survivals in the syncretisms of Islam.''

3. ''The mention of women in the Holy Qur'ān is, in the first place, to

show that men and women are both equal in the sight of God, and that both will enjoy the higher life in the Resurrection. That women, in general, shall have access to Paradise, is made clear in many places . . ." ('Ali, *The Religion of Islam*, p. 295).

4. One of the wives of the Prophet is reported to have complained that all of the references in the Qur'ān were to men, after which both masculine and feminine forms were included in descriptions of the faithful. Ṣadīq Ḥasan Khān, *Ḥusn al-uswa* n.d., p. 117. See also Richard Bell, *The Qur'ān* (1937–39), II, 559, n. 7.

5. This collar of palm-fiber is an interesting variation on the Qur'ānic promise (S 17:13–14) that the fate of every person will be fastened around his neck on the day of resurrection.

6. See discussion below.

7. Ṣadīq Ḥasan Khān, for example, says that the verse could be interpreted to mean that the wives are punished even if they have not sinned (*Ḥusn al-uswa*, p. 90).

8. *al-Tafsîr*, XXIII, 22; cf. Darwaza, *al-Tafsîr*, IV, 200, and Wajdī, *al-Muṣḥaf*, p. 588.

9. *al-Tafsîr*, XII, 972.

10. *al-Tafsîr*, p. 78.

11. See S 18:45, 21:104, 25:27, and 50:43.

12. al-Barzinjī, *al-Ishā'a*, pp. 70 ff; cf. *Mishkāt*, II, 109, 558–59.

13. A.b.Ḥ., III, 176; cf. Bū., LXVII, 110; LXXXVI, 20; and Nas., III, 98, 176.

14. *Tafṣîl al-Nash'a*, p. 41.

15. *Eschatology in Islam*, pp. 112–13.

16. Ahmad A. Galwash in *The Religion of Islam*, for example, puts as his concluding commentary on "The Belief in the Day of Resurrection" what he calls a refutation of the "falsehood of vulgar imputation on Muhammadans who are reported, by some Christian writers, to believe that women have no souls, or, if they have, that they will perish, like those of brutes, and will not be rewarded in the next life" (I, 246).

17. A.b.Ḥ., I, 137. Ṣadīq Ḥasan Khān, *Yaqẓat ulî al-i'tibār*, pp. 70–71, cites some traditions saying that women are in the Fire because they desire the beautiful things of the world and because they are lacking intelligence, in patience in the face of misfortune, and in gratitude. Cf. Khān's *Ḥusn al-uswa,* pp. 107–08.

18. A.b.Ḥ., I, 359; Nas., II, 67, 373.

19. A.b.Ḥ. 2, p. 373.

20. A.b.Ḥ., III, 80.

21. See, for example, A. Perron, *Femmes arabes avant et depuis l'islamism* (1858), pp. 326–34, in which is related the tale of two women already in paradise. Around the one circles a bird gently wafting his wings and provid-

ing sweet breezes, while on the head of the other a bird sits pecking (because, though obedient to the commands of God, on earth she had refused to obey her husband).

22. *al-Rūḥīya*, p. 169.

23. *Ḥayāt al-ukhrá*, p. 25.

24. There are several early Meccan references that imply *ḥūr* but where the word does not appear (S 56:35–38, 78:33, and 37:48–49).

25. *Kitāb aḥwāl al-qiyāma*, p. 111. References to the general description of the *ḥūr* are abundant in the collections of traditions; see, for example, the summary and numerous citations of Ṣoubḥi al-Ṣaleḥ, *La Vie Future,* pp. 38–43.

26. *La Vie Future*, p. 39.

27. *Mishkāt*, II, 624; *Ḥusn al-uswa*, p. 219. Sha'rānī, *Mukhtaṣar*, p. 111, relates that in the period of about a month a man will marry some 1000 *ḥūr*. When he comes to any one of his wives, he will find her a virgin, and his desire for her will return to him with the strength of seventy men.

28. The *Kitāb aḥwāl al-qiyāmah*, p. 112, relates from Ibn Mas'ūd that the angel Gabriel, visiting the Garden, was so dazzled by the shining front teeth of one of the *ḥūr* that he thought he was in the light of God Himself. The virgin then called to him, saying: " 'O entrusted of God! Lift your head! He lifted it, looked at her and said, 'Glory be to God who has created you.' And the virgin said, 'O entrusted of God, do you know for whom I have been created?' He answered, 'No.' Then she said, 'For the one who holds the pleasure [*riḍá*] of God over that of himself.' "

29. "Not a woman hurts her husband here on earth, but that his wife, of the *ḥūr* says: Do not hurt him. May God punish you. He is with you but a short time, and about to leave you to come to us." Abū Ya'lā, *al-Mu'tamad fī uṣūl al-dīn* (1973), pp. 181–72.

30. "Ibn al-'Arabī said, If a woman has several husbands the Prophet said that she will be given the choice and whomever she chooses she becomes his. . . . Umm Ḥabība asked the Prophet, If a woman has two husbands in this world and they die and all are united in the Garden, to whom will she belong, the former or the latter? And the Prophet said, She will belong to the one who treats her better in this world." Sha'rānī, *Mukhtaṣar*, p. 105.

31. *Anwār al-tanzīl* (n.d.), p. 585.

32. *Tafsīr*, I, 233.

33. *Tafsīr al-Manār*, X, 548.

34. 'Ammār, *al-Tafsīr*, p. 197; Ḥijāzī, *al-Tafsīr*, XXVII 27, 138–39; Darwaza, *al-Tafsīr*, III, 105; Wajdī, *al-Muṣḥaf*, p. 716.

35. al-Jammāl, *al-Tafsīr*, IV, 3027.

36. P. 297. 'Ali allows for this interpretation by translating the Qur'ānic phrase *'inna ansha'nāhunna inshā'an* as "surely We have made them grow into a new growth." It is interesting to note that some translations, such as

those of Arberry ("Perfectly We formed them, perfect . . .") and Yusuf 'Ali ("We have created [their Companions] of special creation . . .") would seem to suggest that by the nature of the original creation the *mu'mināt* could not be implied, while others such as Pickthall ("Lo! We have created them a [new] creation") leave room for either understanding.

37. Nas., III, 80; Khān, *Ḥusn al-uswa*, p. 219.

38. Muḥammad Ḥasanayn Makhlūf, *Ḥukm al-Islām*, p. 19.

39. *The Religion of Islam*, p. 298.

40. *al-Ḥujaj*, in *'Alā hāmish al-tafsīr* (1950), pp. 47–49, as summarized in *La Vie Future*, p. 134.

41. *Jāmi' al-bayān* (1954–), XXVII, 13–14.

42. *Jāmi' al-bayān* XIII, 434; XXVII, 13.

43. *al-Kashshāf*, IV, 411.

44. "{. . . in faith, We shall join to them their progeny . . .} meaning by a great and elevated faith, which is the faith of the fathers, have we joined their progeny to their ranks, even though they may not deserve it, as a beneficence [*tafaḍḍul*] to them and their progeny, that We fulfill their happiness and complete their well-being [*na'īm*]" (p. 411).

45. *Majma' al-bayān (1961), XIII, 169; XXVII, 30.*

46. *Tafsīr*, p. 341.

47. *Tafsīr al-Qur'ān al-'aẓīm* (1966), IV, 85; VI, 432. He cites the Prophet as having said: "When a man enters the Garden, he asks about his parents, his wife and his children. He will be told, 'They have not attained your rank.' Then he says, 'O God, I worked for them and for myself,' and it will be ordered that they join him" (6:433). Cf. Ibn Qayyim al-Jawzīya, *Ḥādī al-arwāḥ*, p. 312.

48. The Ḥanbalī theologian Abū Ya'la ibn al-Farrā' in commenting on S 52:21 describes the elevation of children graphically: "Concerning the children of the faithful in the Garden with their fathers: the proof of it is His saying {God has made known that they will follow their fathers because of their faith.} And Abū Hurayra has reported from the Prophet that he said: The little ones are the roamers [*da'āmīs*] of the people of the Garden. When one of them gets hold of the hem of his father's robe he does not let go until it enables him to enter heaven." *Kitāb al-mu'tamad*, pp. 114–15. Cf. A.b.Ḥ., II, 488, in which he says that the little ones [*ṣighār*] are the roamers of the Garden. This rather unusual term seems to suggest that these children will have free access to any of the several dwellings of paradise. See Lane, *Lexicon,* I, pt. 3, p. 883.

49. *Ḥādī al-arwāḥ*, p. 319.

50. *Tafsīr*, XIII, 47.

51. *al-Tafsīr*, VI, 236.

52. Ḥijāzī, commenting on 13:23, says that "their close progeny will be with them, that they may have their companionship, on the condition that

they are worthy of it . . ." (*al-Tafsîr*, XIV, 44), and Muḥammad al-Qāsimī on the same verse says progeny refers specifically to "those who have had faith, proclaimed unicity, and done good deeds" (*Maḥāsin al-ta'wīl*, IX, 3674).

53. In general the theologians and writers have hesitated to predict the fate of one who dies while still in the pre-responsible condition, relying on the words of the Prophet, as in A.b.Ḥ., II, 481: "The Prophet said, 'Not a child is born but he has a community [*milla*].' One time he said, 'Every child is born into the natural condition [*fiṭra*], then his parents Christianize him or Judaize him or turn him into a polytheist.' And when he was asked, 'What about the one who dies before then?' he replied, 'God knows best what happens to them.' "

54. It is extremely difficult, however, to fit these kinds of references into a time sequence; the question of whether or not such children are already in the Garden or must wait for the day of judgment has not been addressed by such traditions.

55. A.b.Ḥ., V, 58.

56. *Bushrá*, p. 76. A similar assurance is suggested in this tradition from the Prophet: "The oldest fetus that has been aborted is more beloved to me than 400 cavalry men all fighting in the way of the Lord!" (al-Ghazālī, *Iḥyā'*, IV, 475).

57. Suyūṭī, *Bushrá*, pp. 75–76. It would make an interesting study to investigate the various versions in which this notion appears in world literature. The ancient Aztecs postulated, for example, that the souls of children who died very young would rest in the heavens and drink from the nourishing Milk Tree, whose limbs are shaped like breasts.

58. Traditions indicating the relationship of a child to a stance of piety or faith, again a fact no doubt determined by the Qur'ānic orientation, sometimes take the simple form of a general consolation to parents that the righteous child has preceded them to the Garden (al-Ghazālī, *Iḥyā'*, IV, 473) and other times more directly relate the child's determination to the circumstance of his or her parents.

59. *al-Dār al-barzakhīya*, pp. 269–70, from Bukhārī, Muslim, Ibn Māja, and Aḥmad ibn Ḥanbal.

60. Khalīfa suggests that other reports indicate that Adam, Gabriel, or Michael will perform this function, which he reconciles by saying that some children will be with them and some with Abraham. Al-Suyūṭī, *Bushrá*, p. 76, places Abraham, whom he calls by the familiar designation al-Khalīl, near the Ṭubba tree and says the children will be found in the lap of Abraham.

61. *Bushrá*, p. 75. Here we find expressed quite clearly the assurance that children (specifically the offspring of Muslims or believers) will be cared for during the intermediate state between death and resurrection. Al-Ghazālī in the *Durra*, MS. p. 34, relates: "In the *Ṣaḥīḥ* [of Bukhārī] it says that the Prophet [on the *mi'rāj*] passed by [Abraham] while he was leaning against the

Bayt al-Ma'mūr, surrounded by the children of Muslims." (The Bayt al-Ma'mūr is the celestial archetype of the Ka'ba.)

62. Some of the more extreme Khawārij held to the belief that until a child had of his own accord accepted Islam, he was not a Muslim, even though his parents were Muslims, and that the children of unbelievers were automatically consigned to the Fire.

63. P. 108. 'Ā'isha is cited as having wept at the funeral of a child out of compassion for what was to happen in the grave, and as having said that as surely as all will be questioned in the hereafter will all be questioned in the grave. Ibn Taymīya, *al-Furqān bayn awliyā' al-Raḥmān wa-awliyā' al-shayṭān* (A.H. 1387), pp. 23–24, reports another *ḥadīth,* however, in which 'Ā'isha is reported to have said that the Prophet listed three groups of persons who will *not* be held accountable for their actions: the non-rational [*al-majnūn*], the boy [*al-ṣaby*] before he reaches puberty, and the sleeper before he awakes. Ibn Taymīya, however, adds that when a child before puberty is able to distinguish between right and wrong, then he will be held accountable.

64. al-Jawzīya, p. 109. Muḥammad Kamāl al-Dīn al-Adhamī, one of the few contemporary writers to comment on the question of children, says that he who dies before he reaches puberty will be given enough life and intellect to comprehend the blessings of the Garden and the punishment of the Fire without his being interrogated about anything. *Kitāb al-tadhkīr*, p. 42.

65. Ṭay., Nos. 2382, 2624; cf. A.b.Ḥ., II, 244, 259, 268. Abū Ḥanīfa was among those who refused to say whether the children of unbelievers would be sent to the Garden or the Fire.

66. I.e. her two children before she married the Prophet.

67. A.b.Ḥ., I, 134. This tradition is cited with some frequency (cf. Ibn Kathīr, *Tafsīr*, VI, 453). The Mu'tazilī 'Abd al-Jabbār Ibn Aḥmad, *Sharḥ al-uṣūl al-khamsa* (1965), p. 480, however, says that it is a unitary example with no corroboration from supporting *ḥadīths*, and as such is unacceptable.

68. Ṭay., No. 2111.

69. *Kitāb al-mu'tamad*, p. 115.

70. Aḥmad Subḥī, *Fī 'ilm al-kalām* (1967), p. 554. The *Kitāb aḥwāl al-qiyāma* describes this role of children as servants in paradise (p. 47). Affirming that the children of Muslims will be in the crops of green birds of the Garden by a mountain of musk until the day of resurrection, it then states that the children of the *mushrikūn* will go around in the Garden but without a place of rest until the resurrection. While they are guaranteed this degree of felicity, however, they must nonetheless be in a position of servitude to those whose faith is proven [*thumma yakhdimūna al-mu'minīn*].

71. See, e.g. A. S. Tritton's discussion of the beliefs of al-Naẓẓām of the Basra school of Mu'tazila: "The children of Muslims and unbelievers will go to heaven and so will animals for no distinction is made between animals, children and lunatics." *Muslim Theology,* p. 94.

72. *Maqālāt*, I, 253–54.

73. He cites al-Bāqillānī, *Tamhīd*, p. 341, as having said it would be justice if God did this.

74. The contemporary Egyptian writer Aḥmad Subḥī agrees with al-Jabbār in saying that all the Mu'tazila believed that God wlll not punish children or make them suffer on the day of resurrection. This, he says, is in harmony with their position on *taklīf* (responsibility): where there is no *taklīf*, there is no judgment and no punishment. He cites Naẓẓām as saying that God would not punish children because that would by definition make Him an oppressor, which He is not, and Bishr as indicating that God has the capacity to punish him would not unless the child were mature and responsible. *Fī 'ilm al-kalām*, p. 176.

75. A.b.Ḥ., III, 9; cf. III, 80.

76. A.b.Ḥ., III, 16.

77. MS pp. 57–58. Cf. *al-Tafsīr al-Qur'ānī* of al-Khaṭīb (XIV, 709–10), in which he says children are in the Garden, forever going around with cups and pitchers of wine, which they fill from flowing springs, filling wine cups of the inhabitants of the Garden when they are empty.

78. The term used in S 52:24 is *ghilmān* and in 56:17 and 76:19 is *wildān*.

79. This assertion is frequently repeated by contemporary Islamic writers such as al-Mubārak ("God will not ask a person about other people's sins and a man will not carry his father's or relative's or children's sins" [*Niẓām*, p. 138]) and Nawfal ("Not a child will pay for his father nor father for his son, nor will children or relatives be able to intercede for him" [*Yawm al-qiyāma*, p. 17]).

80. From Ibn Ḥanbal as cited by Ibn Kathīr, *Tafsīr*, VI, 433.

81. See Ibn Qayyim, *Ḥādī al-arwaḥ*, p. 319.

82. *Muslim Devotions* (1961), p. 31, n. 1. The following prayer is cited in the *Islamic Prayer Book* (1975), pp. 34–35, the *du'ā* for a deceased child: "O Allah! make him cause of reward for us, and recompense in the world to come and let him be an intercessor for us on the day of compensation and his intercession be granted by Thee." (The same prayer, with change of pronoun, is given for both male and female children.)

83. al-Ghazālī, *Iḥyā'*, IV, 475.

84. *Kitāb al-tadhkīr*, p. 53. "The Prophet said, There is not a Muslim who loses three children before they come of age but he will surely enter the Garden or any of the eight gates of the Garden. If a woman loses three (or two) children this will keep her from the Fire."

85. Ḥamid Ibrāhīm Aḥmad and Muḥammad Ḥusaynī al-'Uzbī, *Kaffārāt al-khaṭāya* (1970), p. 43. Cf. al-Adhamī, *Kitāb tadhkir*, p. 53.

86. *Mishkāt* II, 109.

87. 'Ali, *The Religion of Islam*, p. 297.

88. Nawfal, *Ḥayāt al-ukhrá*, p. 106.

89. Ḥamza, *Rūḥīya*, p. 198.
90. *Yawm al-qiyāma*, pp. 120, 142.
91. Padwick, *Muslim Devotions*, p. 284.

APPENDIX C

1. *Muslim Devotions,* p. 38.

2. This division into four realms is still suggested by many modern writers. See the former Shaykh of al-Azhar Muḥammad al-Ṭayr, *Hādī al-arwāḥ*, p. 39, who says prophets and messengers are in the highest rank, *walīs* in the second, those in whom good and evil are mixed in the third, and the errant spirits in the fourth.

3. "Any belief that visitation of the grave is beneficial is akin to taking [the grave] as an idol. . . ." *Kitāb al-radd 'alá'l-ikhnā'ī* (1957), p. 56.

4. See, e.g., his *al-Furqān bayn awliyā' al-Raḥmān wa-awliyā' al-shayṭān.* Taqī al-Dīn al-Subkī, writing in counter-attack to Ibn Taymīya's denunciation of this kind of intercession, cites numerous traditions from the Prophet (with lengthy *isnāds*) in support of Muḥammad's intercessory powers in favor of those who visit his tomb *(Shifā' al-saqām,* pp. 11–25), "It is permissible and desirable to seek help in intercession from the Prophet," says al-Subkī, "as everyone who knows anything about religion has understood until Ibn Taymīya came with his interpolations . . ." (p. 119). He insists that the prophets are all alive in their graves praying (p. 134).

5. *Tafsīr*, I, 306.

6. This was clearly articulated by the current editor of *Majallat al-Azhar*, Dr. 'Abd al-Wadūd Shalabī, in a personal interview April, 1976.

7. Māhir, *Karāmāt*, pp. 89–90. This closeness is understood to be actualized in an even more concrete way at death; the celebration held annually at the tombs of all important saints is called *'urs*, wedding, symbolizing the union [*wiṣāl*] of the spirit of the *walī* with God. See Murray Titus, "Mysticism and Saint Worship in India," *Muslim World,* 12 (1922), 136.

8. *Ḥukm al-Islām*, p. 9.

9. Nawal al-Messiri, "Sheikh Cult in Daḥmīt," M.A. Thesis, American University of Cairo, 1965.

10. In support of the visitation of tombs of the saints in Egypt Muḥammad Su'ād Māhir, *Masājid Miṣr wa-awliyā'uhā al-sāliḥūn* (1971), pp. 44–45, says that the purpose of tomb visitation is to remember the hereafter; according to the Ḥanafīs it should take place on Friday and Saturday, the Shāfi'īs say Thursday evening to Saturday morning, and the Ḥanbalīs do not specify a day. When one visits the graves, says Māhir, he should be busy with prayer and petition.

11. In the city of Cairo itself, of course, many persons actually inhabit the

vast necropolis known as the city of the dead, due in large measure today to the burgeoning of population, which Cairo cannot support.

12. See Sayyid ʻUways, *Ḥadīth ʻan al-thaqāfa* (1970), pp. 123–35. The Waqf ministry since 1961 receives two-thirds of the income from the boxes put by the graves of the *walīs*, the Shaykhs of the mosque the remainder. ʻUways, *Min malāmiḥ al-mujtamaʻ al-Miṣrī al-muʻāṣir* (1965), p. 24.

13. ʻAbd al-Ḥāmid Taḥmāz, *Ḥayātunā wa'l-mawʻid al-majhūl* (1973), pp. 85–86.

14. See, e.g. ʻAbd Allāh al-Ṣadīq, *al-Ḥujaj al-bayyināt fī ithbāt al-karāmāt* (n.d.), pp. 153–56. Al-Ṣadīq relates such incidents as that of a pious man who was removed from his grave after thirty years with no change in the condition of his body, and the report in Spanish newspapers some twenty years ago that opened Arab graves revealed bodies that had not deteriorated even though they had been buried 300 years earlier.

15. "La cité des morts au Caire," *Mardis de Dar el-Salam* (1955; published 1958), p. 11.

16. Sayyid ʻUways, *Min malāmiḥ al-mujtamaʻ al-Miṣrī al-muʻāsir*, pp. 24 ff.

17. Related to the authors by Sayyid ʻUways in a personal interview of May, 1976.

18. Ibid.

19. Māhir, *Masājid Miṣr*, p. 362.

20. J. W. McPherson, *The Moulids of Egypt* (1941).

21. The *mūlid* (*mawlid*) or birthday celebration of Ḥusayn is rivaled only by that of the Prophet Muḥammad in the degree of enthusiasm and celebration expressed by Cairenes.

22. This does not negate the understanding that Ḥusayn, like the other *walīs*, is still present at the place of his tomb and thus accessible to the petitions of believers.

23. Sayyid Khalīl Ibrāhīm, "Waqfatum fī riḥāb al-Ḥusayn," *al-Muslim,* 25 (April 13, 1975), 9.

24. Māhir, *Masājid Miṣr*, p. 116.

25. Māhir, *Karāmāt,* p. 123. This materialization is a phenomenon common to many mystical accounts and recognized by modern spiritualists.

26. Māhir, *Masājid Miṣr,* p. 94. Because her husband, mother, and sons all died, as did her brothers Ḥasan and Ḥusayn, she was in a special position to understand the meaning of suffering and personal loss. Zaynab herself was also taken as a hostage and treated as a booty of war.

27. ʻAbd Allāh Shams al-Dīn, "Fīn riḥāb mawlātinā al-Sayyida Zaynab," *al-Muslim,* 26 (January, 1976), 6–7.

28. Muḥammad Shāhīn Ḥamza, *al-Sayyida Nafīsa* (n.d.), p. 89.

29. For a classic description of the cult of saints in both urban and rural Egypt in the early part of the last century see E. W. Lane, *An Account of the*

Manners and Customs of the Modern Egyptians. Much of the practice that Lane describes one still finds in relatively unchanged form in various parts of Egypt.

30. For a similar description of these saints' tombs earlier in this century see W. S. Blackman, "Some Social and Religious Customs in Modern Egypt," *Bull. Soc. Geog. Egypte,* 14 (1926–27), 47–61.

31. Nawal el-Missiri, "Sheikh Cult," pp. 64–68, suggests that the primary reasons for making a visit and request [*nadr*] to a saint are as follows, in order of incidence: (1) to conceive a child, (2) to recover from illness, (3) to make a safe journey, (4) to succeed in school, (5) to find a job, and (6) to take revenge on enemies.

32. 'Uways, *al-Khulūd fī ḥayāt al-Miṣriyyin al-mu'āṣirīn,* pp. 74–75.

33. See H. B. Barclay, "Study of an Egyptian Village Community," *Studies in Islam,* 3 (1966), 143–66, 201–26.

Bibliography

WORKS IN ARABIC

'Abd al-Jabbār ibn Aḥmad. *al-Uṣūl al-khamsa*. Cairo, 1965.

'Abd al-Raḥmān, 'Ā'isha. *al-Qur'ān wa-qaḍāya al-insān*. Beirut, 1972.

'Abdu, Muḥammad. *Tafsîr al-Qur'ān al-karîm*. Cairo, 1927.

Abū'l-'Azā'im, Muḥammad Māḍī. *Tafsîl al-nash'a al-thāniya*. Cairo, 1973.

Abū Ya'la Ibn al-Farrā'. *Kitāb al-mu'tamad*. Ed. W. Z. Haddad. Beirut, 1973.

al-Adhamī, Muḥammad Kamāl al-Dīn. *Kitāb tadhkîr li'l-marji' wa'l-maṣîr*. Cairo, A.H. 1349.

Aḥmad, Ḥāmid Ibrāhīm and Muḥammad Ḥusaynī al-'Uqbī. *Kaffārāt al-khaṭāya*. Cairo, 1970.

'Alī, Jawād. *Tārîkh al-'Arab*. Baghdad, 1956.

'Ammār, Ḥāfiz 'Īsá. *al-Falsafa al-Qur'ānīya*. Cairo, n.d.

al-'Aqqād, 'Abbās Maḥmūd. *al-Falsafa al-Qur'ānīya*. Cairo, n.d.

'Awaḍayn, Ibrāhīm. "Ta'ammulāt fī al-bayān al-Qur'ānī: al-ṣūra al-Qur'ānīya." *Minbar al-Islām*, 33, no. 10 (October, 1975), pp. 14–23.

'Awwād, Muḥammad. *Ḥayāt al-Islām*. Cairo, n.d.

al-Barzinjī, Muḥammad ibn Rasūl al-Ḥusaynī. *al-Ishā'a li-ishrāṭ al-sā'a*. Cairo, A.H. 1384.

al-Bayḍāwī, 'Abd Allāh ibn 'Umar. *Anwār al-tanzîl wa-asrār al-ta'wîl*. Cairo, n.d.

al-Bayjūrī, Ibrāhīm. *Sharḥ al-Bayjūrî 'alá'l-Jawhara*. Cairo, 1964.

Darwaza, Muḥammad 'Izza. *al-Tafsîr al-ḥadîth*. Cairo, 1962– .

Fā'iz, Aḥmad. *al-Yawm al-ākhir fî ẓilāl al-Qur'ān*. Beirut, 1975.

al-Fandī, Muḥammad Jamāl al-Dīn. *al-Samāwāt al-sab'*. Cairo, 1973.

al-Ghazālī, Abū Ḥāmid Muḥammad ibn Muḥammad. *al-Durra al-fākhira*. Ed. M. Gautier. Leipzig, 1877.

_____. *Iḥyā' 'ulūm al-dīn*. Cairo, A.H. 1334.
Ḥamza, Muḥammad Shahīn. *Ma'a'l-fikr al-Islāmī*. Cairo, 1970.
_____. *al-Ruḥīya al-ḥadītha*. Cairo, 1968.
_____. *al-Sayyida Nafīsa*. Cairo, n.d.
Ḥijāzī, Muḥammad Maḥmūd. *al-Tafsīr al-wāḍiḥ*. Cairo, 1962–69.
al-Ḥūfī, Aḥmad. "Asmā' yawm al-qiyāma fī'l-Qur'ān al-karīm." *Minbar al-Islām,* 32 (July-November, 1974).
Ḥusayn, Muḥammad Muḥammad. *al-Ḥayāt al-rūḥīya*. Cairo, 1960.
Ibn Kathīr, Ismā'īl ibn 'Umar. *Tafsīr al-Qur'ān al-'aẓīm*. Beirut, 1966.
Ibn Taymīya, Taqī al-Dīn. *al-Furqān bayn awliyā' al-Raḥmān wa-awliyā' al-shayṭān*. Cairo, A.H. 1387.
_____. *Kitāb al-radd 'alá al-ikhnā'ī*. Cairo, 1957.
_____. *Qā'ida jalīla fī al-tawassul wa'l-wasīla*. Cairo, A.H. 1374.
Ibrāhīm, Sayyid Khalīl. "Waqfatun fī riḥāb al-Ḥusayn." *al-Muslim,* 25 (April 13, 1975), 9.
'Īsá, 'Abd al-Jalīl. *al-Muṣḥaf al-muyassar*. Cairo, 1962.
Ja'far, Muḥammad Kāmil Ibrāhīm. *Fī al-dīn al-muqāran*. Alexandria, 1970.
al-Ja'farī, Sīdī 'Abd al-Raḥmān ibn Muḥammad ibn Makhlūf al-Tha'ālībī. *Kitāb al-'ulūm al-fākhira fī al-naẓar fī umūr al-ākhira*. Cairo, A.H. 1317.
al-Jamal, Ḥasan 'Izz al-Dīn. *al-Mawt wa'l-ḥayāt*. Cairo, 1973.
al-Jammāl, Muḥammad 'Abd al-Mun'im. *al-Tafsīr al-farīd li'l-Qur'ān al-majīd*. Cairo, 1973.
al-Jawzīya, Ibn Qayyim. *Ḥādī al-arwāh*. Cairo, 1962.
_____. *Kitāb al-rūḥ*. Cairo, A.H. 1357.
al-Kalbī, Hishām ibn Muḥammad. *Kitāb al-aṣnām*. Cairo, 1965.
Khafājī, Muḥammad 'Abd al-Mun'im. *Tafsīr al-Qur'ān al-karīm*. Cairo, 1959.
Khalīfa, Muḥammad 'Abd al-Ẓāhir. *Kitāb al-dār al-barzakhīya*. Cairo, 1973.
Khān, Ṣadīq Ḥasan. *Ḥusn al-uswa*. Cairo, n.d.
_____. *Yaqẓat ulī al-i'tibār*. Cairo, n.d.
al-Khaṭīb, 'Abd al-Karīm. *al-Tafsīr al-Qur'ānī li'l-Qur'ān*. Cairo, 1967–70.
al-Kīk, Muṣṭafá. *Rasā'il ilayhim*. Alexandria, 1972.
_____. *Tanāsukh al-arwāḥ*. Alexandria, 1970.
Kitāb aḥwāl al-qiyāma. Ed. Monitz Wolff. Leipzig, 1872.
al-Kurdī, Sa'īd Ṭah. *al-Mawt fī khidmat al-ḥayāt*. Cairo, n.d.
Līmūd, Ḥāmid Maḥmūd. *Jawhar al-tawḥīd*. Cairo, 1974.
Maghnīya, Muḥammad Jawād. *al-Mahdī al-muntaẓar wa'l-'aql*. Beirut, n.d.
Māhir, Farīd. *Karāmāt al-awliyā'*. Cairo, 1971.
Māhir, Su'ād Muḥammad. *Masājid Miṣr wa-awliyā'uhā al-ṣāliḥūn*. Cairo, 1971.
Maḥmūd, Muṣṭafá. *al-Qur'ān*. Beirut, 1970.
_____. *Riḥlat min al-shak ilá'l-īmān*. Beirut, n.d.
_____. *al-Rūḥ wa'l-jasad*. Beirut, 1974.
Makhlūf, Muḥammad Ḥassanayn. *Ḥukm al-Islām*. Cairo, 1974.

Malḥas, Thurayyā 'Abd al-Fattāḥ. *al-Qiyam al-rūḥīya fī al-shi'r al-'arabī*. Beirut, 1964.

al-Marāghī, Aḥmad Muṣṭafá. *Tafsīr al-Marāghī*. Cairo, 1953.

al-Mawdūdī, Abū'l -A'lá. *al-Ḥadāra al-Islāmīya*. Beirut, n.d.

al-Mubārak, Muḥammad. *Niẓām al-Islām*. Beirut, 1970.

al-Muẓaffar, Muḥsin 'Abd al-Ṣāḥib. *Nihāyat al-kawn bayn al-'ilm wa'l-Qur'ān*. Najaf, 1967.

Nawfal, 'Abd al-Razzāq. *As'ila ḥarija*. Cairo, 1970.

_____. *al-Ḥayāt al-ukhrá*. Cairo, 1965.

_____. *al-Islām dīn wa-dunyá*. Cairo, n.d.

_____. *Ṭarīq ilá Allāh*. Cairo, 1962.

_____. *Yawm al-qiyāma*. Cairo, 1969.

al-Qāsimī, Muḥammad Jamāl al-Dīn. *Maḥāsin al-ta'wīl*. Cairo, 1957–70.

Qazwīnī, Zakariyā' Muḥammad ibn Muḥammad, *Kitāb 'ajā'ib al-makhlūqāt al-mawjūdāt*. Ed. F. Wüstenfeld. Göttingen, 1849.

al-Qurṭubī, Muḥammad ibn Aḥmad, *al-Tadhkira fī aḥwāl al-mawtá wa-umūr al-ākhira*. Cairo, 196?.

Quṭb, Sayyid. *Fī ẓilāl al-Qur'ān. Cairo,* 195?–1959.

_____. *Mashāhid al-qiyāma fī al-Qur'ān*. Beirut, 1975.

Rāḍī, 'Alī 'Abd al-Jalīl. *al-Aḍwa' 'alá'l-rūḥīya*. Cairo, 1961.

_____. *al-Mautá ya'ūdūn*. Cairo, 1975.

Rāzī, Fakhr al-Dīn. *al-Tafsīr al-kabīr*. Cairo, 1934–62.

Riḍā, Muḥammad Rashīd. *Tafsīr al-Manār*. Cairo, 1948–56.

al-Ṣadīq, 'Abd Allāh. *al-Ḥujaj al-bayyināt fī ithbāt al-karāmāt*. Cairo, n.d.

al-Ṣaffār, Ibtisām Markūn. *al-Ta'ābīr al-Qur'ānīya wa'l-bī'a al-arabīya fī mashāhid al-qiyāma*. Najaf, 1966.

Shaltūt, Maḥmud. *al-Islām, 'aqīda wa-sharī'a*. Cairo, 1975.

al-Sha'rānī, 'Abd al-Wahhāb. *Mukhtaṣar tadhkirat al-Qurṭubī*. Cairo, A.H. 1307.

Subḥī, Aḥmad Maḥmūd. *Fī 'ilm al-kalām*. Alexandria, 1967.

al-Subkī, Taqī al-Dīn. *Shifā' al-saqām fī ziyāra khayr al-anām*. Cairo, A.H. 1315.

Suyūṭī, Jalāl al-Dīn. *Bushrá al-ka'īb bi-liqā'i al-ḥabīb*. Cairo, 1969.

_____. *al-Durar al-ḥisān fī al-ba'th wa-na'īm al-janān*. Cairo, n.d.

al-Ṭabarī, Abū Ja'far Muḥammad ibn Jarīr. *al-Jāmi' al-bayān fī tafsīr al-Qur'ān*. Cairo, 1954–

al-Ṭabarsī, Abū 'Alī al-Faḍl ibn al-Ḥasan. *Majma' al-bayān fī tafsīr al-Qur'ān*. Beirut, 1961.

Ṭabāṭabā'ī, Muḥammad Ḥusayn. *al-Mīzān fī tafsīr al-Qur'ān*. Beirut, 1970–

Tahānawī, Muḥammad 'Alā' ibn 'Alī. *Kashshāf iṣṭilāḥāt al-funūn*. Calcutta, 1862.

Ṭahmāz, 'Abd al-Ḥamīd. *Ḥayātunā wa'l-maw'id al-majhūl*. Hamah, 1973.

Ṭanṭāwī Jawharī. *al-Jawāhir fī tafsīr al-Qur'ān al-karīm*. Cairo, 1932–33.
al-Ṭayr, Muṣṭafá Muḥammad. *Hādī al-arwāḥ*. Cairo, 1971.
'Ubayd, Ra'ūf. *al-Insān rūḥ lā jasad*. Cairo, 1964.
'Uways, Sayyid. *Ḥadīth 'an al-thaqāfa*. Cairo, 1970.
——. *al-Khulūd fī ḥayāt al-Miṣriyīn al-mu'āṣirīn*. Cairo, 1972.
——. *al-Khulūd fī al-turāth al-thaqāfī al-Miṣrī*. Cairo, 1966.
——. *Min malāmiḥ al-mujtama' al-Miṣrī al-mu'āṣir*. Cairo, 1965.
Wajdī, Muḥammad Farīd. *al-Muṣḥaf al-mufassar*. Cairo, 1968.

WORKS IN WESTERN LANGUAGES

Abel, A. "Changements politiques et littérature eschatologique dans le monde musulmane." *Studia Islamica*, 2 (1954), 23–43.

'Ali, Maulana Muhammad. *The Religion of Islam*. United Arab Republic: National Publication and Printing House, n.d.

Ali, Syed Ameer. *Life and Teachings of Mohammed*. London: W. H. Allen and Co., Ltd., 1891.

Alwaye, A. M. Mohiaddin. "The belief in the Day of Judgment and its effects on the life of man." *Majallat al-Azhar* (June, 1969), pp. 1–6.

——. "Life after death—in the conception of Islam." *Majallat al-Azhar* (October, 1974), pp. 1–6.

Andrae, Tor. *Les Origines de l'Islam et le Christianisme*. Paris: Adrien-Maisonneuve, 1955.

Arberry, A. J. *Revelation and Reason in Islam*. London: George Allen and Unwin, Ltd., 1957.

——. *The Seven Odes: the first Chapter in Arabic Literature*. London: George Allen and Unwin, Ltd., 1957.

Asin Palacios, M. *Islam and the Divine Comedy*. London: John Murray, 1926.

Azzam, 'Abd al-Rahman. *The Eternal Message of Muhammad*. New York: Devin-Adair Co., 1964.

Baljon, J. M. S. *Modern Muslim Qur'ān Interpretation*. Leiden: E. J. Brill, 1961.

Barclay, H. B. "Study of an Egyptian Village Community." *Studies in Islam*, 3 (1966), 143–66, 201–26.

Bell, Richard. "The Men on the A'raf." *Muslim World*, 22 (1932), 43–48.

——. *The Origin of Islam in its Christian Environment*. London: Macmillan and Co., 1926.

——. *The Qur'ān*. Edinburgh: T. and T. Clark, 1937–39.

Berthels, E. "Die Paradiesischen Jungfrauen im Islam." *Islamica*, 1, (1925), 263–87.

Bevan, A. A. "The Beliefs of Early Mohammedans Respecting a Future

Existence." *Journal of Theological Studies* (October, 1904), 20–36.

Blackman, W. S. "Some Beliefs among the Egyptian Peasants with Regard to *'afārīt*." *Folklore*, 35 (1924), 176–84.

______. "Some Social and Religious Customs in Modern Egypt." *Bull. Soc. Geog. Egypte*, 14 (1926–27), 47–61.

Bowker, J. W. "Intercession in the Qur'ān and the Jewish Tradition." *Journal of Semitic Studies*, 11 (1966), 69–84.

Brandon, S. G. F. *Man and his Destiny in the Great Religions*. Toronto: Univ. of Toronto Press, 1962.

Bravmann, M. M. *The Spiritual Background of Early Islam*. Leiden: E. J. Brill, 1972.

Browne, E. G. *A Literary History of Persia*. Cambridge: Univ. Press, 1969.

Calverly, E. E. "Doctrines of the Soul (*nafs* and *rūḥ*) in Islam." *Muslim World*, 33 (1943), 254–64.

Carra deVaux, Le Baron. *La Doctrine de l'Islam*. Paris: Gabriel Beauchesne and Co., 1909.

Caton-Thompson, Gertrude. *The Tombs and Moon Temple of Hureidha (Hadhramaut)*. Oxford: Univ. Press, 1944.

Chelhoud, Joseph. *Les Structures du Sacré chez Les Arabes*. Paris: G.-P. Maisonneuve et Larose, 1964.

Corbin, Henri. *Terre Celeste et Corps de Resurrection*. Paris, 1960.

Dietrich, E. L. "Die Lehre von der Reinkarnation im Islam." *Zeitschrift für Religions und Geistesgeschichte*, 9 (1957), 129–49.

Doughty, Charles M. *Arabia Deserta*. Cambridge: Univ. Press, 1888.

Eklund, Ragnar. *Life between Death and Resurrection According to Islam*. Uppsala: Wiksells Boktryckeri-A.-B., 1941.

Elder, E. E. *A Commentary on the Creed of Islam*. New York: Columbia Univ. Press, 1950.

______. "al-Ṭahāwī's 'Bayān al-sunna wa'l-jamā'a'." *The Macdonald Presentation Volume*. Princeton: Princeton Univ. Press, 1933. Pp. 131–44.

Evrin, M. Sadeddin. *Eschatology in Islam*. Istanbul: Institute of Advanced Islamic Studies, 1960.

Fakhry, Majid. *A History of Islamic Philosophy*. New York: Columbia Univ. Press, 1970.

Fakim, Hussein. "Change in Religion in a Resettled Nubian Community, Upper Egypt." *International Journal of Middle East Studies*, 4 (1973), 163–77.

Faris, Nabih Amin. *The Antiquities of South Arabia* (A Translation of al-Ḥamdānī's *al-Iklīl* 8). Princeton: Princeton Univ. Press, 1938.

______. *The Book of Idols*. Princeton: Princeton Univ. Press, 1952.

Finegan, Jack. *The Archeology of World Religions*. Princeton: Princeton Univ. Press, 1965.

Frazer, J. G. "On Certain Burial Customs as Illustrative of the Primitive

Theory of the Soul.'' *Journal of the Anthropological Institute*, 15 (1886), 64–104.

Galwash, Aḥmad. *The Religion of Islam*. Doha, Qatar, 1973.

Gardet, Louis. *Dieu et la Destinée de l'Homme*. Paris: Librarie Philosophique, J. Vrin, 1967.

______. *L'Islam, Religion et Communauté*. Paris: Desclé de Brouwer, 1970.

Gautier, Lucien, ed. and tr. *Ad-Dourra al-Fakhira, la Perle Précieuse*. (Arabic text of Abū Ḥāmid al-Ghazālī.) Leipzig: G. Kreysing, 1877.

Henniger, Joseph. ''La Religion Bédouine Préislamique.'' *L'Antica Società Beduina*. Ed. F. Gabrieli. Rome: Centro di Studi Semitici, 1959. Pp. 115–40.

Ḥishād, 'Antar Aḥmad. ''Al-īmān bi-yawm al-ākhar and its Effect on Character.'' *Majallat al-Azhar* (April, 1975), pp. 314–20.

Hitti, Philip K. *History of the Arabs*. London: Macmillan and Co., 1960.

Hodgson, M. G. S. ''A Note on the Millenium in Islam.'' *Millenial Dreams in Action*. Ed. S. L. Thrupp. The Hague: Mouton, 1962. Pp. 218–19.

Horovitz, J. ''Muhammeds Himmelfahrt.'' *Der Islam*, 9 (1919), 159–83.

Iqbal, Muhammad. *The Reconstruction of Religious Thought in Islam*. Lahore: Sh. Muhammad Ashraf, 1962.

Islamic Prayer Book. Lahore: Sh. Muhammad Ashraf, 1975.

Izutsu, Toshihiko. *The Concept of Belief in Islamic Theology*. Tokyo: The Keio Institute of Cultural and Linguistic Studies, 1965.

______. *Ethico-Religious Concepts in the Qur'ān*. Montreal: McGill Univ. Press, 1966.

______. *God and Man in the Koran*. Tokyo: The Keio Institute of Cultural and Linguistic Studies, 1964.

Jacob, Georg. *Altarabisches Beduinenleben nach den Quellen Geschildert*. Berlin: Mayer and Müller, 1897.

Jenkinson, E. J. ''The Rivers of Paradise.'' *Muslim World*, 19 (1925), 151–55.

Kamali, Sabih Ahmad, ed. and tr. *Al-Ghazali's Tahafut al-Falasifah*. Lahore: Pakistan Philosophical Congress, 1963.

Kensdale, W. E. N. ''The Religious Beliefs and Practices of the Ancient South Arabians.'' A lecture given to the Philosophical Society, University College, Ibadan on December 16, 1953.

Khan, Muhammad Zafrullah. *Islam, its Meaning for Modern Man*. New York: Harper and Row, 1962.

Kirkbride, Diana. ''A Stone Circle in the Deserts of Midian: Cryptic Carvings from the Wadi Rum.'' *The Illustrated London News*, August 13, 1960, pp. 262–63.

Knight, G. A. F. ''Bridge.'' *Encyclopaedia of Religion and Ethics* II (1953), pp. 848–857.

Künstlinger, David. ''Einiges über die Namen und die Freuden des Kurānischen Paradieses." *Bulletin of the School of Oriental and African Studies*, 6 (1930–32), 617–32.

______. "Eschatologisches in Sura 111." *Orientalistische Literaturgeitung*, 41 (1938), 407–10.

Lammens, H. "Les Santuaires Préislamites dans l'Arabie Occidentale." *Mélange de la Faculté Orientale de l'Université St. Joseph de Beyrouth*, 11 (1926), 39–173.

Lane, E. W. *An Account of the Manners and Customs of the Modern Egyptians* (1833, 34 and 35). London, 1846.

______. *An Arabic-English Lexicon*. Parts 6–8 Ed. Stanley Lane-Poole. London: Williams and Norgate, 1863–93.

Lane-Poole, Stanley. "Death and Disposal of the Dead (Muhammedan)." *Encyclopaedia of Religion and Ethics* IV (1935), pp. 500–502.

Latif, Syed Abdul. *The Mind Al-Qur'an Builds*. Agapura, Hyderabad: The Academy of Islamic Studies, 1952.

Legrain, Léon. "Archeological Notes: In the Land of the Queen of Sheba." *American Journal of Archeology*, 38 (1934), 329–37.

Lyall, C. J. *Translations of Ancient Arabian Poetry*. London: Williams and Norgate, 1885.

McCarthy, Richard J. *The Theology of al-Ash'arî*. Beirut: Impremerie Catholique, 1953.

Macdonald, D. B. "The Development of the Idea of Spirit in Islam." *Muslim World*, 22, no. 1 (January-April, 1932), 25–42.

______. "Immortality in Mohammedanism." *Religion and the Future Life*. Ed. E. H. Sneath. New York: Fleming H. Revell Co., 1922.

Macdonald, J. "The Angel of Death in Late Islamic Tradition." *Islamic Studies*, 3 (1964), 485–519.

______. "The Creation of Man and Angels in the Eschatological Literature." *Islamic Studies*, 3 (1964), 285–308.

______. "The Day of Judgment in Near Eastern Religions." *Indo-Iranica*, 14 iv (1961), 33–53.

______. "The Day of Resurrection." *Islamic Studies*, 5 (1966), 129–97.

______. "Paradise." *Islamic Studies*, 5 (1966), 331–83.

______. "The Preliminaries to the Resurrection and Judgment." *Islamic Studies*, 4 (1965), 137–79.

______. "The Twilight of the Dead." *Islamic Studies*, 4 (1965), 55–102.

McPherson, J. W. *The Moulids of Egypt*. Cairo, 1941.

Makino, Shinya. *Creation and Termination*. Tokyo: The Keio Institute of Cultural and Linguistic Studies, 1970.

Margoliouth, D. S. "Mahdi." *Encyclopaedia of Religion and Ethics* VIII (1953), pp. 336–340.

Massignon, Louis. "La Cité des Morts au Caire." *Mardis de Dar el-Salam*

1955 (published 1958), pp. 5–20.

______. "L'Idée de l'Esprit dans l'Islam." *Eranos-Jahrbuch*, 13 (1945), 277–82.

______. "Recherche sur la Valeur Eschatologique de la Légende des VII Dormants chez les Musulmanes." *Actes 20e Cong. Int. des Or.* (1938), pp. 302–03.

______. "Les 'Sept Dormants,' Apocalypse de l'Islam." *Analecta Bollandiana*, 68 (1949), 245–60.

______. "Time in Islamic Thought." *Man and Time*. Ed. J. Campbell. New York: Bollingen, 1957. Pp. 108 ff.

Maudoodi, Sayyed Abul A'la. *The Ethical Viewpoint of Islam*. Lahore, 1953.

______. *Towards Understanding Islam*. Lahore: Islamic Publications Ltd., 1960.

Meier, Fritz. "The Ultimate Origin and the Hereafter in Islam." *Islam and its Cultural Divergence: Studies in Honor of Gustave E. von Grunebaum*. Ed. G. L. Tikku. Urbana: Univ. of Illinois Press, 1971. Pp. 96–112.

el-Messiri, Nawal. "Sheikh Cult in Daḥmīt." Unpublished M.A. thesis, American University of Cairo, 1965.

Nasr, Seyyed Hossein. *Science and Civilization in Islam*. Cambridge, MA: Harvard Univ. Press, 1968.

Nicholson, Reynold A. *A Literary History of the Arabs*. Cambridge: Univ. Press, 1962.

Nöldeke, Th. "Arabs (Ancient)." *Encyclopaedia of Religion and Ethics* I (1955), pp. 659–673.

O'Shaughnessy, Thomas. *Muhammad's Thoughts on Death*. Leiden: E. J. Brill, 1969.

______. "The Seven Names for Hell in the Koran." *Bulletin of the School of Oriental and African Studies*, 24 (1961), 444–65.

Padwick, Constance E. *Muslim Devotions*. London: S.P.C.K., 1961.

Perron, A. *Femmes Arabes avant et depuis l'Islamisme*. Paris: Librarie Nouvelle, 1858.

al-Qāḍī, Imam 'Abd al-Raḥīm ibn Aḥmad. *The Islamic Book of the Dead (Daqā'iq al-akhbār fī dhikr al-janna wa'l-nār)*. Tr. 'Ā'isha 'Abd al-Raḥmān. Norwich, England: Diwan Press, 1977.

Quasem, Abdul. *The Ethics of al-Ghazali*. Malaysia: Central Printing Sendirian Berhad, 1975.

Rahbar, Daud. *God of Justice*. Leiden: E. J. Brill, 1960.

Refoulé, F. "Immortalité de l'Âme et Resurrection de la Chair." *Revue de l'Histoire des Religions*, 163 (1963), 11–52.

Robson, James. "Is the Moslem Hell Eternal?" *Muslim World*, 28 (138), 386–96.

______. ed. and tr. *Mishkāt al-Masābīḥ* (of al-Baghawī). Lahore: Muhammad Ashraf, 1960.

Rosenthal, Franz, ed. and tr. *The Muqaddimah* (of Ibn Khaldūn). London: Routledge and Kegan Paul, 1958.

______. "On Suicide in Islam." *Journal of the American Oriental Society*, 66 (1946), 239–59.

Rüling, J. B. *Beiträge zur Eschatologie des Islam*. Leipzig: Otto Harrassowitz, 1895.

Ryckmans, G. "Les Religious Arabes Prêislamiques." *Histoire Général des Religions*, 4 (1947), 307–32.

El-Ṣaleḥ, Ṣoubḥi. *La Vie Future selon le Coran*. Paris: Librarie Philosophique J. Vrin, 1971.

al-Samarrai, Qassim. *The Theme of Ascension in Mystical Writings*. Baghdad: National Printing and Publishing Co., 1968.

Shaltout, Mahmoud. "The Source of Immortality in Islam." *Majallat al-Azhar,* 31 (1959–60), 37–42, 69–75.

Siddiqi, Abdul Hamid. "Religion of the Pre-Islamic Arabs." *Iqbal,* 16 i (1967), 73–83.

Smith, Jane I. "Concourse Between the Living and the Dead in Islamic Eschatological Literature." *History of Religions,* 19, no. 3 (1980), 224–36.

______. *The Precious Pearl* (A translation of Abū Ḥāmid al-Ghazālī's *Kitāb al-Durra al-Fākhira fī Kashf 'Ulūm al-Ākhira*). Missoula, Montana: Scholars Press, 1979.

______. "The Understanding of *nafs* and *rūḥ* in Contemporary Muslim Considerations of the Nature of Sleep and Death." *Muslim World*, 49, no. 3 (1979), 151–62.

Smith, Jane I. and Haddad, Yvonne. "Women in the Afterlife: The Islamic View as Seen from Qur'ān and Tradition." *Journal of the American Academy of Religion*, 43, no. 1 (1975), 39–50.

______. "Afterlife Themes in Modern Qur'ān Commentary." *Journal of the American Academy of Religion* Supplement (December 1979), 699–720.

Smith, Margaret. *Rābi'a the Mystic*. Cambridge: Cambridge Univ. Press, 1928.

______. "Transmigration and the Sufis." *Muslim World*, 30 (1940), 351–57.

Smith, Wilfred C. *The Meaning and End of Religion*. New York: Macmillan and Co., 1963.

Smith, W. Robertson. *The Religion of the Semites*. New York: Schocken Books, 1972.

Sourdel, Dominique. "Le Judgment des Morts dans L'Islam." *Sources Orientales*, 4 (1961), 177–206.

Taylor, John B. "Some Aspects of Islamic Eschatology." *Religious Studies,* 4 (1968), 57–76.

Titus, Murray T. "Mysticism and Saint Worship in India." *Muslim World,* 12 (1922), 129–41.

Tritton, A. S. "Man, *nafs, ruh, 'aql*." *Bulletin of the School of Oriental and*

African Studies, 34 (1971), 491–95.

______. "Muslim Funeral Customs." *Bulletin of the School of Oriental and African Studies*, 9 (1937–39), 653–61.

______. *Muslim Theology*. London: Luzac and Co., 1947.

______. "Spirits and Demons in Arabia." *Journal of the Royal Asiatic Society* (1934), pp. 715–27.

Watt, W. M. *Free Will and Predestination in Early Islam*. London: Luzac and Co., 1948.

______. "The Muslim Yearning for a Savior: Aspects of Early 'Abbāsid Shī'ism." *The Savior God*. Ed. S. G. F. Brandon. Manchester: Univ. Press, 1963.

Wellhausen, J. *Reste Arabischen Heidentums*. Berlin: Georg Reimer, 1897.

Wensinck, A. J. *The Muslim Creed*. New York: Barnes and Noble, Inc., 1965.

Widengren, Geo. *The Ascension of the Apostle and the Heavenly Book*. Uppsala: Univ. of Uppsala, 1950.

Wolff, Monitz, ed. and tr. *Muhammedanische Eschatology (Kitāb Aḥwāl al-qiyāma*, anonymous). Leipzig: F. A. Brockhaus, 1872.

Younis, M. Abdel Moneim. "The Religious Significance of Mi'raj." *Majallat al-Azhar* (November 1967), pp. 5–9.

Index